Legacy and Legitimacy

Black Americans and the Supreme Court

Rosalee A. Clawson and
Eric N. Waltenburg

TEMPLE UNIVERSITY PRESS
Philadelphia

TEMPLE UNIVERSITY PRESS
1601 North Broad Street
Philadelphia PA 19122
www.temple.edu/tempress

Copyright © 2009 by Temple University
All rights reserved
Published 2009
Printed in the United States of America

♾ The paper used in this publication meets the requirements of the American
National Standard for Information Sciences—Permanence of Paper for
Printed Library Materials, ANSI Z39.48-1992

Library of Congress Cataloging-in-Publication Data

Clawson, Rosalee A.
Legacy and legitimacy : black Americans and the Supreme Court /
Rosalee A. Clawson and Eric N. Waltenburg.
p.   cm.
Includes bibliographical references and index.
ISBN 978-1-59213-902-6 (cloth : alk. paper)
ISBN 978-1-59213-903-3 (pbk. : alk. paper)
1. United States. Supreme Court—Public opinion.   2. African Americans.
3. African Americans—Politics and government.   4. Mass media and
public opinion—United States.   5. African Americans—Civil rights.
I. Waltenburg, Eric N., 1965–   II. Title.
KF8748.C425 2008
347.73'2608996073—dc22   2008014334

2   4   6   8   9   7   5   3   1

In loving memory of Addie Barrett
—Rosalee A. Clawson

For T.S. and S.S.
—Eric N. Waltenburg

Contents

Preface

It's an interesting exercise to consider the history of an intellectual endeavor. This particular one had its origins in a graduate proseminar course on American politics taught by Eric Waltenburg about 10 years ago. One of the sections in that course dealt with the Supreme Court's role in the American political system, and a reading in that section used experimental tests to examine the Court's capacity to confer legitimacy upon a policy. The question held a strong attraction for Waltenburg, a student of the courts, and the methodology seemed to him to provide tremendous leverage in answering it. The problem was that Waltenburg had no background in experimental design, so he talked to Rosalee Clawson. Along with experimental methodology, Clawson's areas of research expertise include public opinion, the media and politics, and race and politics. It didn't take too long before we realized that combining our interests would yield a rich vein of analysis to mine. And so we began digging.

We were egged on in our endeavors by Leah Kegler, our undergraduate research assistant, who quickly proved herself worthy of coauthorship on a couple of conference papers and journal articles. That research appeared in *American Politics Research* and *Political Behavior,* and we appreciate the permission of those journals to draw on that work here. A special thanks to Leah for cogently pointing out that our various papers and articles addressed a common theme—the special relationship between black Americans and the Supreme Court—and that fully exploring that theme was a study deserving presentation in a book. Taking our cue from our undergraduate friend and colleague, then, we focused our attention and energy on producing that study. Leah went on to earn a masters in public affairs from the University of Texas at Austin and to work for the Bush administration (much to Clawson's dismay and Waltenburg's delight).

We also had a graduate student co-author, Neil Strine, on part of our work, and we appreciate his assistance with our media analysis. That work was published in the *Journal of Black Studies,* and we are grateful for the journal's permission to present the research again here. Neil is now an assistant professor of political science at Bloomsburg University.

Our primary goal in this book is to systematically examine the nature and consequence of the unique historical relationship African Americans have with the Supreme Court. We conceptualize that relationship as a reservoir of support that allows the Court to legitimize policies in the eyes of black Americans—allows it, in other words, to shape black public opinion so that it is more likely to fall in line with the Court's position on a given policy. Public opinion, however, is a complex phenomenon. First, it is moderated by a variety of forces, most notably media framing and attitudes toward and about groups. And, second, when it comes to public opinion toward the Court and its decisions, it is remarkably difficult to sort out the exact nature of the effects. That is, does the Court's policy affect public opinion about the policy, or does the policy affect public opinion about the Court? This complexity, in turn, requires a wide variety of analytical procedures in order to cobble together a systematic understanding. Consequently, we use a multi-method approach to explore the relationship between black public opinion and the Court.

This book would not have come to fruition without the help of many, many people. It has been a true pleasure to work with Alex Holzman, the director of Temple University Press, and we thank him for his support of this project. Other folks at Temple are worthy of note, including Elena Coler, the senior production editor, who was efficient and timely in response to queries. Jennifer Burbridge and Matthew Kull also provided able assistance, and Jane Barry provided helpful copyediting suggestions. Two anonymous reviewers offered discerning feedback, and we greatly appreciate the careful attention they gave our manuscript.

We were exceedingly fortunate to have our research supported by the National Science Foundation (SES #0331509). Paul Wahlbeck shepherded us through the Small Grants for Exploratory Research application process, and we thank him for his assistance. We also greatly appreciate our co-principal investigator, Katherine Tate, who provided us with much insight and advice. The Purdue University College of Liberal Arts (CLA) provided funding at key junctures, including several Research Incentive Grants. In particular, Howie Zelaznik was helpful in obtaining support from CLA. Corey Back and Jessie Morefield, both from the CLA Business Office, lent us their expertise at a moment's notice. The Department of Political Science also provided support for our endeavors. In fact, the head of the department at the time, Bill Shaffer, heroically took on extra teaching duties so we could be on research leave the same semester. We owe Bill big, as he reminds us every now and again.

Over the years, we have had several outstanding students help us with this research in addition to Leah and Neil. Much of our experimental research would have been impossible without the outstanding assistance of Tricey Wilks, a Purdue undergraduate. She hounded—we mean recruited—virtually every black student on campus to participate in our experiments. Her energy and enthusiasm, not to mention her talent, ensured that our experiments went off without a hitch. Two College of Liberal Arts Dean's Scholars, Maria Hetzer and Cory Driver, also provided able research assistance. Two graduate students, Terri Towner and Katsuo Nishikawa, were not only first-rate research assistants; they also kept Clawson from being too uptight. (Waltenburg says just barely so.)

We are indebted to Larry Baum for reading and commenting on the entire manuscript (during his sabbatical, if we recall correctly). Words cannot express our appreciation for Larry, a wonderful scholar, teacher, mentor, and friend. Many others read chunks of our research, including Greg Caldeira, John Clark, James Gibson, Judson L. Jeffries, Will McLauchlan, Rich Pacelle, Leigh Raymond, Evelyn Simien, Elliot Slotnick, Lester Kenyatta Spence, and Katherine Tate. We thank them for their insightful comments and for their encouragement. Our dear colleague Jay McCann deserves a special shout out for his hands-on assistance with the "sensitivity tests" conducted in Chapter 6 and his general willingness to answer methodological questions. Rorie Spill Solberg and Zoe Oxley provided us with helpful feedback on our experimental stimuli; they should also be commended for listening to us kvetch about this project as it dragged on longer than we intended.

A number of other colleagues discussed the project with us, some on too many occasions to count. We thank Pat Boling, Aaron Hoffman, Jim Kuklinski, Jay Morris, Glenn Parker, Suzie Parker, Bert Rockman, Keith Shimko, Bruce Stinebrickner, and Laurel Weldon for their support. Several colleagues let us collect data in their classes, including Ann Clark, Janet Day, Liz Frombgen, Will McLauchlan, and Laurel Weldon. We appreciate their willingness to let us recruit their students as subjects in our experiments. Finally, from helping us schedule experiments to solving computer problems to making wisecracks at key moments, Michelle Conwell was a huge help throughout this project. We would never have pulled this book together without her assistance.

On a more personal note, Rosie owes a huge thanks to the loves of her life, Des Smith and Zo Clawson-Smith. She wouldn't have been able to finish this book without the fabulous babysitting services of her mom, Janice Clawson. Her family deserves kudos for their support over the years: Dale and Janice Clawson; Tammy, Mike, and Jared Harter; Jill, Scott, Liv, and Sadie Castleman; and her Cleveland Cousins. Eric is especially thankful for Julie, who always patiently listened to him gripe about the project that would not end. (By the way, she's always right.)

After thanking all these people, we have realized we've done nothing. Everyone named here (and probably many others we've overlooked) deserves credit for the book, while we should be blamed for any errors.

1

Legitimacy and
American Democracy

In 1954 the "Let Robeson Sing" campaign was in full voice, bombarding the U.S. State Department with letters and petitions calling for the reinstatement of Paul Robeson's passport. President Eisenhower warned against military intervention in Southeast Asia. Before year's end, he authorized an emergency program to train the South Vietnamese army. The Communist Control Act went into effect, virtually outlawing the Communist party in the United States. Meanwhile, the Senate censured Joseph McCarthy, the nation's most notorious "red-baiter." West Germany regained its sovereignty. The first issue of *Sports Illustrated* appeared. Elvis Presley began his Sun recording sessions. A new nemesis for Bugs Bunny, the Tasmanian Devil, made his debut. Puerto Rican nationalists opened fire from the gallery of the U.S. House of Representatives, wounding five congressmen. U.S. consumerism got a shot in the arm as the nation's first shopping mall opened in Southfield, Michigan. RCA began mass production of the first color television set; sporting a 12-inch screen, it was priced at $1,000. A month or so later, Swanson and Sons contributed to the nation's television culture by putting the first TV dinner on sale. The Ohio State

Buckeyes won their second national championship in college football, their first under legendary coach Woody Hayes. Hank Aaron recorded his first major league home run; he went on to hit 754 more, setting a career record that stood until 2007. Roger Bannister broke the holy grail of track records, running the mile in less than four minutes. Contrary to the predictions of some medical experts, the effort did not kill him. His record stood for less than two months. Mary Church Terrell, the first president of the National Association of Colored Women, died, and Oprah Winfrey was born. Ellis Island closed after 63 years of operation, during which more than 20 million immigrants passed through its halls looking for a new and better life. And the Supreme Court decided *Brown v. Board of Education of Topeka,*[1] offering that same possibility to black Americans.

The unanimous *Brown* opinion was announced by Chief Justice Earl Warren early on the afternoon of May 17. Sitting at the Court Chamber's raised mahogany bench and flanked by his black-robed brethren, he read it aloud. It was short (merely 11 pages), and it took him only 30 minutes to deliver (Patterson 2001, 65). *Brown's* brevity, however, should not be used as a metric of the scope of its effect, for within those 11 pages and 30 minutes were the seeds for the elimination of state-created and -sanctioned second-class citizenship for black Americans. In *Brown* the Court declared that separate was inherently unequal, and although the decision itself focused narrowly on public education in the United States, its logic would be used to extirpate state-contrived apartheid throughout the nation (Kelly, Harbison, and Belz 1991, 591). Through a series of decisions predicated on *Brown* over the next two decades, that end was all but achieved (see Chapter 2). This effect alone affirms Judge Lewis Pollak's assertion that the *Brown* opinion was "probably the most important American governmental act of any kind since the Emancipation Proclamation" (quoted in Higginbotham 1996, xxxi).

But *Brown* and the associated Supreme Court decisions of the 1950s and 1960s did more than eradicate the vestiges of slavery jurisprudence in the United States; they also seem to have created a reservoir of good will toward the Court among African Americans, a reservoir that appears deep enough to endure the high court's

LEGACY AND LEGITIMACY

much more tepid support for black political and legal interests since the 1970s (see Chapter 2 for a detailed discussion of this doctrinal shift). Analysis presented by Gibson and Caldeira (1992) confirms this point. Using cohort analysis, they performed a rough test to determine whether different eras of black litigation success before the Court affected the level of commitment black Americans have to the Court as an institution—in short, their *diffuse support* for it. Dividing a black national sample into three age cohorts, they found that those blacks who came of political age during the glory days of the Warren Court era (birth years from 1933 to 1953) showed the highest level of diffuse support. On the other hand, blacks who were socialized either prior to the Warren Court era or after the Warren Court revolution had significantly lower levels. Thus, the Court's decisional behavior with respect to *Brown* and its progeny seems to have given rise to a legacy of legitimacy among black Americans (see Gibson and Caldeira 1992; Gibson, Caldeira, and Spence 2003b; Hoekstra 2000 for more systematic discussions of residual loyalty for the Court).

Legitimacy Theory and Pluralism

That the U.S. Supreme Court appears to enjoy a legacy of legitimacy among black Americans has important implications for the American political system.[2] Legitimacy is fundamental to the maintenance and operation of all political regimes. Without it, leaders and governmental institutions alike lose their political authority—that is, the mass public's acceptance of their right to rule. This aspect of the concept of legitimacy is particularly important in a pluralist democracy such as the United States, for these systems are prone to political cleavage and stress. Any political system's constituents place demands upon it—indications of what is desired, needed, perhaps required by society. But, by definition, a pluralist system's constituents regularly lodge competing demands. As those demands are met, winners and losers are created, placing stresses upon the political system. As these stresses accrue, the system can begin to lose its organizational vitality, and its constituents may begin to divest it of their support. A crucial force to counteract this entropy is a pluralist system's legitimacy.

Legitimate institutions and political actors are endowed by their constituents with an authoritative mandate to render judgments for the polity. Thus, legitimacy contributes to the vitality and persistence of pluralist systems. First, when the regime promulgates rules or mandates that are accepted, legitimacy can stimulate greater public approval or support, thereby augmenting the system's vitality. And, second, it permits pluralist systems to periodically (perhaps even regularly) disappoint some of their constituents. To be sure, authorities can rely on persuasion, appeals to self-interest and/or tradition, even coercion to effectuate society's rules and mandates, but in the long run these forces of compliance are inefficient and unreliable. Instead, "the most stable support will derive from the conviction on the part of the member that it is right and proper for him to accept and obey the authorities and to abide by the requirements of the regime" (Easton 1965, 278).

According to Easton (1965), the bedrock of this invaluable legitimacy is diffuse support. Conceptually, it is enduring, the product of political socialization, and not given to seismic or rapid changes. "Except in the long run, diffuse support is independent of the effects of daily outputs. It consists of a reserve of support that enables a system to weather the many storms when outputs cannot be balanced off against inputs of demands" (Easton 1965, 273; see also Easton and Dennis 1969). Diffuse support can stimulate greater public approval for the system, facilitating its persistence. Furthermore, diffuse support is a principal ingredient in a pluralist system's ability to meet the stresses that inevitably arise when members are asked to accept policies or rules that they do not want. As Easton nominally defines it, diffuse support "forms a reservoir of favorable attitudes or good will that helps members to accept or tolerate outputs to which they are opposed or the effect of which they see as damaging to their wants" (1965, 273). Citizens, of course, vary in their levels of diffuse support, both for the overall political system and the institutions that compose it.

Theoretically, diffuse support gilds policies with legitimacy, increasing their level of support and augmenting the system's vitality. Legitimate institutions enjoy the sustained confidence of their constituents that they have an authoritative mandate to make policies. Consequently, "the people to whom [a policy] is intended to apply or who are affected by it, consider that they must or ought to obey it" even if they oppose it (Easton 1965, 132). In simplest terms, legitimate political institutions govern constituents who believe that the institution has the right to rule. Thus, institutions with diffuse support are able to promulgate policies that, first, can rally support and contribute to the vitality of the regime and, second, can cut against the preferences of their constituents and still be accepted or tolerated. In the end, then, the bonds of loyalty to the political regime established by diffuse support for the system and its institutions work to regulate the political conflict intrinsic to pluralism and permit or facilitate the persistence of the system (Easton 1965, 273).[3]

In the United States, which institution most effectively regulates pluralist conflicts and rallies support for the regime? The research literature points toward the Supreme Court. Relative to other institutions, it has the greatest capacity to legitimize policies (see, for example, Clawson, Kegler, and Waltenburg 2001; Hoekstra 1995; Mondak 1990, 1991, 1992, 1994). And, consistent with Legitimacy Theory, this capacity likely stems from its institutional credibility. The Court enjoys remarkably high and stable levels of abstract mass approval compared with the presidency and Congress (Mondak and Smithey 1997). Moreover, at the individual level, citizens with greater levels of diffuse support are more likely to agree with its decisions. Mondak (1990, 1991), for example, uses experimental analyses to show that attitudes toward the high bench affect one's evaluations of its outputs (see also Bartels 2003; Clawson, Kegler, and Waltenburg 2003; Hoekstra 1995). This research literature, however, has been nearly silent on the Court's image among black Americans and its capacity to influence their opinion (but see Gibson and Caldeira 1992; Gibson, Caldeira, and Spence 2003b). This is not a trivial omission.

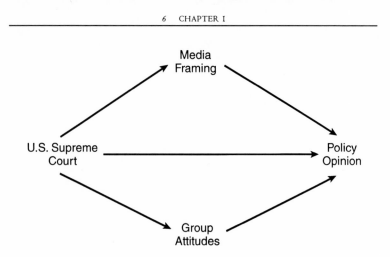

Figure 1.1 The Legitimizing Capacity of the U.S. Supreme Court

It must also be noted that the Supreme Court does not operate in a political vacuum. It is responsive to interest groups, such as the National Association for the Advancement of Colored People (NAACP), that strategically push cases through the judicial system. And since the Court does not actively pursue media coverage, the interpretation of its rulings is largely shaped by journalists. Furthermore, citizens are not empty vessels, simply waiting to be filled by the Court's pronouncements. Citizens' reactions to the Court's rulings are often filtered through a web of standing judgments, particularly their attitudes toward politically important groups in society.

We begin with the premise that the Court can wrap its cloak of legitimacy around its rulings. The Court has a greater capacity to pull citizens toward its policy pronouncements than other political institutions. Furthermore, citizens with higher levels of diffuse support for the Court are more likely to agree with its policies. This direct legitimizing effect is illustrated in Figure 1.1 by the arrow running from the Supreme Court to Policy Opinion. But we also assert that the Court's ability to legitimize policies is moderated by how the media cover its decisions. In other words, whether the Court can pull citizens in its direction is at least partially dependent on the media's framing of its rulings, as illustrated by the arrow from the Supreme Court to Media Framing to Policy Opinion. Citizens' predispositions also matter. In particular, citizens' group attitudes act as an anchor moderating the influence of the Court's rulings. This is illustrated by the arrow running from the Supreme Court to Group Attitudes to Policy Opinion. Below, we bring various pieces of evidence to bear in support of this conceptualization of the legitimizing capacity of the U.S. Supreme Court.

Black Americans, the Political System, and the Supreme Court

Like so much else in the study of American politics, conclusions about the Court's legitimizing effect have been drawn with little or no regard for the attitudinal differences between blacks and whites. And yet it is well documented that black Americans have distinct and identifiable attitudes toward a variety of institutions and social policies (see, for example, Kinder and Winter 2001; Secret, Johnson, and Welch 1986; Tate 1994; Tuch and Sigelman 1997). Most of the research examining mass attitudes toward the Court, as well as the experimental analyses demonstrating the Court's legitimizing capacity, has failed to include adequate numbers of black subjects, thereby rendering the extension of their findings to black Americans suspect and leaving a significant gap concerning public opinion and the Court.

The gravity of this gap in the discipline's understanding of the Court's role in the political system should not be underestimated. African Americans are the nation's largest racial minority and a potent political interest. Thus, how they react to a policy articulated by the Court may have important ramifications for the political system's overall performance and stability. Furthermore, their relationship with the Court has been historically unique. Its decisions in the middle decades of the twentieth century and the heavy weight of its institutional credibility, for example, likely contributed to white Americans' grudging acceptance of policies aimed at alleviating racial discrimination. The Supreme Court, more than any other political institution, may affect African Americans' belief in the system's right to rule and their overall support for the regime.

Historically, black Americans have enjoyed only tenuous footing in the political system. Constitutionally guaranteed the right to vote in 1870, their actual employment of the franchise was effectively denied until well into the twentieth century. It is little wonder, then, that black representation in the elective branches of all levels of government has been historically anemic. From 1870 to 1900, on average fewer than three blacks served in each Congress. This, however, was not the nadir of their representational presence. Over the course of the next three decades, no black was seated at all. In 1929 a black representative returned to the halls of Congress, but it took 40 more years before blacks began to consistently hold 10 or more seats. Even today, blacks occupy only 7% of seats on the Hill; yet they account for better than 13% of the nation's population. The picture is no brighter in either the 50 state legislatures or the nation's executive branches. Between 1975 and 2001, for example, on average blacks never constituted more than 8% of state legislators. Until Senator Barack Obama's run, no black has ever been a viable electoral threat in a presidential election, and only two black Americans have ever been elected a state's governor. Within the federal bureaucracy, blacks have enjoyed a greater numerical presence; yet until recently they have not occupied positions of genuine policy-making authority.

This dearth in black representation has had deleterious effects on the formulation and implementation of substantive policies of interest to African Americans and their attitudes toward the broader political system. To put it concretely, black citizens are substantively better represented by black legislators (Lublin 1997). Indeed, a raft of research literature has concluded that the minority composition of a legislature affects its substantive outputs (Herring 1990; see, however, Tate 2003). Black legislators have different policy preferences than whites and are apt to introduce different bills than their white counterparts (Bratton and Haynie 1999; Haynie 2001). Consequently, the historical paucity of black legislators reduced the likelihood that issues of concern to black Americans would be raised, let alone addressed in legislation.

The low incidence of "black-centric" policies emerging from Congress, the federal bureaucracy, and state legislatures, however, is hardly the most consequential deficiency resulting from the insubstantial levels of black representation in the political branches. It is very likely that their trivial number has also had negative repercussions on black Americans' support for, and confidence in, the political system. Studies have shown that the presence of black political officials, and the membership in the governing coalition that this presence signifies, is positively related to black political participation (Bobo and Gilliam 1990) and attitudes about the political regime. Gilliam (1996), for example, finds that blacks who were core members of a large urban governing coalition "were significantly more likely to . . . have more confidence in local government" (76).

Similarly, in her study of the effects of black and female representatives, Mansbridge (1999) finds that blacks who are represented by blacks are more apt to perceive the system and its outputs as legitimate. In their eyes, the presence of members of their race in the policy-making process yields a sense of inclusiveness that contributes to the system's legitimacy. As she writes, "This feeling of inclusion makes the polity democratically more legitimate in one's eyes" (651).

Tate (2003) makes a parallel point when she suggests that the symbolic representational value of blacks in government may be of much greater importance than their substantive accomplishments. Using the Congressional Black Caucus (CBC) as an example, she avers that although its substantive accomplishments may be modest, its presence is far from irrelevant. The CBC, by giving voice to black interests, ensures that "in the marketplace of ideas and ideologies," blacks are heard, and their concerns are knowledgeably and sensitively represented. The CBC prevents blacks from being marginalized in American politics and society (110). It guarantees that African Americans are symbolically represented and thereby increases the system's legitimacy in their eyes.

Given these findings, then, the obverse would seem likely. That is, the historically small number of black political officials should militate against black confidence in and support for the political system. Indeed, the terrible history of blacks in the United States creates a severe challenge to black support for the political process.

Even today, their meager presence in the regime and concomitantly limited capacity to urge the full and sensitive representation of black interests would hardly seem able to generate a sense of inclusiveness great enough to overcome that legacy and enhance the system's legitimacy in their eyes. And yet African Americans accept the political system as legitimate. They believe that the regime has an authoritative mandate to rule (Tate 2003). What explains this?

One significant force contributing to the legitimacy of the American political system for blacks is the Supreme Court. Certainly throughout the middle third of the twentieth century, the Court was the principal defender of black minority rights in our majority-rule democracy. As such, the Court has been the source of great substantive accomplishments for African Americans. After all, it was the Court that routed out the last vestiges of slavery jurisprudence and triggered the full realization of blacks' humanity and citizenship. Not surprisingly, black Americans greeted these substantive achievements with euphoria. Following the Court's *Brown* decision, for example, Harlem's *Amsterdam News* proclaimed, "The Supreme Court decision is the greatest victory for the Negro people since the Emancipation Proclamation" (quoted in Patterson 2001, xiv), while the novelist Ralph Ellison wrote, "The court has found in our favor and recognized our human psychological complexity and citizenship and another battle of the Civil War has been won" (quoted ibid., xiv).

Symbolically, the Court has been the exclamation point to the voice for black interests and has had a tremendous effect on the polity's legitimacy in their eyes. The appointment of Thurgood Marshall as the nation's chief lawyer, and then his elevation to the Supreme Court itself, ensured that black Americans would have a surrogate directly participating in the nation's great battles over black legal and political rights. The fact that an African American was present and possessed of full status in the judicial process throughout the latter third of the twentieth century enhanced the legitimacy of the Court's outputs for blacks. "Having had a voice in the making of a particular policy, even if that voice is through one's representative and even when one's views did not prevail, also makes that policy more legitimate in one's eyes" (Mansbridge 1999, 651). Marshall's presence on the high bench and the substantive accomplishments of black petitioners before the Court also helped to guard against feelings of black marginalization. They encouraged the sense that blacks were included in the process, had a voice, and were meaningful players in American society. "This feeling of inclusion in turn makes the polity more legitimate in one's eyes" (ibid.; see also Tate 2003).

In the final analysis, then, for blacks in the American political system, this may be the most important "political" function of the Court. Although its capacity to bring about significant social change appears to be modest at best (Rosenberg 1991), the Court does contribute to the integrity and legitimacy of the political system. In the case of black Americans, this is no inconsequential accomplishment. Whereas their experiences in the rest of the system give them little reason to invest it with an authoritative right to rule, African Americans' historical relationship with the Court helps to engender among them a more trusting and efficacious orientation toward politics and political affairs. In accordance with Legitimacy Theory, then, we assert that the Court contributes to the political system's legitimacy and stability in the eyes of black Americans. Their attitudes toward and responses to the U.S. Supreme Court present a highly consequential and intriguing landscape, one worthy of detailed and systematic analysis.

The Data and Scope of the Book

Our goal in this book is to explore the attitudes of African Americans toward the Supreme Court and the Court's effect on black public opinion, oriented by a theoretical perspective that explains these attitudes and this effect in terms of Legitimacy Theory. That is, black Americans' attitudes toward the Court as an institution are largely stable and the product of historical experience, while the Court's ability to affect black public opinion is a function of its institutional credibility among the black public. The Court, of course, does not operate in a vacuum, and citizens are not simply blank slates. Thus, we also investigate the moderating influence of group attitudes and media framing. In some instances, we compare black and white public opinion. The data we use to examine this complicated relationship are drawn from three sources.

Experimental Data

One type of data is derived from a series of experimental analyses conducted between the fall of 1999 and the fall of 2001. Our subjects were students—black and white—from Purdue University. We chose to conduct experiments because of the leverage they provide for establishing the effects of different forces on our variables of interest. With random assignment of subjects to conditions and experimenter manipulation of the independent variables, experimental research designs are an excellent way to establish causal relationships (Aronson et al. 1990; Kinder and Palfrey 1993). There is a cost to establishing this leverage, however; experiments often depend on unrepresentative samples, weakening the generalizability of the results. We relied on convenience samples of college undergraduates. Although our samples are not representative of the nation as whole, they *do* vary in important ways—they are not just "college sophomores" (Sears 1986).

Archival Data

We also draw upon archival data. Because knowledge of the Court and its policies conditions an individual's responses to it (Franklin and Kosaki 1995), it is important to take soundings of the Court's portrayal in the media. Indeed, the role of the media may be particularly important to understanding public evaluations of the Court, since it, unlike other policy makers, is largely dependent upon others to disseminate its policy pronouncements to the mass public. Accordingly, we collected data on framing of the *Adarand v. Pena*[4] affirmative action decision in both the black and the mainstream press.

National Survey Data

Finally, we used data on public evaluations of the Supreme Court originally collected in the 1987 General Social Survey (GSS), the 1996 National Black Election Study (NBES), and the 2003 Blacks and the U.S. Supreme Court Survey (BSCS). These survey data are particularly useful for our purposes. The 1987 GSS oversampled blacks (Davis and Smith 1972–1998), and it includes the five questions that constitute the Caldeira and Gibson (1992) measure of diffuse support for the Court. Thus, we have the most direct and valid sounding available on public attitudes toward the U.S. Supreme Court as an institution. The NBES is a full-coverage stratified random sample of the national black electorate (Tate 1996).[5] It includes information on an array of basic political, social, and demographic forces. Using data from a large national sample of blacks, we are able to conduct a full analysis of black opinion. Finally, the BSCS is a panel survey that was put into the field to take soundings on the attitudes of a national representative sample of black Americans both before and after the Court issued its decisions in the University of Michigan affirmative action cases (Clawson, Tate, and Waltenburg 2003).[6] Including measures of attitudes toward affirmative action policy, diffuse support for the Court, and racial identification, this unique data source yields substantial intellectual payoffs. It allows us to measure the change in blacks' opinion of affirmative action policy and the Court in response to an actual Court decision, and, most importantly, it permits us to trace the relationship between attitudes toward the Court and opinions on a specific policy it has articulated.

Overview of the Book

In combination, these data provide a rich palette with which to paint a portrait of the relationship between black Americans and the Supreme Court. As in all relationships, of course, a history underlies the attitudes and responses of the parties involved. Accordingly,

Chapter 2 tells the story of the power of the Court, but it is also a story of black relations with and responses to the Court. The Supreme Court was a significant force in black Americans' movement toward fuller political and legal equality. Yet it must be remembered that it is a reactive institution, and if not for efforts by blacks, spearheaded by the NAACP, the Court would not have had a leading hand in producing these salutary ends. In short, the Court was the site for significant and substantive victories for black interests, but black Americans were fully engaged and involved in producing these outcomes. Their litigation successes from the 1940s into the 1970s helped to form a reservoir of diffuse support for the Court that conditioned black attitudes toward it and its outputs. In this chapter we explore in some detail how this reservoir took shape.

Chapter 2 establishes that the Court has played an epochal role in protecting and defining black Americans' political and legal rights. As a result, black Americans have invested the Court with a reservoir of institutional legitimacy (see Gibson and Caldeira 1992; Gibson, Caldeira, and Spence 2003b). But to what effect? Legitimacy Theory suggests that the Court should be able to legitimize policies among African Americans. Indeed, that the Court can influence white public opinion in the direction of a policy that it articulates is fairly well documented (see Clawson, Kegler, and Waltenburg 2001; Gibson 1989; Hoekstra 1995; Hoekstra and Segal 1996; Mondak 1990, 1991, 1992, 1994; Stoutenborough, Haider-Markel, and Allen 2006). But is this true for black Americans? In Chapter 3 we put that question to the test. Through experiments, we show that the Court has a relatively greater capacity to move black and white opinion alike in the direction of an affirmative action policy attributed to it than an identical policy attributed to the bureaucracy.

The legitimizing capacity of the Court, however, is not unmoderated. In Chapter 3 we show that group-centric forces condition the Court's effect. Other research has demonstrated that the Court's influence is somewhat contingent on the characteristics of the individuals exposed to its message (Hoekstra 1995; Hoekstra and Segal 1996; Mondak 1990, 1992; Stoutenborough, Haider-Markel, and Allen 2006). One force that might affect the Court's influence and is exogenous to the individual is the framing effect of the media (but see Mondak 1994). Indeed, framing is ubiquitous in American politics, and no institution's policies are more susceptible to framing effects than are the Court's. Unlike the president, Congress, or state governors, for example, the Court does not actively attempt to shape public opinion regarding its policies. Instead, it leaves it to others to frame its decisions. As a consequence, how the media frame the Court's actions likely affects the levels of support for the Court itself as well as its rulings. Caldeira, Gibson, and Baird (1998), for example, suggest that the media's portrayal of judicial institutions tend to expose individuals to a series of symbols reinforcing the courts' legitimacy. The possible effect of the media may be all the more consequential for the attitudes of black Americans, since the black media are appreciably different from their mainstream counterparts (see Owens 1996; Wilson 1991; Wolseley 1990). Do these differences carry over to the black press's coverage of a Supreme Court decision? In Chapter 4 we present the results of a content analysis of black and mainstream press coverage of the 1995 *Adarand v. Pena* decision. This analysis uncovers systematic differences. The black press tended to cast the decision as a dramatic setback to affirmative action and appeared to use the decision to mobilize black support for affirmative action policies. The mainstream press, on the other hand, was more likely to frame *Adarand* in apolitical or legalistic terms and tended to present affirmative action as an instance of reverse discrimination.

But do these different frames affect public opinion? More concretely, does the Court's legitimacy-conferring capacity vary with the different media frames? In Chapter 5 we take up this question. Using stimuli we created based on the coverage of the *Adarand* decision, we show that the different media frames have a significant effect on the Court's ability to effect agreement with its policy, for both black and white subjects.

Legitimacy Theory suggests that there is a positive relationship between black Americans' levels of diffuse support for the Court and the intensity of their agreement with a policy attributed to it. In Chapter 6, we use the GSS and NBES survey data to analyze the effect of various levels of diffuse support on blacks' willingness to accept Court rulings that cut contrary to their interests. We find a relationship that is consistent with Legitimacy Theory. That is, blacks with higher levels of diffuse support are more likely to adopt positions consistent with Supreme Court decisions *even when those decisions are inconsistent with conventional black interests.*

The relationship we examine in Chapter 6, however, is dynamic and possibly reciprocal (see Gibson, Caldeira, and Spence 2003b). As a result, using the cross-sectional data of the GSS and NBES leaves it unclear whether diffuse support for the Court affects support for its decisions or vice versa. In Chapter 7, we draw upon panel data from the 2003 BSCS to examine black Americans' reactions to the Supreme Court and its rulings in the University of Michigan affirmative action cases. The nature of these data allows us to trace the relationship between African Americans' attitudes toward the Court and their opinion on the affirmative action policy it articulated. We show that, overall, black Americans' view of affirmative action is consistent with the Court's policy and, most importantly, that their attitude toward the policy did not affect their support for the Court.

Finally, in Chapter 8 we build upon our discussion and findings. Here, we take stock of our evidence and summarize some useful comparisons of black and white attitudes. We discuss the implications of our findings for the legitimizing capability of the U.S. Supreme Court, the role of the mass media in a democratic society, and the centrality of group attitudes in American politics. We close with a discussion of areas for future research.

2

Blacks, Civil Rights,
and the Supreme Court

In the American constitutional system, the responsibility for protecting minority rights against infringements by political majorities has traditionally fallen on the Supreme Court. Indeed, in outlining his rationale for judicial power in *Federalist 78*, Alexander Hamilton writes that the judiciary must have the capacity to check legislative encroachments on individual rights; otherwise those rights would be constantly vulnerable to "those ill humours which the arts of designing men sometimes disseminate among the people" (Wills 1982, 397).

> By a limited constitution I understand one which contains certain specified exceptions to the legislative authority. . . . Limitations of this kind can be preserved in practice no other way than through the medium of the courts of justice; whose duty it must be to declare all acts contrary to the manifest tenor of the constitution void. Without this, all the reservations of particular rights or privileges would amount to nothing. (Wills 1982, 394)

Of the various political, social, racial, and regional minorities in the United States, no other has relied as consistently on, or tied its political fate as intimately to, the Supreme Court as black Americans. To them, the Court has offered the most direct and effective means of fulfilling the Declaration of Independence's assertion of full political and legal equality. Throughout the greater part of the past century, the Court was the primary policy arena in which black Americans could compete and win. As such, it was the location of their greatest political triumphs, and it was the institution, by virtue of their presence in its membership, where they had the greatest voice. One result: the Court appears to enjoy a special legacy of legitimacy among black Americans. Laying out the foundations of that legacy is the objective of this chapter.

It is a tale without constant direction, in no small part because political leaders and the nation have varied greatly over time in their support for the political and legal rights of black Americans. As a consequence, the Court has been both black Americans' most effective champion and their most potent adversary. One need only mention *Dred Scott* to bring this latter point into sharp relief.[1]

To describe the ebb and flow of the Court's protective role, and its consequences for black attitudes toward the judiciary, we fix our attention on the quest for civil rights. This focus necessarily gives short shrift to other areas in which blacks have significant interaction with the judiciary, but we believe that describing the struggles, triumphs, and reversals in this one area goes a long way toward laying out the contours of black Americans' experiences with the Court more generally.

The constitutional keystone to black Americans' pursuit of civil rights consists of the three Reconstruction Amendments. How the guarantees provided by these amendments have been interpreted and implemented has a determinative bearing on the legal place of blacks in American society. We pick up the thread of our tale shortly after their ratification.

Reconstruction and the Construction
of Jim Crow

At the close of the Civil War, Republicans in Congress believed that the Reconstruction Amendments effectively guaranteed equality of civil rights for black Americans (or at least black men). They did so by integrating the freedmen into the national social and political order on the basis of legal equality. The Thirteenth Amendment prohibited slavery. The Fourteenth Amendment conferred national and state citizenship upon blacks, and it provided national guarantees of civil rights protections. Finally, the Fifteenth Amendment established the right not to be discriminated against on racial grounds when voting. In combination, the three amendments were thought to empower black Americans to protect their own civil rights in the political system. By the end of the nineteenth century, however, northern political interest in implementing and enforcing the legal equality guaranteed in those amendments was flagging, and the Supreme Court's decisional behavior followed suit. The Reconstruction Amendments' promise, therefore, was held in abeyance.

For the Court, the slippage in support for black political and legal rights ironically began with a case that did not directly involve any black litigants. In 1869 the Louisiana state legislature enacted a law that incorporated the Crescent City Live Stock Landing and Slaughterhouse Company, granting it a monopoly over the slaughtering trade in New Orleans. Within a few years, the monopoly had driven from business all the competing butchers in the city. Faced with the loss of their trade and livelihood, the non-monopoly butchers banded together in the Butchers' Benevolent Association and brought suit against the monopoly, arguing that its operation violated their Fourteenth Amendment guarantees of citizenship and due process by denying them their right to earn a living.

In the *Slaughterhouse Cases*,[2] the Court disagreed with this interpretation of the Fourteenth Amendment. It ruled that the amendment guaranteed only *national* rights of citizenship—that is, those rights that owe their existence exclusively to the national government.

These rights, however, constitute a very small and explicitly defined bundle of guarantees and protections. The full body of the rights of citizens (such as the right to earn a living) extend beyond those rights that can be directly traced to the national government, its laws, and the Constitution. And as such they antedate the formation of the national government, and thus are attributes of state citizenship. These, averred the Court, the Fourteenth Amendment did not speak to, and, therefore, the national government was impotent to protect them (see Schwartz 1993, 159–60). Given this interpretation, the Court refused to countenance the power of the national government to act as a "perpetual censor upon all legislation of the States, on the civil rights of their own citizens" (83 U.S. 36, 78). In other words, the Court ruled that it was not within the scope of national governmental powers to regulate and protect both national and state civil rights. Black Americans were guaranteed that national power could be used to ensure that their national civil rights were not undermined, but they were dependent upon state authorities to safeguard their rights as state citizens—a flimsy protection at best.

The debilitating effect on civil rights protections of the Court's respect for state prerogatives is better seen in *U.S. v. Cruikshank*[3] and the *Civil Rights Cases*.[4] In *Cruikshank* Chief Justice Waite began to give shape to a "state-action theory"[5] of the Fourteenth Amendment, pointing out that the Amendment "adds nothing to the rights of one citizen as against another. It simply furnishes a federal guaranty against any encroachment by the States upon the fundamental rights which belong to every citizen as a member of society" (92 U.S. 542, 554). In the *Civil Rights Cases,* decided almost ten years after *Cruikshank,* the Court put meat on the bones of that theory when it struck down the Civil Rights Act of 1875 because the act was directed against private discrimination rather than state action. Five cases came to the Court, challenging the enforcement of the act against innkeepers, theater owners, and a railway company. They were consolidated and decided together. Justice Bradley held for the Court, first, that the Fourteenth Amendment prohibited only state discriminatory action. "It is state action of a particular character that is prohibited. Individual invasion of individual rights is not the sub-

ject matter of the amendment" (109 U.S. 3, 11). Second, the Thirteenth Amendment (the other constitutional foundation on which
Congress built the 1875 act) only abolished slavery; it did not pro-
hibit private racial discrimination. "It would be running the slavery
argument into the ground to make it apply to every discrimination
which a person may see fit to make as to the guests he will entertain,
or as to the people he will take into his coach or cab or car, or admit
to his concert or theater, or deal with in other matters of intercourse
or business" (109 U.S. 3, 24–25).

The consequences of the Court's ruling in the *Civil Rights Cases*
were profound. For one thing, the judicial nullification of the Civil
Rights Act halted legal gains for racial equality. No appreciable positive movement in that area would be made until the twentieth
century (Schwartz 1993, 166). Worse still, the majority's ruling reinforced racist attitudes and provided the legal rationale for "Jim Crow
laws requiring the separate treatment of blacks and whites in public
accommodations" (O'Brien 1995, 1300). Indeed, within four years
of Justice Bradley's decision, Florida had enacted the first such law.
Other states in the Deep South quickly followed suit, and in the
coming decade the policies were stamped with judicial approval.

The Supreme Court's and the nation's nearly full retreat from
the cause of civil rights equality for black Americans is best exempli-
fied in *Plessy v. Ferguson*.[6] In 1892 Homer Plessy, one-eighth black,
boarded a whites-only car in a train bound for New Orleans. The
conductor, enforcing a Louisiana law that required separate but equal
railroad accommodations for black and white passengers, removed
Plessy to the car reserved for blacks. Plessy eventually sued, claiming
that the Louisiana statute violated his Fourteenth Amendment equal
protection rights. When the case arrived in the Supreme Court, a
majority of the justices found no constitutional objection to the state
law requiring separate facilities for the races, as long as both races
were furnished with equal accommodations. With this, the "separate
but equal" doctrine was born, legitimizing racial classifications. Jim
Crow ruled the South and cast a shadow over much of the North.

Ironically, that same doctrine would eventually serve to pry apart
the structure of racial discrimination in the twentieth century. The

failure to implement the equality *Plessy* required provided the opening: by the 1930s the NAACP had formulated a legal strategy that emphasized that aspect of the ruling. Simply put, it would challenge the existence of unequal facilities, believing that the cost to the states of maintaining substantially equal dual systems would be prohibitive, causing segregation to collapse under its own weight[7] (see Davis and Clark 1994, 64–68; Schwartz 1993, 188–89).

The Destruction of Jim Crow

At the beginning of the twentieth century, a racial caste system was firmly entrenched throughout the South, its tentacles reaching north into the border states. Before the dawn of the next century, however, the legal foundations supporting that system would be razed. The achievement of civil rights equality for black Americans was not automatic or painless, nor is it fully complete. But after a slow and uncertain start, the legal drive for the equalization of black rights became nearly irresistible. And just as Supreme Court decisions had rationalized and legitimized the construction of Jim Crow, it was the Court's interpretations that helped to tear that edifice down.

Foundations

Kelly, Harbison, and Belz (1991, 581; see also Vose 1967, 40) note that even in the extremely racist atmosphere of the early twentieth century, the flame of civil rights had not completely guttered out.[8] Between 1910 and 1917, the Court invalidated peonage laws as a violation of the Thirteenth Amendment, struck down "grandfather laws" that disenfranchised blacks by extending the vote only to those whose ancestors had been eligible to vote in 1866, and found unconstitutional local ordinances prohibiting blacks from moving into white neighborhoods.[9] Just as important, though, were other political, cultural, and legal developments in the first half of the twentieth century, which added fuel to the flickering embers and lit the way for the substantial civil rights gains of black Americans in the 1950s and 1960s.

The collapse of King Cotton as the backbone of the South's regional economy—beginning immediately after World War I and culminating with the massive economic dislocation of the Great Depression—led to heavy black migration to the North, a movement that had potent political consequences. The northern migration was not a general exodus; rather, it was effectively a selective movement of blacks from areas where they were politically disenfranchised to areas where they could exercise their political rights and where their growing numbers and votes purchased some genuine political clout (McAdam 1982, 77, 79–80). By the 1930s, blacks joined with other groups to block a Supreme Court nominee and then unseat several senators who had supported the confirmation. "These demonstrations of political strength, coupled with the continuing flow of migrants northward, had, by 1936, firmly established blacks as an electoral force to be reckoned with" (McAdam 1982, 80).

The Depression era also saw a realignment in political affiliations. Blacks broke their historical alliance with the Republican party and joined Franklin D. Roosevelt's New Deal coalition, becoming one of the key components in FDR's landslide victory. This, in turn, paid material dividends, as it "yielded [blacks] positions in the lower ranks of the federal bureaucracy, access to WPA jobs and welfare rolls, and admission to public housing projects" (Kelly, Harbison, and Belz 1991, 582).

Black Americans' presence in the North and their new alliance with the Democrats also had policy consequences beneficial to black interests. In 1924 the southern states' electoral votes accounted for 90% of all the votes won by the Democratic presidential ticket. By 1936, that proportion had dropped to a mere 23% (McAdam 1982, 82). From this point on, Democratic presidential candidates no longer felt themselves to be dependent upon the electoral votes of the southern states to win the White House. Instead, their electoral coalition was built primarily in the North, where the support of black Americans was crucial. McAdam (1982) notes that in both 1944 and 1948, had blacks reversed the votes they gave the two major party candidates, the election outcomes would have changed. Consequently, maintaining the electoral support of the large black minority in the North was emphasized, even at the cost of disaffecting white voters in the South, a fact "registered dramatically in the 1948 campaign when Truman, running on what for the time was a radical civil rights platform, emerged victorious, despite the active opposition of much of the southern wing of the party" (McAdam 1982, 82).

Events growing out of World War II and its aftermath also enhanced the political and social position of black Americans. Wartime labor shortages opened up positions in unions and trade associations. Condemnation of Nazi atrocities cast a bright and unflattering light on the unequal and racist treatment of black Americans at home—so much so that FDR created the Fair Employment Practices Commission and prohibited racial discrimination in the defense industries. Following the war, President Truman created a Committee on Civil Rights and quickly submitted legislation to Congress proposing to enforce civil rights. The Cold War battle with the Soviet Union for the allegiance of emerging Third World countries made American racism an embarrassing and effective propaganda weapon for the Communists. Likewise, the adoption of the United Nations Charter in 1948, with its declaration of human rights, allowed black Americans to call attention to their unequal position in American society. Both phenomena brought the issue of black civil rights into mainstream political debate.

But certainly it was the NAACP's formation in 1909 that was the most important impetus for the civil rights gains of black Americans.[10] It signaled the rise of a black professional and white-collar class who adhered to a tightly focused goal regarding black rights. It also helped to launch a concerted effort to use the federal judiciary in African Americans' pursuit of legal and political equality.

Tushnet (1987) asserts that from the outset the NAACP took as its *raison d'être* the elimination of the legal subordination imposed by the "separate but equal" rule of *Plessy v. Ferguson*. Because "separate but equal" was a constitutional doctrine articulated by the Supreme Court, it was natural that the NAACP would pursue a legal strategy in order to extirpate it. Accordingly, shortly after its formation, the association created a legal redress committee. By 1915 it was active in nearly every case before the Court that involved the issue of black civil rights (Vose 1967, 39). As noted above, it met with some success there.

Reflecting the achievements of its litigation effort, the NAACP's 1926 *Annual Report* noted that activity in the federal courts, "where the atmosphere of sectional prejudice is notably absent," would be the best strategy for the pursuit of black rights (quoted in Tushnet 1987, 1). For one thing, successes in the judiciary would be more definite than victories elsewhere. Legislative successes can quickly turn into costly defeats if policies are implemented contrary to congressional designs (see Waltenburg 2002). "Legal victories in the cause of civil rights . . . could be 'built upon'" (quoted in Tushnet 1987, 1).

To this end, the NAACP developed plans for a coordinated litigation campaign. By early 1930, its strategy was finalized. A permanent staff position for litigation was created, and the decision was made to pursue selective litigation to secure favorable precedents and mobilize the black community (Tushnet 1987, 13–14). A propitious confluence of events occurred: the black civil rights leadership was poised to aggressively pursue their interests through litigation at the very moment when the Supreme Court became demonstrably more supportive of those goals.

Days of Inspiration

In 1937 a sea change occurred in the Court's decisional behavior.[11] Prior to that year, it had been a staunch defender of conservative economic and property rights against legislation permitting trade unionism, regulating the economy, and protecting civil liberties. Following 1937, economic rights no longer occupied a preferred position. Instead, the Court took it upon itself to become the guardian of individual rights against legislative encroachments (Schudson 1998). In particular, the Court became leery of governmental invasions of the rights of discrete and insular minorities (see Schwartz 1993, 260–61). As Justice Black noted in *Korematsu v. U.S.*,[12] "all legal restrictions which curtail the civil rights of a single racial group are immediately suspect. That is not to say that all such restrictions are unconstitutional. It is to say that courts must subject them to the most rigid scrutiny" (323 U.S. 214, 215).

That requirement for "rigid scrutiny" produced what Schwartz (1993, 261) contends are the most important decisions protecting individual rights during the 1940s and 1950s—those involving racial discrimination. The Court and American democracy owe these progressive decisions in no small part to black Americans, who presented the Court with the opportunity to render them (Schudson 1998). Black Americans waged a protracted litigation campaign of successive lawsuits based on securing the equal protection of individual rights guaranteed by the Constitution. The campaign had multiple targets—racist obstacles to the right to vote, state-supported segregation in housing patterns, Jim Crow laws more generally, and segregation in education (Tushnet 1987, 135)—and it eventually paid dividends.

A daunting obstacle to black Americans' full achievement of their political and legal rights was their effective impotence in the political system. Recall that the framers of the Reconstruction Amendments believed that the guarantees embodied in those amendments would enable black Americans to protect themselves through the democratic process. Upon the amendments' ratification, black Americans could not be enslaved. They could be denied neither their rights as citizens nor their due process guarantees. And, finally, to ensure that the political system could not be used against their interests, they were guaranteed a voice in it through a right to vote that could be neither denied nor abridged on account of their race.

Despite the Reconstruction Amendments' intentions, however, the democratic process and black Americans had barely a blushing acquaintance. In the "Confederate South" during the 1930s and 1940s, fewer than 3% of eligible black voters participated in elections (Davis and Clark 1994, 112), not because of a lack of interest, but because of legal machinations—the white primary, poll taxes, and literacy tests—designed to muzzle black Americans in the electoral process, and buttressed by the threat and use of violence and economic reprisal. Each had to be eliminated in turn.

The white primary was a particularly effective and ingenious device.[13] Because of the dominance of the Democratic party in the deep South, its primary winner was certain to win the general election. Consequently, the only vote that mattered was the Democratic party primary vote, and here blacks were effectively disenfranchised. In order to participate in the Democratic primary, one had to be a member of the Democratic party. But the Democratic party in those states prohibited blacks from being members. Thus, blacks had no voice in the choice of elected officials, no weapon to challenge an oppressive social and political order. It was a catch-22 worthy of Joseph Heller.

Black civil rights leaders cast about for a case to challenge the legality of the white primary, and in *Smith v. Allwright*[14] they appeared to have it. In 1940 Lonnie Smith, a black Texan, was denied the right to vote in the Texas Democratic primary because he was not a member of the party. Smith sued the party in federal district court for denial of his voting rights, but, consistent with Supreme Court precedent,[15] that court and the circuit court of appeals denied the relief he sought on the grounds that the Texas Democratic party was a private organization and therefore could include or exclude anyone it chose. Within a year, however, fissures appeared in this bulwark against black electoral participation. In 1941, in *U.S. v. Classic*,[16] the Court ruled that where state primaries are integral to the election of federal officials, the federal government may step in and regulate them, suggesting that the guarantees of the Fifteenth Amendment might be extended to state primary elections as well. Building on the *Classic* precedent, the NAACP appealed *Smith v. Allwright* to the Supreme Court. In its decision, the Court struck down Texas's white primary as a violation of the Fourteenth and Fifteenth Amendments, ruling that although political parties are private organizations, they are entrusted by the state with such a crucial public and governmental function that denying blacks the opportunity to participate in their selection procedure was state action within the meaning of the Fifteenth Amendment. Therefore, black Americans' exclusion by the party was unconstitutional (see Kelly, Harbison, and Belz 1991, 595).

In 1937 the Supreme Court ruled that poll taxes did not violate the Fourteenth and Fifteenth Amendments,[17] triggering an effort to get the states and Congress to abolish the taxes (O'Brien 1995). By the early 1960s, that effort had proven quite successful. All but five southern states[18] had eliminated them, and with the ratification of the Twenty-Fourth Amendment in 1964, Congress banned poll taxes in all federal elections. Finally, in *Harper v. Virginia State Board of Elections,*[19] the Supreme Court incorporated the Twenty-Fourth Amendment's prohibition of poll taxes, thereby eliminating them in the handful of state and local elections where they were still in use.

Literacy and other qualification tests were perhaps the most effective method of disenfranchising blacks. Typically, they required the ability to read and write (to the satisfaction of white registrars) in order to become a registered voter. The Court had passed on their constitutionality in 1915, ruling that a literacy requirement for voting was certainly within the purview of state power.[20] As recently as 1959, it had not deviated from that position.[21] Still, the Court was aware that the tests could be used to deny blacks their right to vote—indeed, there was overwhelming historical evidence that they were designed for just that purpose. First established in the 1890s, these laws were predicated on the fact that in the states where the tests were applied, the overwhelming majority of blacks were illiterate, while only a relatively small proportion of whites were.[22] Still in use in the 1960s, the tests had helped to depress the rates of black registration to trivial levels.[23] Black leaders tried a number of tactics to increase the rates of black registration. Martin Luther King, for example, led voter registration drives in the South; a group of black leaders established "Citizenship Schools" designed to equip voting-age blacks with the knowledge necessary to pass the tests.[24] Yet it would require congressional action and Supreme Court countenance to overcome these "legal" barriers to black voting.

In 1965 Congress passed the Voting Rights Act. Enacted under the "appropriate measures" clause of the Fifteenth Amendment, the act forbade all qualifications or prerequisites to voting designed to deny or abridge the right to vote on account of race. It specifically prohibited literacy tests, knowledge or understanding tests, proof of moral character, and proof of qualification by voucher in states or political subdivisions where less than 50 percent of the voting-age population was registered to vote or had voted as of the presidential election of 1964. Of course, the 50 percent requirement was a thinly veiled rebuke to states using the qualification tests for discriminatory effect. The statute was applicable only to six southern states,[25] Alaska, and 26 counties in North Carolina. It signaled Congress's "'firm intention' to rid the country of racial discrimination in voting" (Pritchett 1984, 344), and in *South Carolina v. Katzenbach*[26] the Court upheld the constitutionality of Congress's intention.

The act had a dramatic effect. Within seven years, black registration had climbed 27.3 percentage points, from 29.3% to 56.6%, in the southern states covered by it (Pritchett 1984). Nonetheless, the act was and remains controversial. Renewed in 1970, the revised act banned literacy tests nationwide (upheld in *Oregon v. Mitchell*).[27] Renewed again in 1975, the revision made permanent the ban on literacy tests and required bilingual voting information. It was renewed in 1982 for 25 more years (see Pritchett 1984, 342–46). Finally, in 2007 President George W. Bush signed a second 25-year reauthorization.

Securing a meaningful electoral voice for black Americans was only one front in the war for legal and political equality. Contemporaneous with their battles for voting rights, civil rights leaders were also litigating to knock down the walls of segregated housing, to clip the wings of Jim Crow in interstate transportation, and to abolish segregation in the nation's public schools. In 1948 the Court decided the racial covenant cases,[28] ending judicial support for privately drawn contracts barring blacks from owning or occupying private property and eliminating a legal impediment to integrated neighborhoods. Moving the Court to this point, however, was neither a direct nor a simple task.

In 1917 the Supreme Court held that a Louisville ordinance establishing segregated residential zoning was a violation of the Fourteenth Amendment's due process clause.[29] The ruling, however, did not throw open the gates to integrated housing in Louisville, or anywhere else. Instead, white property owners (northern and southern alike) maintained segregated residential patterns by establishing racial covenants that bound white property owners to sell only to other whites. Nine years later, in *Corrigan v. Buckley*,[30] the Court stamped this tactic with judicial approval. Consistent with its state-action doctrine, the Court ruled that these covenants were merely *private* agreements and therefore did not fall within the scope of the Fourteenth Amendment. This was all to change in 1948.

J. D. Shelley, a black man, bought a parcel of land in a St. Louis neighborhood covered by a restrictive covenant barring owners from selling their property to members of the "Negro or Mongoloid race." Louis Kraemer sought and obtained an injunction prohibiting Shelley from taking possession of the property. This was the beginning of *Shelley v. Kraemer*[31] and the beginning of the end of restrictive covenants.

When *Shelley v. Kraemer* reached the Supreme Court, the NAACP, counsel for Shelley, asked the Court to reconsider its 1926 *Corrigan* precedent. Eighteen *amicus curiae* briefs, including one filed by the United States, supported the NAACP position (O'Brien 1995, 1314–15). Writing for a unanimous Court, Chief Justice Vinson honored the request. With a nod to the state-action doctrine, he ruled that restrictive covenants were not per se unconstitutional. "We conclude . . . that the restrictive agreements, standing alone, cannot be regarded as violative of any rights guaranteed . . . by the Fourteenth Amendment" (334 U.S. 1, 13). Rather, it was their enforcement by state agencies that ran afoul of constitutional protections. "[I]n granting judicial enforcement of the restrictive agreements . . . the states have denied petitioners the equal protection of the laws" (334 U.S. 1, 20).

The removal of racial segregation in interstate transportation began just prior to World War II, with *Mitchell v. U.S.*,[32] and continued in 1950 with *Henderson v. U.S.*[33] As was the case in the housing scenario, the Court had to work its way around the state-action wall it had erected in the *Civil Rights Cases*. Here, however, the Court did not rely on clever judicial parsing. Instead, it rested its decision on Congress's interstate commerce power[34]—a prelude to the Court's use of that instrument to break down private discrimination more generally.

Although housing and transportation were early examples of the use of the judiciary to effectuate integration, education was the centerpiece of black Americans' efforts (spearheaded by the NAACP) to eradicate their second-class citizenship. The challenges facing the campaign to integrate America's public school systems are almost poetically displayed in the tortuous route traversed by the *Brown* ruling and its eventual implementation. The Court was deeply split over the constitutionality of segregation when *Brown* first appeared on its docket in 1951. In the hope of attaining unanimity—and its expected ameliorative effect on widespread southern and white resistance—the vote was held over until 1954. The resulting unanimous opinion was purchased at the price of compromise among the justices and with the expectation of appreciable public resistance. In the face of these political considerations, the Court's opinion was intentionally quite narrow, and the question of effectuating the policy articulated in *Brown* was held over for one year (see O'Brien 1995, 1317–20, 1328–29, 1340–42; Patterson 2001, ch. 3). Even then the Court articulated a desegregation policy of "all deliberate speed" (*Brown v. Topeka Board of Education, II,* 349 U.S. 294 [1955]) that resulted in glacial progress for over a decade.

The roots of a segregated educational system were deep and extensive. At the end of World War II, *de jure* segregated school systems prevailed in the South and existed in many communities in the North. Indeed, 18 states had statutes mandating segregated systems, while six others allowed segregation at the discretion of local school boards (Kelly, Harbison, and Belz 1993, 585).

The NAACP began its attack on segregated educational systems by challenging the separate but equal accommodations made to black students in institutions of higher education in the South. In *Sweatt v. Painter*[35] (1950) and *McLaurin v. Oklahoma State Regents*[36] (1950), the Court held that the separate facilities provided for black law and graduate students were decidedly *not* equal and therefore violated the equal protection clause of the Fourteenth Amendment. More importantly, the Court took the first tentative steps in undermining the *Plessy*-based "separate but equal" precept for segregated educational institutions by suggesting that there were intangible aspects of education (at least higher education) that prevented separate from being equal.[37]

The *Sweatt* and *McLaurin* successes spurred efforts to extend the desegregation campaign to elementary and secondary schools. And in the epochal *Brown v. Board of Education of Topeka*[38] (1954), a unanimous Court ruled that "[s]eparate educational facilities are inherently unequal" (347 U.S. 483, 495), in the process striking down *Plessy* and invalidating legalized apartheid in these systems as well. Schwartz (1993) points out that there is little practical difference between the adverse psychological effects of segregation in educational systems and segregation elsewhere. This point was lost on neither the civil rights community nor the federal judiciary, and in short order *Brown* became the springboard from which the civil rights community launched attacks on state laws using racial classifications to segregate state-owned or -operated facilities of all kinds.

The path of adjudication was well blazed. Typically, it would begin with a federal district court ruling that *Brown* invalidated the contested instance of segregation. If the district court decision then found its way to the Supreme Court, that body would affirm the decision without opinion. Occasionally, a lower court might find some constitutional justification for the segregated institution. In that case the Supreme Court would remand the decision to the lower court for further proceedings not inconsistent with the *Brown* ruling (see Kelly, Harbison, and Belz 1991, 591). The movement of cases along this path witnessed the abolition of segregated municipal beaches and golf courses, city bus lines, and courthouses and courtrooms.[39] Indeed, armed with the *Brown* precedent, the civil rights community had managed to use litigation to all but eliminate *state-contrived* discrimination by the end of the 1960s.

Eliminating *private* discrimination was not so simple. *Brown* rested upon the Fourteenth Amendment's prohibition of *states'* denying persons within their jurisdiction the equal protection of the laws. Consequently, the *Brown* precedent could not be used to regulate the private dealings of citizens with one another. For that matter, there was no automatic constitutional provision that the Court could use to remove the private vestiges of black Americans' second-class citizenship. In the *Civil Rights Cases,* the Court had declared that the Fourteenth Amendment regulated only state action. That precedent still stands. Moreover, there is ample evidence in congressional debates surrounding the Civil Rights Act of 1875 (the legislation struck down in the *Civil Rights Cases*) that only 10 years after its ratification, legislators doubted that the Fourteenth Amendment gave Congress the power to reach individual discriminatory action (see Schwartz 1993, 167). Since the nineteenth century, then, blacks had regularly been denied seats in restaurants and hotel accommodations simply because of their color, and the *Brown* decision was not going to change that.

Where the federal judiciary could not take the lead in routing out private discrimination, Congress would step into the breach. The Civil Rights Act of 1964 guaranteed equal access to all public accommodations under Congress's interstate commerce power.[40] It did not take long for this use of the commerce power to be challenged. Nor did it take long for the Supreme Court to find for Congress. Within a year of the law's enactment, the Court decided *Heart of Atlanta v. U.S.*[41] and *Katzenbach v. McClung,*[42] declaring "that Congress could pass the law under its commerce power and a law under that power was not subject to the 'state action' limitation" (Schwartz 1993, 278). Thus, by the decade's close, the Court and Congress had effectively demolished the distinction between state and private discriminatory action and all but eliminated segregated public accommodations at all levels.

Remedy and Affirmative Action

Kelly, Harbison, and Belz (1991) note that the late 1960s saw a profound change in the basic goals and orientation of the civil rights movement. With its historical objective—the elimination of racial classification and discrimination in public institutions—largely met, "black leaders began to redefine equal rights with reference to the distribution of social and economic benefits in society" (609). They called for positive state action to overcome decades of past racial discrimination. Civil right leaders argued that simply breaking down segregated institutions could not achieve genuine equality. Rather, remedial and compensatory programs were necessary for blacks to obtain full citizenship in the American political and social system. Moreover, the achievement of this goal was not to be gauged by the elimination of segregated institutions, but through quantifiable measurement of actual levels of black participation in political, social, and economic endeavors (Kelly, Harbison, and Belz 1991, 603–4). In short, the civil rights movement changed its objective to the creation of affirmative action policies, and here again the federal judiciary was instrumental in the process.

Judicial forays into affirmative action were pioneered in the area of education in no small part because of southern efforts to frustrate *Brown*'s requirement of integration. Southern states shut down their public school systems, repealed compulsory school attendance laws, and passed "freedom of choice" plans that would allow a pupil to select his or her own school. As a consequence, 10 years after *Brown* 98% of black students remained in all-black schools (Orfield and Lee 2004). These statistics were not lost on the civil rights movement. Reacting to them, it pressed the federal government to establish plans that would effect the full implications of *Brown*.

In 1966 the Department of Health, Education, and Welfare (HEW) responded by issuing a set of "desegregation guidelines" that included a variety of means to achieve integrated schools, among them closing certain schools, voluntary transfer of students to schools where they would be a racial minority, and busing (see Kelly, Harbison, and Belz 1991, 605). The Supreme Court greeted the HEW guidelines enthusiastically, handing down rulings[43] that ultimately "decided that desegregation must be thorough, comprehensive, immediate, and, that in segregated urban school systems, courts could transfer students to other neighborhoods [i.e., busing] to end school segregation" (Orfield and Lee 2004, 18).

The success of the civil rights movement in first knocking down state-constructed and -supported barriers to equal educational opportunities for blacks and then formulating positive remedial plans for integration eventually ignited efforts to pursue the same outcomes in the economic sphere. The Civil Rights Act of 1964 created an Equal Employment Opportunity Commission (EEOC). It obliged firms above a minimum size to eliminate past discriminatory employment practices and empowered the EEOC to investigate individual complaints. Meanwhile, the Department of Labor's Office of Contract Compliance adopted rules that required private employers doing business with the federal government to take remedial action, here defined as the employment of minorities at statistical levels commensurate with their representation in the population.

As was the case with the HEW guidelines, the Court responded positively to the new employment requirements. In fact, it confirmed and extended them. Notable here was the Supreme Court's 1971 decision *Griggs v. Duke Power Company*,[44] in which Chief Justice Burger, for a unanimous Court, articulated the "disparate impact theory." Simply put, the Court held that even ostensibly racially neutral employment criteria were unlawful if they operated in a way that imposed disproportionate barriers to the employment of minorities. As Burger put it, "good intent or the absence of discriminatory intent does not redeem employment procedures . . . that operate as 'built-in headwinds' for minority groups" (401 U.S. 424, 432). In the Civil Rights Act of 1964, Congress had defined racial discrimination as the intentional unequal treatment of individuals on the basis of race. In *Griggs,* the Court went a step further: racial discrimination could take place, and consequently must be corrected, even in the absence of intent (see Kelly, Harbison, and Belz 1991, 609).

The Republican Court's Slow Retreat

The 1970s saw the high-water mark for the cause of black Americans' political and legal equality before the Supreme Court. Early in that decade the Court first endorsed,[45] and then all but required wherever necessary,[46] the hugely unpopular device of busing (see Epstein, Spaeth, and Walker 1994, table 8.11). In 1979 it found that intentional discrimination, as opposed to state-ordered racial separation, was cause enough to require that whole school systems undergo ameliorative integration plans.[47] That same year it also found discriminatory intent in the allocation of teachers.[48] As noted above, the 1971 *Griggs* decision opened wide the door to minority challenges of race-neutral employment criteria. In its 1978 *Bakke*[49] decision, the Court formally approved the use of racial classifications to pursue result-oriented affirmative action in higher education. It did so by recognizing that racial classifications may be constitutionally valid if used for a benign purpose. "[T]he state has a substantial interest that legitimately may be served by a properly devised admissions program involving the competitive consideration of race and ethnic origins" (438 U.S. 265, 320). In 1979 it extended this finding of constitutionality to private programs designed to remedy past racial discrimination in the workplace.[50] And finally, in 1980, the Court sanctioned the use of a racial quota system in the assignment of federal construction contracts.[51]

According to Kelly, Harbison, and Belz, "The affirmative action decisions of the late 1970s can hardly be regarded as the work of a conservative Court" (1991, 668). The record was by no means one of unsullied success: two cases decided in the first half of that decade severely checked the integrationist movement. In *San Antonio Independent School District v. Rodriquez*,[52] the Court refused to find a constitutional obligation for equality in school-financing plans. One year later, in *Milliken v. Bradley*,[53] it refused to order a metropolitan area (Detroit) to merge its urban and suburban school systems to enable inter-district busing in order to achieve a better racial balance in the districts' schools. *Milliken* was the first key Supreme Court decision to back away from *Brown* (see Patterson 2001, 177–81). Even *Bakke*, while supporting the principle of affirmative action, imposed limits on its use—most obviously the Court's refusal to recognize that past racial discrimination justified the use of racial quotas. Other developments just below the surface of the Court's published decisions were cause for alarm within the civil rights community. As the 1970s gave way to the 1980s, those developments grew teeth.

To begin with, there was a wholesale and ideologically monotonic change in the Court's composition. Richard Nixon's ascent to the presidency and his appointment of Warren Burger as Chief Justice in

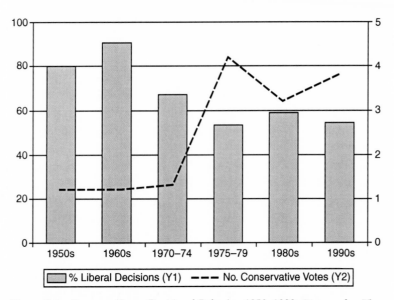

Figure 2.1   Supreme Court Decisional Behavior, 1953–1999. *(Data are from The United States Supreme Court Judicial Database, 1953–1997 Terms, Harold Spaeth [1999], principal investigator [ICPSR 9422].)*

1969 signaled the beginning of an unbroken string of 10 Republican appointments to the Supreme Court. By the time President Clinton named Ruth Bader Ginsburg an associate justice in 1993, every Democratic appointee to the high bench who had ushered in the civil rights revolution in the 1950s and 1960s had been replaced. Consequently, the conservatism that was barely visible in the decisions of the late 1970s was in fact building like a thunderhead throughout the decade. It would pour by the end of the next decade.

This development is evident in the voting data for the justices (Fig. 2.1). In the 1950s the Court decided 80% of its desegregation and discrimination cases in a liberal direction. In the 1960s its support for the liberal claimant in these and in affirmative action cases increased to 91%. Then began the serial Republican nominations. Already by the mid-1970s, four Republican justices had mounted the bench,[54] and the Court's tendency to arrive at a liberal decision had dropped to 67%; by the end of the decade, it had fallen to just over 50%. Perhaps more ominous still was the increasing incidence of conservative votes being cast in these cases (i.e., the number of individual justices in any given case who cast a vote against the civil liberties claimant). In the 1950s and 1960s, desegregation, affirmative action, and anti-discrimination causes won easily in the Court. On average, just over one conservative vote per decision was recorded. By the 1980s, the frequency of conservative votes per decision had tripled. To put it in more concrete terms, civil rights claimants were winning their cases in Court with fewer and fewer votes to spare. The interests of black Americans in the Court were on thin ice.

Second, the nation entered an extended period of economic dislocation. Between 1977 and 1981, the "misery index," a measure of stagnating economic performance,[55] averaged 16.6—an unprecedented level. (From 1960 to 1976, it averaged only 11.0; from 1982 to the present, 11.1.)[56] As a consequence of the economy's dismal performance, public support for remedial policies aimed at correcting past racial discriminations dropped (see Steeh and Krysan 1996, fig. 3). After all, it is one thing for racial majorities to support affirmative action programs when jobs are plentiful; it is another thing altogether to support them when jobs are scarce and the perception takes root that a job opportunity is jeopardized by a program benefiting a racial minority. This sentiment was perceived and echoed by the Reagan administration as it pursued an anti–quota enforcement policy. Once three Reagan appointees joined the bench and William Rehnquist was elevated to Chief Justice, the Court was ready to follow suit.[57]

Thus, by the late 1980s, there was at best tepid public support for affirmative action policies among whites (see Steeh and Krysan 1996), an executive branch with little interest in enforcing or expanding the economic or political rights of black Americans, and a Supreme Court in arguably its most conservative incarnation since the Taft era of the 1920s. All the elements of a perfect storm were in place. In 1989 the storm broke.

In that year alone, the Rehnquist Court handed down three decisions that left the defenders of civil rights bloodied and alarmed. In *Wards Cove Packing Company v. Atonio*,[58] the Court undercut the solid legal and constitutional foundation for race-conscious employment programs that had stood since 1971. It did so by severely limiting the reach of the disparate impact theory of *Griggs*, thereby making it much more difficult for litigants claiming discrimination to prove their case. Prior to *Wards Cove*, employers who hired a disproportionately large share of non-minority employees had to prove that the job qualifications they were using were in fact necessary for carrying out the job.[59] Following *Wards Cove*, the burden of proof fell on the employee.

In *City of Richmond v. J. A. Croson*,[60] the Court struck down the Virginia capital's minority set-aside program—modeled after the federal program the Court approved nine years earlier in *Fullilove*. In her opinion for the Court, Justice O'Connor raised the bar yet again for the defenders of affirmative action programs in the courts by employing a "strict scrutiny" standard to gauge the constitutionality of state and local affirmative action programs. Under this standard only the most narrowly tailored affirmative action programs aimed at actual victims of past discrimination would survive constitutional challenge.

Finally, in *Martin v. Wilks*[61] Chief Justice Rehnquist, for a narrow majority, held that white employees who had not been parties to the original action instituting an affirmative action program could sue and challenge that program years after it had gone into effect. Thus, *Wards Cove* and *Martin* made it easier for majority white employees to attack affirmative action programs, while *Wards Cove* and *Croson* respectively made it more difficult for private employers and states and localities to defend them.

The 1989 decisions showed a skeptical if not actually hostile Court where affirmative action was concerned. And yet one year later Justice Brennan managed to cobble together a fragile majority to uphold a federal affirmative action program in *Metro Broadcasting v. FCC*.[62] He did so by holding the federal government to "intermediate scrutiny," a standard of review far more lenient than the standard the Court used to evaluate state and local programs. Under this standard, if the government's program was aimed at an important objective and if the race-based classification system was substantially related to the achievement of that objective, then the federal program would pass constitutional muster.

Thus, by 1990 the Court had created a context in which all but federal affirmative action programs were on thin ice. Within five years, federal programs were there as well. In the interim the Court had changed again, and not to the advantage of the civil rights movement. The two great champions of civil rights and affirmative action, Justices Brennan and Marshall, had retired, replaced by Bush appointees Souter and Thomas, respectively. And although Democratic appointees filled the next two Court vacancies, the loss of Brennan and Marshall was enough to leave the *Metro Broadcasting* precedent vulnerable. In *Adarand v. Pena*[63] that vulnerability was exploited.

Adarand concerned the validity of the use of minority preferences in federal construction programs, and specifically the payment of bonuses to prime contractors if at least 10% of the prime contract was subcontracted to minority-owned businesses. As in *Croson,* Justice O'Connor wrote the opinion for a five-justice majority. In it she eliminated the disjuncture between *Croson* and *Metro Broadcasting* by ruling that the use of *all* race-based preferences must be examined under strict scrutiny standards. "[W]e hold today that all racial classifications, imposed by whatever federal, state, or local governmental actor, must be analyzed by a reviewing court under strict scrutiny" (515 U.S. 200, 225).

Thus, the Rehnquist Court held affirmative action policies at *all levels* to exquisitely demanding standards. To be sure, *Adarand* did not sound the death knell for affirmative action policy. Indeed, Justice O'Connor took pains to assert that the Court's application of the strict scrutiny standard would not automatically prove fatal to all affirmative action policies. *Adarand,* though, was the final bolt in a mechanism that made affirmative action programs far easier to attack and far more difficult to sustain. The decision imposed a substantial barrier to the creation and expansion of affirmative action programs at all levels.

This final point is well illustrated by the disparate fates of the two University of Michigan admissions programs: the law school program, which was found constitutional,[64] and the undergraduate program, which was not.[65] The Court found that the law school program passed constitutional muster because race was considered as only one of several criteria with the goal of achieving a diverse student body, an end in which the state institution had a compelling interest. This was not the case for the undergraduate program. The Court ruled that it operated in such a way that race was determinative in the admissions process. Since race worked to result in nearly automatic admission rather than simply to yield the assertedly compelling interest of educational diversity, the program was not narrowly tailored and therefore was voided under the Court's strict scrutiny standard of review.

In defense of its undergraduate program, the university contended that the crush of applications for undergraduate admission made the narrow, individualized law school process untenable, and that only through quantification such as that at issue could racial diversity be guaranteed. The Court would have none of it. "Respondents contend that 'the volume of applications and the presentation of applicant information make it impractical for [LSA] to use the . . . admissions system' upheld by the Court today in *Grutter*. . . . But the fact that the implementation of a program capable of providing individualized consideration might present administrative challenges does not render constitutional an otherwise problematic system. . . . Nothing in Justice Powell's opinion in *Bakke* signaled that a university may employ whatever means it desires to achieve the stated goal of diversity without regard to the limits imposed by our strict scrutiny analysis" (539 U.S. 244, 269–70). In short, the Court recognized that diversity was a compelling state interest, but mere appeals to efficiency in pursuit of that interest would not be permitted to expand the boundaries of what might constitute an acceptable affirmative action policy. Race-based programs were permissible, but race could not act as the determinative criterion.

Conclusions and Points of Departure

The U.S. Supreme Court was a (perhaps the) pivotal defender of black political and civil rights throughout the middle third of the twentieth century. It may be, therefore, that blacks, more than any other racial or ethnic group, hold the Court in uniquely high regard. Yet the Court's support for black political and legal rights has not followed a constant path. In the 1950s and 1960s it was a strong defender of black interests, but over the past quarter-century it has become a much less reliable advocate. Consequently, we would not necessarily expect black Americans' mass attitudes toward the Court to be static. Blacks socialized during the period when the Court was moving away from its role of defender of black interests might well voice less favorable views than other black cohorts. Ideally, we would have longitudinal survey data from large, representative samples of black Americans (not to mention random samples of non-black Americans for comparison purposes) dating from the advent of scientific polling to examine the evolution of black Americans' mass attitudes toward the Court. Unfortunately, those data simply do not exist. What we can do, however, is build a circumstantial case drawing upon published studies and public opinion surveys conducted over the last four decades.[66]

The mid-twentieth century was a halcyon period for the achievement of black civil rights, and clearly the Supreme Court was instrumental in many of the triumphs. Hoekstra's research (2000) suggests that this era of litigation success should have built up a reservoir of good will toward the Court among blacks, and our reading of extant studies supports this expectation. Hirsch and Donohew (1968) use post-election survey data from 1964 collected by the University of Michigan's Survey Research Center to examine black attitudes toward the high bench. Among the survey respondents who had paid attention to the Court in recent years, 72% of blacks had positive attitudes toward the Court, whereas 71% of whites had negative attitudes. This basic relationship held even in the face of controls for education, income, partisanship, efficacy, and geographic area. Thus, at a time when the Court was handing down rulings in favor of black interests, blacks had considerably higher levels of support for the Court than did whites.

For black Americans the 1970s marked a period of some notable litigation success in the Court, but also some telling failures; it was no longer the stalwart guarantor of their legal and political interests.

We might expect that in the aggregate black attitudes toward the Court would undergo some change, and empirical research appears to bear this out. Studies by Handberg and Maddox (1982) and Sigelman (1979) show that the high levels of support blacks exhibited in the 1960s had decayed somewhat by the end of the 1970s. Conducting a multivariate analysis, Handberg and Maddox (1982) found that blacks and minorities put more trust in the Court than whites did in 1972. By 1976 this finding had reversed, with whites viewing the Court as more trustworthy than did blacks (Handberg and Maddox 1982). Handberg and Maddox speculated that these data illustrate "Black America's increasing awareness that the [Burger] Court was no longer the active defender of minority rights it had been in the Warren era" (1982, 339). Sigelman reached a similar conclusion. Drawing upon aggregated General Social Survey data collected between 1973 and 1977, he found few differences between blacks and whites in their level of confidence in the Supreme Court, but: "Whatever racial difference existed . . . was in the direction of greater confidence in the Court among whites than blacks" (Sigelman 1979, 116). Thus, the evidence suggests that by the late 1970s, black were no longer more positive toward the Court than whites and were probably even less so.

In 1987, early 2001, and June of 2003 (Caldeira and Gibson 1992; Clawson, Tate, and Waltenburg 2003; Gibson and Caldeira 1992; Gibson, Caldeira, and Spence 2003b), black Americans were surveyed regarding their institutional support for the Court. The results of these soundings on black attitudes shed further light on the relationship between the fortunes of black litigation before the Court and black opinion. Specifically, the survey data illustrate that black Americans' levels of support for the Court are affected by its outputs, but that "[p]rior attitudes do spill over into current evaluations" (Hoekstra 2000, 97). The reversal of fortunes in the GOP Court era had their effect. Across all three surveys, in the aggregate blacks were appreciably less supportive of the Court than their white counterparts. At the same time, however, there is evidence of substantial residual loyalty, born of the high bench's strong support for black political and legal rights during the middle decades of the past century. Among blacks with the highest levels of diffuse support, the greatest share came of political age during the Warren Court era (1953–1969).[67]

This brief review of the research literature suggests that black Americans' support for the Court is not insensitive to its outputs. When the Court articulated policies promoting and protecting their political and legal rights, African Americans espoused favorable attitudes toward and confidence in the Court as an institution. As the Court changed from a staunch defender of black political and legal rights to a lukewarm guardian at best, empirical studies showed that black public trust in it decayed somewhat. "Still," as Gibson, Caldeira, and Spence aver, "African Americans seem at least moderately committed to the Supreme Court" (2003b, 543). Decisions of the 1950s and 1960s—and in particular *Brown,* which has taken on almost talisman-like qualities among the black public (see Clawson, Tate, and Waltenburg 2004)—gave the Court a foundation of support that is not easily shaken even by a torrent of decisions contrary to their interests.

Institutional support is likely a necessary condition for an institution to legitimize controversial policies (Caldeira and Gibson 1992). The preceding discussion lays bare the unique historical relationship between African Americans and the Supreme Court, and the resulting legacy of legitimacy. Can the Court dip into this well of legitimacy and persuade black Americans to favor or at least accept its outputs? The next chapter directly addresses this question as we draw upon experimental data to gauge the Court's legitimizing capacity among African Americans.

3

Establishing the Supreme Court's
Legitimizing Capacity

Can the Supreme Court legitimize controversial policies among African Americans? Based upon the logic of Legitimacy Theory, the answer would seem to be a resounding *yes*. Legitimacy Theory holds that an institution's reservoir of good will generates public support for a policy it articulates even in the face of forces that might work against the policy's acceptance. Institutions with deep reservoirs of loyalty are able to pull constituents' preferences in their direction when they articulate particular policies and be confident that citizens will abide by their policies even without coercive measures. In contrast, institutions with anemic levels of loyalty are much more limited in their ability to influence public opinion.

The Supreme Court would appear to stand in remarkably good stead on this score. As we noted in Chapter 1, a raft of research has documented that it enjoys exceptionally high and stable levels of abstract mass approval and has a relatively greater capacity to confer legitimacy on a policy than other institutions do (Gibson 1989; Hoekstra 1995; Hoekstra and Segal 1996; Marshall 1989; Mondak 1990, 1991, 1992, 1994; Mondak and Smithey 1997).

Returning to the question at hand, however, it must be noted that these attributes of the Court can only be assumed for minority groups in our society. The bulk of the studies that build the case for the Court's legitimacy-conferring capacity have been done with little or no regard for the presence of adequate numbers of minority subjects. Consequently, in the case of African Americans, the resounding *yes* of Legitimacy Theory is better stated as a cautious *probably*.

In this chapter we present the results of an experiment in which we put the Court's capacity to legitimize policies among black Americans to a direct test. Specifically, we examine black opinions on a pro–affirmative action Supreme Court ruling. Since blacks generally support affirmative action, we made this a more challenging test of the Court's legitimizing ability by assessing black reactions to an affirmative action program that clearly constitutes a quota system—a type of affirmative action policy on which blacks have more mixed views (Entman and Rojecki 2000, ch. 7).

We also analyze the Court's legitimizing capacity among whites on this controversial issue. While existing research demonstrates the Court's influence over white public opinion, our experiment provides a particularly demanding test of Legitimacy Theory. If the Supreme Court can confer legitimacy on a highly contested, inflammatory issue like quotas, that suggests that it has a great deal of power to shape public opinion in many policy arenas.

Examining both black and white reactions enables us to make direct comparisons, which in turn allows us to more fully understand and appreciate black attitudes toward the Supreme Court. In the case of both races, we show that when a policy is attributed to the Court, subjects express greater support than when the same policy is attributed to another political actor. We discuss these findings in greater detail below, following a description of our research designs— between-subjects experiments with black and white subjects. Then we examine behavioral compliance with the Court's ruling, present evidence illustrating the effect of group-centric forces on public attitudes, and discuss the broader implications of the Court's ability to legitimize policies. In the concluding section, we take stock of our findings.

Research Design and Hypotheses

To examine whether the Supreme Court's legitimizing capacity affects both black and white Americans, we conducted separate between-subjects experiments, one with blacks and one with whites. Experiments, with their random assignment of subjects to conditions and experimenter control over the treatment, are an excellent way to address this issue (Aronson et al. 1990; Kinder and Palfrey 1993). In each experiment, black and white subjects were asked to read a "newspaper article" that attributed a pro–affirmative action ruling to either the Supreme Court or the Department of Education, and then complete a questionnaire.

We recruited our subjects through somewhat different processes. In the case of white participants, we used 99 students enrolled in political science courses at Purdue University during the fall 1999 semester. Although it is quite easy to recruit white students for political science experiments by going into college classrooms, the small number of black students on campus makes it difficult to collect data on black attitudes in this manner. Instead, we advertised widely across campus, offering $10 to African Americans for participation in a "study of political attitudes." Thanks to fliers, word of mouth, and a diligent undergraduate research assistant, we found 129 black subjects during the fall semester of 2001. These subjects reported to the Department of Political Science lounge to read the newspaper story and complete the survey. After finishing the questionnaire, they were paid and asked to sign a log indicating that they had received the payment.

The use of experiments often raises the question of generalizability—the proverbial "college sophomore" issue (Sears 1986). We rely on convenience samples of college students at Purdue University. Although our samples are not random, our subjects vary in important ways. In Table 3.1 we present some basic political and social characteristics of our subjects and compare them with black respondents in the 1996 National Black Election Study (NBES; see Tate 1996) and white respondents in the 2000 National Election Study (NES; see Burns et al. 2000).

TABLE 3.1   DEMOGRAPHIC AND POLITICAL CHARACTERISTICS
OF PARTICIPANTS: LEGITIMIZING CAPACITY STUDY

	2001 Black Participants (*N* = 129)	1996 NBES (*N* = 1,216)	1999 White Participants (*N* = 99)	2000 NES White Respondents (*N* = 1,393)
Sex				
Male	33%	36%	60%	44%
Female	67	64	40	56
Median age	20	37	21	46
Median income	$41,000–60,000	$25,000–30,000	$61,000–80,000	$50,000–64,999
Education				
Less than high school		13%		8%
High school		28		27
Some college	94%	39	100%	30
College graduate or more	6	21		34
Party identification				
1 = Strong Democrat	24%	49%	3%	16%
2	33	21	5	14
3	22	15	15	14
4 = Independent	18	7	20	12
5	2	4	25	14
6	1	2	23	15
7 = Strong Republican		2	8	15
Interest				
1 = Not interested	9%	24%	5%	14%
2	14		10	
3	14		9	25
4 = Somewhat interested	29	45	23	
5	18		19	38
6	9		18	
7 = Very interested	7	31	15	23

Note: The National Election Study (NES) and the National Black Election Study (NBES) use a branching and fully labeled measure of party identification. Our measure was a 7-point scale labeled at its midpoint and endpoints. The NES measures political interest on a fully labeled 4-point scale, while our interest item was a 7-point scale labeled at its midpoint and endpoints. The NBES does not include a general interest in politics question, but does contain an item measuring interest in political campaigns on a 3-point scale. Because of rounding, numbers may not sum to 100%.

Given that both samples are college-based, it is not surprising that our subjects are younger, wealthier, and better educated than national cross-sections. Our black participants are also more likely to be Independents and less likely to be "strong Democrats" than the NBES sample. Nevertheless, our black respondents are still overwhelmingly identified with the Democratic rather than the Republican party. There is a great deal of variation in political interest among our black subjects, which reflects the variability among the greater black population.[1] Finally, like the NBES, we have significantly more females than males in our sample. The majority of our white subjects, on the other hand, are male (60%),[2] and they are substantially more Republican than a representative sample of U.S. citizens, with better than 50% indicating an affinity for the GOP. Although our white subjects were enrolled in political science courses, they were not uniformly interested in politics. Indeed, student interest in politics mirrors quite closely the interest of Americans generally.[3]

Our reading of the extant experiment-based analyses made us especially mindful of issues of internal and external validity (Aronson et al. 1990). We believe our experiments are particularly well designed in this regard. In terms of internal validity, we created strong experimental manipulations to ensure that the subjects paid attention to, and thought about, the source of the policy decision. We informed the subjects that we were interested in learning how people gather political information from the media and asked them to read (fictitious) newspaper stories that they were told had appeared in the *New York Times*. Each newspaper article had a prominent headline attributing the policy decision to either the Department of Education or the Supreme Court. We presented our subjects with a specific alternative source of the policy to guard against the possibility that the control group would attribute the policy to the Court (for a similar strategy see Hoekstra 1995; Mondak 1990, 1992, 1994). The story described an affirmative action case, the ruling in the case, and the ramifications of the ruling. Aside from the attribution of the policy decision, the stories were identical in length, facts presented, and writing style. (Appendix A displays the experimental stimuli.)

We were also concerned with issues of external validity. To ensure that our experiments had "mundane realism" (Aronson et al. 1990, 70), our articles were carefully constructed to mirror actual newspaper stories on Supreme Court rulings (see Spill and Oxley

2003). In addition, we based the articles on facts drawn from a recent circuit court decision; however, we reversed the decision, indicating in our story that the Court had ruled in favor of a quota-based affirmative action policy in a Boston public high school. In the case of our white subjects, we did this to provide a stringent test of our hypothesis. If the Supreme Court can confer legitimacy on an inflammatory policy like quotas, that suggests that the Court has significant power to influence white public opinion on other controversial issues. This particular stimulus also provides an effective test for our black subjects: although blacks generally support affirmative action, they are less supportive when it comes in the form of quotas (Entman and Rojecki 2000). In our data, the overall mean level of support for affirmative action is 3.82 (sd = 1.02) for blacks and 2.44 (sd = 1.02) for whites, both on 5-point scales, with higher scores indicating greater support for affirmative action.

After reading the newspaper article, the subjects were asked to complete a questionnaire. To ensure that the stories were carefully read and processed (and to reinforce our cover story), participants were asked to indicate whether the article was well-written and whether they gained new information from it. The heart of the questionnaire, though, concerned the subjects' level of agreement with the policy, using a 5-point scale, with 1 representing "strong disagreement" and 5 denoting "strong agreement" with the decision of either the Supreme Court or the bureaucracy. We anticipated that the source of the affirmative action policy would affect the intensity of our subjects' support for it. More concretely, we hypothesized that subjects exposed to the Supreme Court condition would be more supportive of the pro–affirmative action decision.

Other factors besides the source of the policy may shape opinion, including diffuse support for the Court, group attitudes, and political predispositions. To measure diffuse support, we took the mean of five items that tap citizens' respect for the Court as an institution. This measure, originally developed by Caldeira and Gibson (1992; see also Gibson and Caldeira 1992), is the most valid sounding of the public's institutional commitment to the Court.[4] We would expect diffuse support for the Court to lead to greater agreement with the policy pronouncement in both conditions because affirmative action in education is so closely linked to decisions made by the Court (see Chapter 6 for elaboration on this point).

Many observers have commented on the group-centric nature of public opinion (Conover and Feldman 1981; Converse 1964; Dawson 1994, 2001; Nelson and Kinder 1996; Tate 1994). Decades of empirical research have demonstrated that social groups are central to the way many citizens think about politics; group loyalties and enmities strongly influence political perceptions and evaluations. Many public policies disproportionately affect members of certain social groups, and opinions about these policies depend in large part on citizens' attitudes toward the groups involved. Affirmative action is no exception. It is an issue that is popularly understood to pit blacks against whites (Entman and Rojecki 2000). Therefore, we predicted that our subjects' support for the pro–affirmative action ruling would be affected by their attitudes toward blacks and whites as social groups. To measure affect toward the two groups, we asked subjects to place themselves on 11-point feeling thermometers, with higher numbers representing more positive emotions toward blacks and whites.

Finally, we controlled for citizens' political predispositions. Research shows that white Democrats are generally more supportive of affirmative action (Sears et al. 1997). Tate's (1994) work, however, shows that party identification and ideology are not significant predictors of black attitudes toward the policy. Nevertheless, given the importance of these political predispositions to opinion on public policies generally, we chose to include them in the analysis.

Research Findings: Blacks

To begin our examination of the legitimizing capacity of the U.S. Supreme Court, we conducted an independent samples *t*-test. Can the Court legitimize a quota-based affirmative action policy among African Americans? Based upon the results of the *t*-test, the short answer is yes. It is able to throw its cloak of legitimacy around its policy pronouncement for black citizens. More precisely, the Court increases the intensity of black support for the affirmative action policy by about one-third of a point, from 3.67 to 3.97 ($p \leqslant .05$).

To examine the Court's legitimizing capacity under multivariate conditions and to test our hypotheses that diffuse support, group attitudes, and political predispositions affect support for affirmative action, we conducted an ordered logit regression. The results are displayed in Table 3.2. In the Supreme Court condition, blacks are significantly more likely to support the policy than they are in the Education Department condition ($\beta = .68$, $p \leqslant .05$). To state the matter concretely, when the policy is attributed to the Court, the likelihood that blacks *strongly agree* with it increases by 13%,[5] evidence that the Court intensifies already existing black support. Moreover, in the face of multivariate controls, the effect of the Court is noteworthy.

To be sure, our regression analysis showed that the source of the policy was not the only force affecting black support for affirmative action. Black citizens are influenced by group-centric effects (a point we elaborate on in a later section). Blacks who have strong emotional ties to their own racial group are 9% more likely to strongly agree with the policy. Meanwhile, group-centric attitudes toward whites have nearly the opposite effect. The likelihood that blacks who feel especially close to whites strongly agree with the quota-based policy drops by 5%.

Consistent with Legitimacy Theory, the institutional credibility of the Court also stands out. Black subjects with greater levels of diffuse support for the Court are more likely to agree with its policy pronouncement and exhibit more intense agreement with affirmative action. Higher levels of diffuse support increase the probability of blacks strongly agreeing with the policy by 5% ($\beta = .48$, $p \leqslant .11$). Finally, as with Tate's earlier research (1994), neither party identification nor ideology has a statistically significant effect on our black subjects.

Research Findings: Whites

Existing studies show that the Court has the ability to legitimize policies among white citizens. But here we have set up a particularly

TABLE 3.2 EXPLAINING BLACK SUPPORT FOR THE SUPREME COURT RULING

Variable	β	Predicted Probability				
		SD	D	U	A	SA
Stimulus (1 = Supreme Court, 0 = Otherwise)	.68** (.35)	−.01	−.04	−.08	.00	.13
Attitudes toward blacks	.33*** (.13)	−.01	−.03	−.05	.00	.09
Attitudes toward whites	−.14* (.10)	.00	.02	.03	.00	−.05
Diffuse support for the Court	.48* (.30)	.00	−.02	−.03	.00	.05
Party identification	.23 (.16)	.00	−.02	−.03	.00	.05
Ideology	−.15 (.16)	.00	.01	.02	.00	−.03
N		120				
Log likelihood		−145.23				
χ^2		16.76				
Percent correctly predicted		46%				
Pseudo R^2		.13				
Cut 1		−.08 (2.04)				
Cut 2		1.74 (1.94)				
Cut 3		3.11 (1.94)				
Cut 4		5.32 (2.00)				

Note: Table entries are ordered logit coefficients with standard errors in parentheses, unless otherwise noted. One-tailed significance tests: *p ≤ .15, **p ≤ .05, ***p ≤ .01. Level of agreement/disagreement: SD = "strongly disagree"; D = "disagree"; U = "undecided"; A = "agree"; SA = "strongly agree."

tough test of the Court's power: can it legitimize a quota-based affirmative action program among whites? Quotas are a hard sell for white Americans, violating the dearly held value of individualism—the belief that a person should be evaluated based on individual characteristics, not group membership. The results of our analysis suggest that, indeed, the U.S. Supreme Court can pull whites toward its views on a controversial issue. An independent samples t-test shows that the Court increases the intensity of white support for the affirmative action policy by just under three-fifths of a point, from 2.15 to 2.73 ($p \leq .01$). This is a larger change than the one-third of a point for black Americans, although whites are starting at a lower level of support, allowing more room for movement.

The Court's ability to influence white Americans' opinions holds up under multivariate conditions (see Table 3.3). Even when controlling for diffuse support, group attitudes, and political predispositions, whites are significantly more likely to support the quota policy in the Supreme Court condition than in the Education Department condition ($\beta = 1.11$, $p \leq .01$). To be precise, the Court has a positive and statistically secure effect on white attitudes toward affirmative action. The likelihood that white subjects in the Court condition agree with the policy increases by 15%. Thus, the Court's effect is notable even in a multivariate context.

As expected, our regression analysis showed that the source of the policy was not the only force affecting white support. As with our black subjects, whites are affected by group-centric considerations. Whites who feel especially warm toward blacks are 13% more likely to agree with the affirmative action policy. In contrast, the likelihood that whites who identify closely with their own race agree with the policy drops by 5%, although this effect does not attain statistical significance.

The institutional credibility of the Court has a marginal influence on white attitudes toward the policy. White subjects with greater levels of diffuse support for the Court were more likely to agree with its pro–affirmative action ruling: higher levels of diffuse support increase the probability of agreement by 5% ($\beta = .52$, $p \leq .13$). Finally, contrary to some of the extant literature (see Sears et al. 1997), ideology and party identification seem to have no effect on our white subjects.

Extensions

That the U.S. Supreme Court can affect white opinion is fairly well documented (see Franklin and Kosaki 1989; Gibson 1989; Hoekstra 1995; Hoekstra and Segal 1996; Johnson and Martin 1998; Mondak

TABLE 3.3   EXPLAINING WHITE SUPPORT FOR THE
SUPREME COURT RULING

Variable	β	Predicted Probability				
		SD	D	U	A	SA
Stimulus (1 = Supreme Court, 0 = Otherwise)	1.11** (.42)	−.11	−.13	.08	.15	.01
Attitudes toward blacks	.49** (.19)	−.09	−.11	.06	.13	.01
Attitudes toward whites	−.21 (.18)	.04	.05	−.03	−.05	.00
Diffuse support for the Court	.52* (.30)	−.03	−.04	.02	.05	.00
Party identification	−.12 (.20)	.02	.02	−.01	−.02	.00
Ideology	−.16 (.23)	.02	.03	−.01	−.03	.00
N	95					
Log likelihood	−111.27					
χ^2	25.53					
Percent correctly predicted	51%					
Pseudo R^2	.29					
Cut 1	1.06 (2.02)					
Cut 2	3.84 (2.06)					
Cut 3	4.63 (2.07)					
Cut 4	7.51 (2.23)					

Note: Table entries are ordered logit coefficients with standard errors in parentheses, unless otherwise noted. One-tailed significance tests: *$p \leq .15$, **$p \leq .01$.

1990, 1991, 1992, 1994; Stoutenborough, Haider-Markel, and Allen 2006). Here we bolster these findings by showing that the Court can even move white opinion on an extremely controversial issue, such as a quota-based affirmative action program. The results of the experiments presented in this chapter indicate that the Court can affect black opinion as well. Moreover, its persuasive effect among blacks appears to be comparable to its effect among whites.

Aside from demonstrating the Court's legitimizing capacity among African Americans, however, the analysis presented here suggests several points that deserve further attention. First, the Court's ability to affect professions of support is only one aspect of its legitimizing capacity, and arguably the least important (see Eagly and Chaiken 1993; Zanna and Rempel 1988). As Caldeira (1991) points out, professions of support (the measures used to gauge legitimization in the experiments) do not necessarily coincide with behaviors. Consequently, we have no clear indication of the Court's ability to legitimize by encouraging behavioral compliance. Yet in terms of Legitimacy Theory and the performance of a regime, an institution is of little consequence unless its legitimizing capacity has a beneficial effect on behavioral intentions. Second, the finding that group-centric effects were at play in both experiments suggests that group attitudes might moderate the Court's persuasive effect. Finally, that the Court appears to be able to legitimize policies among African Americans raises questions about its role and representational theory. We address each of these points in turn.

Behavioral Compliance

Why should a policy pronouncement emanating from the judiciary be more likely to enjoy behavioral compliance than an identical policy emanating from some other governmental agency? The answer likely exists in the special relationship the judiciary has with the Constitution. Segal, Spaeth, and Benesh (2005) point out that the judiciary—the U.S. Supreme Court in particular—occupies a rather implausible position in the political system inasmuch as it is the sole political institution without power to *compel* obedience with its policy choices, yet its policies are the least likely to incite disobedience: "though our courts lack coercive capability, they are nonetheless the most authoritative of our governmental decision-making bodies" (5). Segal and his coauthors go on to suggest that the explanation for the curious nature of the courts lies in, among other things, Americans' beliefs about the Constitution and the mythology surrounding courts and judging.

For most Americans, *constitutionalism* is effectively a secular religion. Accordingly, we invest tremendous legitimacy in policy choices and actions that have the trappings of constitutionality. In short, if a policy is deemed constitutional, the likelihood that the mass public will support it or at least tolerate it increases dramatically. This raises two obvious questions. First, who or what determines a policy's constitutionality? And, second, why should we as a nation abide by that agency's determination?

With respect to the first question, Murphy and his colleagues (2003) point out that the Constitution vests interpretive authority in a matrix of shared powers. Thus, Congress can enact laws that are "necessary and proper" only with a valid understanding of what is constitutional. Article II charges the president with protecting, preserving, and defending the Constitution, an impossible task without the ability to form a notion about what the Constitution means. And Article III gives the federal courts jurisdiction over all cases arising under the Constitution. To adjudicate these cases assumes a power to interpret constitutional law. Clearly, then, there is no definitive *textual* statement concerning which institution prevails when collisions over constitutional meaning occur as each institution acts according to its constitutional warrant (see Murphy et al. 2003, 274).

If the Constitution is a bit cryptic when it comes to interpretive preeminence, to most Americans there is far less ambiguity. History, tradition, and practice have come together to place the power of deciding what is and what is not constitutional in the hands of the judiciary, especially in the domain of civil rights and liberties (Murphy et al. 2003, 284). As John Marshall famously put it in *Marbury v. Madison* (1803): "It is emphatically the province and duty of the judicial department to say what the law is" (5 U.S. 137, 177). In other words, the judiciary's word *is* the law (see Segal, Spaeth, and Benesh 2005, 5), a theme reaffirmed a century and a half later in *Cooper v. Aaron* (1958). There, in the face of open resistance by the governor and legislature of the state of Arkansas to its desegregation order in *Brown*, the Court unanimously ruled that "[*Marbury*] declared the basic principle that the federal judiciary is supreme in the exposition of the law of the Constitution, and that principle has ever since been respected by the Court and the Country as a permanent and indispensable feature of our constitutional system" (358 U.S. 1, 18). This, in turn, leads us to the second question.

Given the stakes involved in the judiciary's power to declare what the law is, what the Constitution means, why is it that judicial decisions are generally accepted or at least consented to? A likely answer is that the judiciary, especially the Supreme Court, has managed to assume a position where there is virtually no light between itself and the Constitution. Segal, Spaeth, and Benesh (2005) write that many Americans perceive judges as deciding cases "dispassionately, impartially, and objectively" (4). In other words, many Americans believe that the justices do not decide cases according to their own ideological predilections or political biases. Instead, they simply lay the law alongside the Constitution and make sure that the former squares with the latter—in the process declaring what the law says and what the Constitution means. This is the *myth* of courts and judging (see Segal, Spaeth, and Benesh 2005). Given that judges are simultaneously legal technicians and high priests of the Constitution, their decisions are legitimate because they are simply statements of the Constitution. Policy pronouncements emanating from the courts are policy pronouncements emanating from the Constitution. They are one and the same—according to the myth. It is to be expected, then, that a policy articulated by the Supreme Court will enjoy greater behavioral compliance than a policy articulated by a bureaucratic agency. After all, the Court's policy automatically possesses a constitutional imprimatur; the bureaucracy's policy awaits one.

This is not to say that the Court's statement of policy will settle the issue for all citizens for all time. *Plessy,* for example, did not put the issue of racial discrimination to rest, as the NAACP's legal strategy and the twentieth-century civil rights movement demonstrate. A Court ruling, compared with decisions from other institutions, is able to put a lid on the level of intolerance a given policy will engender. It may carve out political cover for other policy-making institutions to act (a point we return to in greater detail in Chapter 8). And, identified so closely with the Constitution, the Court's ruling may provide the political space necessary for large, consequential segments of society to accommodate themselves to the new political order. All of these possibilities are quite consistent with Legitimacy Theory.

To examine whether the Court's legitimizing capacity extends to behavioral compliance, we designed our experiments to measure whether the source of the policy neutralized intentions to protest by asking subjects who *disagreed* with the policy pronouncement if they would engage in political activity to express their displeasure. By examining the behavioral intentions of only those subjects who disagreed with the policy, we are able to assess whether identifying the Court as the source of the policy makes people who should be more apt to protest less likely to do so than they would be if the policy were articulated by some other political actor. This strategy, however, had some pernicious effects on our samples. It reduced the sample size for whites from 99 to 69, and it rendered an experiment on the black sample impossible, since only 15 black subjects disagreed with the policy. Thus, our analysis below is based solely on our white subjects.

To measure behavioral intentions, participants were asked if they would be willing to write a letter to the newspaper, write a letter to their congressional representative, participate in a campus demonstration, participate in a demonstration in front of the Supreme Court or the Education Department, or contribute to an interest group that promotes their (anti-ruling) position.[6] Subjects indicated their responses on a 3-point scale ranging from "not willing at all" (1) to "very willing" (3). We computed a mean from those five items to create our measure of behavioral intentions.[7]

When explaining behavioral intentions, we expected that subjects' interest in politics would be an important explanatory factor. We hypothesized that subjects who are uninterested in politics would not be affected by the experimental manipulation, their apathy leaving them unwilling to participate regardless of the circumstances. Subjects who are interested in politics should be more likely to participate, but their tendency to action would be moderated by the source of the policy. Subjects who read that the policy was the child of the bureaucracy would profess a greater propensity to protest than subjects who believed that the Supreme Court fostered it.

TABLE 3.4   EXPLAINING BEHAVIORAL INTENTIONS TOWARD
AFFIRMATIVE ACTION POLICY: WHITE SUBJECTS

Variable	Coefficient	SE
Stimulus (1 = Supreme Court, 0 = Otherwise)	.29	.31
Attitudes toward blacks	−.02	.06
Attitudes toward whites	−.07*	.04
Diffuse support for the Court	.04	.04
Party identification	−.10	.11
Ideology	−.05	.07
Interest	.19**	.07
Stimulus by Interest	−.16*	.09
Constant	2.10**	.64
N	66	
Adjusted R^2	.09	

Note: Table entries are unstandardized regression coefficients and standard errors. *$p \leq .10$; **$p \leq .01$.

In other words, interested subjects would foresee greater compliance when the policy was attributed to the Supreme Court because of the Court's greater legitimacy and their own increased likelihood of accepting its authoritative decisions.[8]

To test our hypotheses concerning behavioral compliance, we conducted a regression analysis. The model included all of the forces for the ordered logit estimates of white support discussed above, as well as a measure of interest in politics and a policy attribution condition by interest interaction. As displayed in Table 3.4, there is a main effect of interest on participation, such that subjects who are more interested in politics are more likely to participate than those subjects who are uninterested ($\beta = .19$, $p \leq .01$). The interaction of condition and interest in politics, however, is of greater note. Delving into this relationship shows that a Supreme Court ruling does not have much impact on those who are not particularly interested in politics. In contrast, interested subjects were *less likely* ($\beta = -.16$, $p \leq .06$) to say that they would protest against the affirmative action policy *when the Supreme Court was its source* (Fig. 3.1). To put

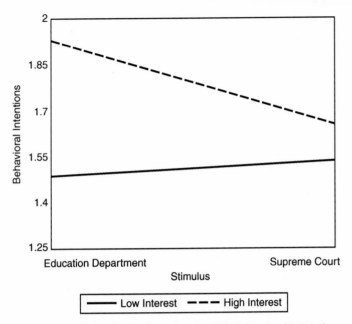

Figure 3.1   Effects of Stimulus at Low and High Levels of Political Interest

it in concrete terms, when the Supreme Court speaks, it discourages those most likely to protest from protesting.

Group-Centrism

Since affirmative action has clear racial connotations, we expected that perceptions of it as a policy would be affected by attitudes toward racial groups. Our experimental data confirmed this expectation. Aside from this direct effect on attitudes toward the policy itself, however, it is also quite possible that group-centric forces moderate the effect of the source of the policy. That is, the legitimizing influence of the Court might vary with an individual's attitudes toward the groups seen as linked to the policy it articulates—in particular toward blacks, the racial subgroup most closely identified with affirmative action (Kinder and Sanders 1996; Nelson and Kinder 1996). To explore this possibility, we conducted a separate

TABLE 3.5 THE MODERATING EFFECTS OF GROUP-CENTRISM:
WHITE SUBJECTS

Variable	Coefficient	
Stimulus (1 = Supreme Court, 0 = Otherwise)	.18	(1.66)
Attitudes toward blacks	.22	(.18)
Stimulus by Attitudes toward blacks	.77**	(.33)
Attitudes toward whites	.00	(.20)
Stimulus by Attitudes toward whites	−.56*	(.32)
Diffuse support for the Court	.55	(.34)
Party identification	−.10	(.21)
Ideology	−.16	(.24)
N	95	
Log likelihood	−108.65	
χ^2	30.77	
Percent correctly predicted	53%	
Pseudo R^2	.31	
Cut 1	1.04	(2.14)
Cut 2	3.90	(2.18)
Cut 3	4.72	(2.20)
Cut 4	7.76	(2.36)

Note: Table entries are ordered logit regression coefficients with standard errors in parentheses. One-tailed significance tests: *p ≤ .10; **p ≤ .05.

analysis where we interacted the experimental condition with our measures of group affect. This analysis was conducted only on white subjects: there was simply not enough variation in the group affect measures among our black subjects to perform the interaction analysis.

The results (Table 3.5) indicate that group-centric forces do have a bearing on the persuasive effect of the Court. The policy attribution condition is only slightly moderated by attitudes toward whites ($\beta = -.56$, $t = -1.76$), yet there is a significant interaction between policy attribution condition and attitudes toward blacks ($\beta = .77$, $t = 2.30$, $p \leq .05$). To unpack this interaction, we computed the predicted probabilities of our subjects agreeing and disagreeing with the affirmative action policy in each policy attribution condition for "hot" and "cold" attitudes toward blacks. This analysis revealed that the Court had only meager effects on subjects who were "cold" toward blacks, moving them, for example, from a .58 probability of disagreeing with the pro–affirmative action ruling in the Education Department condition to a .50 probability of disagreeing with it ($\Delta = .08$) in the Supreme Court condition. It is not particularly surprising that whites who indicate a strong dislike for blacks are not moved by the Supreme Court decision. Even though the survey was anonymous, "social desirability" pressures make it uncomfortable for those respondents who do not like blacks to admit their antipathy (Weisberg, Krosnick, and Bowen 1989). Therefore, subjects who *did reveal* their aversion to blacks are probably quite committed to their views, making them immune to the weight of the Court ruling. In contrast, subjects who had warmer feelings toward blacks were more likely to support the policy when it was attributed to the Court, dropping from a .56 probability of disagreeing to a .39 probability ($\Delta = .17$).

This is further evidence of the "group-centric" nature of American public opinion. In relative terms, the Supreme Court is a strong and credible persuasive source. It enjoys stable and high levels of public support, and it appears to be able to tap a large reservoir of "political capital" that can be replenished (Mondak 1992; Mondak and Smithey 1997). But even this unique institution's influence on the American public is not unalloyed. Like so much else in the realm of American public opinion, it is moderated by attitudes toward social groups. Such attitudes structure and condition the Court's legitimizing capacity. We will remain mindful of these group-centric effects throughout this study.

Representation

Our findings concerning the Court's capacity to legitimize policies among African Americans speak to larger questions of public support for political officials, policies, and institutions. The United States is and always has been a heterogeneous society composed of different groups with different interests. As a democratic regime, its ability to function as a political system ultimately depends upon a variegated public's general embrace, or at least toleration, of its policies. Democratic theory suggests, and empirical studies show, that a crucial element in this support is the public's perception of representation among the political institutions, in the decision-making process, or both (see, for example, Barrett-Howard and Tyler 1986; Mansbridge 1999; Pitkin 1967; Tate 2003; Tyler 1990; Tyler and Mitchell 1994). On this score, however, the Court comes up short among African Americans. They are without a clear symbolic representative on the bench, yet the Court is able to legitimize policies among them.

To be sure, Justice Clarence Thomas, the present occupant of the so-called black seat, shares black Americans' racial identity; in simple terms, he is their *descriptive* representative (Pitkin 1967). But in order to be *symbolically* representative, officials must also act so that the represented accept them and believe in them as their symbolic presence in the decision-making process (see Pitkin 1967, ch. 4). Pitkin explains, "The existence of [symbolic] representation is to be measured by the state of mind, the condition of satisfaction or belief, of certain people" (1967, 106). Here, Justice Thomas falls short. He is an archconservative whose behavior on the bench places him squarely at odds with the majority of black Americans on issues of civil rights, racial equality, and criminal justice (Dawson 2001, 83). Consequently, most black Americans neither accept him nor believe in him as their symbolic representative. Black elites perceive him as an "Uncle Tom," a sellout, and a fool (see Chapter 4), while the black public can hardly be said to hold him in high regard. An analysis of feeling thermometer ratings from the 1996 NBES (see Tate 1996) shows that Thomas is rated less favorably than any other black leader, including Louis Farrakhan, Jesse Jackson, Kweisi Mfume, Carol Moseley Braun, and Colin Powell.

The Supreme Court's capacity to legitimize a policy is clearly a strong force. Since the Court possesses neither the purse nor the sword, it must rely on institutional credibility to gain citizen acquiescence to its decisions. Accordingly, determining the parameters of its legitimizing capacity is fundamental to developing a full understanding of the Court's power in our democratic system. And here the analysis presented in the chapter has taken an important step. Over the past decade, several studies have examined the Court's legitimizing effect (see, for example, Hoekstra 1995; Hoekstra and Segal 1996; Mondak 1990, 1991, 1992, 1994; Stoutenborough, Haider-Markel, and Allen 2006). We are the first to demonstrate that this capacity extends to those who are not symbolically represented on the high bench.

To the extent that the Court convinces elements of the public that they should accept policies they might be hesitant about, it performs an invaluable service in our political system. One of the hallmarks of American society is its heterogeneity, and this places stress on our politics. Convincing disparate groups holding disparate attitudes to abide by policies they may disagree with is crucial to the efficient and successful functioning of the political system. And here the Court comes to the fore. Invested with substantial institutional credibility, it can knit these disparate groups and attitudes together. Structurally, it would be impossible for the Court to symbolically represent all the different elements of American society—and apparently it need not. Our research indicates that the Court can legitimize policies among those who are unlikely to see themselves as symbolically represented on the bench.

Conclusion

We began this chapter by asking whether the Court can legitimize policies among African Americans. Our study shows that indeed this is the case: when the Supreme Court rules on a quota-based affirmative action program, it is able to pull black Americans in the direction of its opinion. We argue that this is an especially compelling finding, since blacks lack a symbolic representative on the Court.

Likewise, the Court influences white public opinion, even when asked to bestow legitimacy on a highly contested issue like quotas in public schools. Whites are moved toward more support of (or at least less opposition to) the quota policy when it is articulated by the Court rather than the Education Department. Furthermore, politically engaged whites who disagree with the pro-quota ruling are less likely to say they will protest against the policy when it is attributed to the Supreme Court. Thus, the Court brings whites into greater behavioral compliance.

We also examine group-centric effects. For both black and white subjects, positive feelings toward black Americans lead to greater support for the quota ruling. At a much more modest level, positive feelings toward whites encourage greater disagreement with it. Moreover, we find that group attitudes moderate the effect of the Court's ruling for our white subjects. Whites who dislike blacks are not moved by the Supreme Court's pronouncement, whereas whites who are warmer toward blacks are more likely to support the policy when it is attributed to the Court.

Aside from the characteristics intrinsic to the individuals "receiving" the Court's message, however, there are other forces that likely moderate the Court's legitimizing effect. In particular, media framing may influence the public's response to a policy articulated by the Court. Studies have shown substantively important differences between the mainstream and black presses (Wolseley 1990). Do these differences affect the presses' coverage of the Supreme Court, and, if so, do the differences affect the Court's legitimizing capacity? In Chapters 4 and 5, we turn our attention to these points.

4

Different Presses,
Different Frames

Black and Mainstream Press Coverage
of a Supreme Court Decision

The U.S. Supreme Court carefully protects its image as an apolitical guardian of the Constitution. Steeped in tradition and rigidly controlling its exposure to the press and the public, the Court perpetuates the myth that it is the sole institution empowered to protect and interpret that sacred text. This is a double-edged sword. On one hand, the Court's image-protecting silence certainly contributes to its remarkably stable and high levels of abstract mass approval (Marshall 1989; Mondak and Smithey 1997), and this in turn amplifies its relatively greater ability to dress policies in the cloak of legitimacy (see Chapter 3 as well as Gibson 1989; Hoekstra 1995; Hoekstra and Segal 1996; Mondak 1990, 1991, 1992, 1994). On the other hand, that the Court actively engages neither the press nor the public renders its articulation of policy vulnerable to the framing effects of interested parties.

Framing is ubiquitous in the American political system (Gamson 1992; Nelson and Kinder 1996). When policies are articulated, interested elites attempt to cast the relevant issue in terms most favorable to their own objectives. Obviously, the battle of frames takes place among the elites, but it is the attitudes of the general citizenry that are the target of this contest. Frames are "storylines" that tell the public what the essence of the issue is and what the controversy is about; in short, they are *constructions* of the issue (Entman 1993; Gamson and Lasch 1983; Gamson and Modigliani 1987; Iyengar 1991; Kellstedt 2000; Nelson, Clawson, and Oxley 1997; Pan and Kosicki 1993). "Elites wage a war of frames because they know that if their frame becomes the dominant way of thinking about a particular problem, then the battle for public opinion has been won" (Nelson and Kinder 1996, 1058).

Nelson and Kinder (1996) note that this "war of frames" takes place in a variety of theaters—editorials, columns, political talk shows, the coverage of daily events in newspapers, on television, or in radio broadcasts, and, most directly for policy makers, speeches, debates, and press conferences. The Court, however, does not use these direct avenues. Indeed, where other policy makers (e.g., members of Congress, the president, governors) actively attempt to shape public opinion, the Court largely abandons the field, leaving it to others to frame its decisions for the mass public. Consequently, the press and television play an especially pronounced role in influencing public knowledge about the Court's articulation of policy (Franklin and Kosaki 1995).

Oddly, few published studies have systematically examined the media's role in shaping public attitudes regarding the Court's policies. Existing studies have shown that the media's coverage of the Court is qualitatively different from its coverage of the presidency and Congress. Reporting on the Court is more selective and episodic (Graber 1993), with little or no effort to reexamine an issue at a later date to determine whether or not the "landmark decision" actually had the consequences projected for it (Shaw 1981). Often the coverage leaves the public with an incomplete or skewed image of the Court's business. For one thing, the media concentrate on civil rights and First Amendment questions (Franklin and Kosaki 1995; O'Callaghan and Dukes 1992). For another, coverage tends to be result-oriented, focusing on the winners and losers in a given case rather than providing information on the broad issues underlying it or paying appropriate attention to the role of the judiciary in the political process more generally (Shaw 1981). And, finally, television reporting in particular (the primary source of the public's knowledge of the Court and its business) tends to be wrong. In no small part this is a consequence of oversimplified coverage of the Court, which leads to misplaced emphases on certain types of Court outputs and inaccurate reporting of Court actions. For example, Slotnick and Segal (1998) find that Court denials of *certiorari* are often described as instances of the Court's *upholding* a lower court ruling, suggesting that the Court had reached a decision on the merits of the case, when in fact it had done no such thing.

At the same time, there are tantalizing suggestions that the media frame the Court's policies. Davis (1994) finds that litigating parties engage the media assigned to the Court in the hope of drawing attention to their position (also see Towner, Clawson, and Waltenburg 2006). And it is quite possible that these same media-savvy groups will seek out the press and television to frame the Court's policies, once made, to their own advantage. Caldeira (1986) notes that the people who pay the most attention to the Court are also most likely to regard it as apolitical in its decision-making. He speculates that this is the result of media framing. Gibson, Caldeira, and Baird (1998) go further, suggesting that the media's portrayal of the courts (including the U.S. Supreme Court) contributes to the generally high esteem in which the public holds the judiciary. As they put it, "To know the courts is to love them, because to know them is to be exposed to a series of legitimizing messages focused on the symbols of justice, judicial objectivity, and impartiality" (345). In short, mainstream media coverage of the Court and its decisions tends to emphasize the view that the justices rely heavily on the law, original intent, literal meaning, and precedent, as opposed to their own values, when they render their decisions. Since public knowledge about the Court is largely determined by the press, it stands to reason that those who are most knowledgeable are influenced by the apolitical frame (on this point, see Casey 1974; Murphy and Tanenhaus 1968; Murphy, Tanenhaus, and Kastner 1973). Today, however, a wealth of specialized media outlets—electronic and print—are aimed at relatively narrow segments of the American population. And it may well be that not all these media cover (i.e., frame) the Court and its decisions in the same way or to the same effect.

A noteworthy exemplar of the specialized media is the black press.[1] Born in antebellum America, it has been present on the media landscape for well over 150 years. Originally, black journalism was almost totally committed to a cause—abolition. Consequently, it has a long-established pedigree of protest and crusades. Even today, the black press tends to be protest-oriented, editorializing for social causes such as civil rights and integration. At the same time, however, Wolseley (1990) points out that not all black publications are strictly dedicated to crusading for social causes especially significant to African Americans. Like the mainstream press, some black publications have financial profit as their chief goal.

Cause-oriented or not, the black press now exists "primarily to report the news of the black population, . . . to give space to their own and others' opinions on many racially oriented matters, to promote the activities of the society in which they exist, to present advertisers with a billboard or a spoken message, and to be advocates of the black population" (Wolseley 1990, 5–6). In a sense, then, the black press perceives itself as a corrective force, making up for the incidental (and often negative) treatment the mainstream media generally give black and other minority affairs. As Wolseley avers, "readers look to the [black] press to find out 'what really went on' when a news story about blacks breaks" (1990, 198; also see Huspek 2004; Jacobs 2000). As a result, much of the detailed content in the black press is not found elsewhere, even though the story may have been covered in the mainstream media. Indeed, the detailed attention given to the "black angle" is the most dramatic difference between the black press and the mainstream media (Wolseley 1990, 201).

But does the black press frame the Court's decisions differently than the mainstream media? To answer that question, we focus on mainstream and black media coverage of the Supreme Court's 1995 *Adarand v. Pena* decision.[2] Involving affirmative action, the case commanded a relatively substantial amount of public attention among both black and white Americans. Moreover, elites on either side of the affirmative action debate perceived the Court's decision as an important indicator of the policy's legal and political future, and they went to some lengths to cast the Court's decision in terms most favorable to their interests. Thus, we believe *Adarand* is an excellent case for examination.

Although *Adarand* involved a Hispanic rather than an African American litigant, we have chosen to focus on the coverage and framing effects of the black press for several reasons. First, as noted above, the black press has a well-established legacy in American journalism and a long record of concentrating its coverage on racial matters. Second, it is unlikely that the black press would have given *Adarand* short shrift. Because of the historical legacy of discrimination, African Americans are especially sensitive to and supportive of governmental programs promoting affirmative action. Indeed, Kinder and Winter's (2001) data show that 56% of black respondents support hiring preferences for blacks, while only 13% of white respondents do so. Finally, on this specific issue black opinion and Hispanic opinion were quite similar. In an ABC News/*Washington Post* poll administered shortly after the *Adarand* decision was handed down, well over 50 percent of both black and Hispanic respondents disagreed with the ruling.

In the next section we review *Adarand v. Pena* and then turn to a content analysis of the mainstream and black press coverage of the Court's ruling. For the mainstream media, we examine coverage in the *New York Times,* the *Washington Post,* and the *Los Angeles Times.* For the black press, we examine reports in a wide range of newspapers, including the large-circulation *New York Amsterdam News, Philadelphia Tribune,* and *Baltimore Afro-American* and many smaller papers (see Appendix B for a complete list). In the last section we speculate on the effect of the differences we found and offer some concluding remarks.

Adarand Constructors, Inc. v. Pena

Decided in 1995, *Adarand* began as an "ideological cause" case. Earlier that same year, the high court had applied the doctrine of "strict scrutiny"[3] to invalidate a municipal racial set-aside program (see Chapter 2).[4] With that ruling in hand, conservative groups began looking for a case that would present the Court with the opportunity to apply that same standard to federal race-conscious programs. When Randy Pech, owner-operator of Adarand Constructors, lost a guardrail subcontract on a highway project in Colorado, despite making the lowest bid, those groups had their case.

In 1989 the U.S. Department of Transportation awarded the prime contract for a highway construction project through the San Juan National Forest to Mountain Gravel and Construction Company. Mountain Gravel then solicited bids from subcontractors for the guardrail portion of the contract. Under the terms of the federal contract, Mountain Gravel could receive additional compensation if it awarded the subcontracts to "socially or economically disadvantaged" businesses. Gonzales Construction Company was certified as such a business enterprise, and Mountain Gravel awarded the subcontract to Gonzales, despite Adarand's lower bid. Further, Mountain Gravel's chief estimator submitted an affidavit stating that Mountain Gravel would have accepted Adarand's bid had it not been for the additional payment it received by hiring Gonzales instead. Adarand sued, claiming that the federal statute that permitted the subcontracting clause discriminated on the basis of race in violation of the equal protection component of the Fifth Amendment's due process clause, thereby triggering the Court's strict scrutiny test.

Writing for a bare 5–4 majority, Justice Sandra Day O'Connor agreed. "We hold today that all racial classifications, imposed by whatever federal, state, or local governmental actor, must be analyzed by a reviewing court under strict scrutiny. In other words, such classifications are constitutional only if they are narrowly tailored measures that further compelling governmental interests" (515 U.S. 200, 220). Since the lower courts had not examined the facts of the case under this heightened standard of review, the majority ordered the case remanded for further consideration in light of the strict scrutiny test the Court had just announced.[5]

Both sides of the affirmative action debate initially responded to *Adarand* with charged emotion, contending that it marked a "crossing of the Rubicon" for the Court and the nation on racial policies.

The advocates of affirmative action projected *Adarand* as ushering in a period in which the national government would look very much as it did in the late nineteenth and early twentieth centuries: "That is, pretty much without people of color as part of it" (J. Clay Smith, quoted in Coyle 1995, sec. A). Opponents rejoiced. Senator Phil Gramm, for example, hailed the ruling as "a major step toward the end of quotas and set-asides in America and a return to merit as a basis of decision making in America."[6]

These polar views present an excellent opportunity to systematically examine how the Court's *Adarand* policy was constructed by different media outlets. It is to that examination that we now turn.

Media Coverage of *Adarand*

The varying missions and characteristics of the media lead us to suspect that there will be important differences in the way the mainstream press and the black press cover Supreme Court decisions on affirmative action.[7] Using Lexis-Nexis for the *New York Times,* the *Washington Post,* and the *Los Angeles Times* and Ethnic Newswatch for the black press, we downloaded all the stories about the *Adarand* decision that appeared between June 13 and July 31, 1995. The *Los Angeles Times* published 10 articles on the topic, while the *Washington Post* and the *New York Times* each ran 11, for a total of 32 articles; the 22 black newspapers carried 47 relevant articles during the period under investigation.

The selection of our time period, newspaper sources, and content deserves some comment. First, we restricted our analysis to June and July of 1995 because media coverage of *Adarand* tapers off after July, and the stories that mention *Adarand* thereafter are tangential to the actual decision. Second, we compare the coverage of large-circulation, mainstream "papers of record" to a wide variety of black papers (Appendix B). This ensured a large enough number of stories to allow systematic, quantitative analysis. An alternative would have been to compare and contrast the coverage of the mainstream and black newspapers from the same city. A "matched pair" strategy of this sort, however, would not have provided us with the desired quantitative leverage. The Court is covered spottily, and although some large metropolitan newspapers maintain Washington bureaus, many do not have the expertise or resources to cover the arcane pronouncements of the Supreme Court, taking cues instead from the papers we examine. Most importantly, we did compare the coverage of the *Los Angeles Times, New York Times,* and *Washington Post* to their local black counterparts; our findings for this select group are substantially unchanged, bolstering our confidence in the generalizability of our results. Finally, we rely on both news stories and editorials/opinion pieces. They are certainly different vehicles in the mainstream press; however, the distinction is not nearly as clear in the black press. Therefore, we note in the text when the mainstream press's editorials and news stories diverge.

Characteristics

The mainstream media's tendency toward event-oriented coverage is often noted (Martindale, 1986; Shaw 1981). Therefore, we hypothesized that the mainstream press would focus primarily on the content of the Supreme Court ruling and less on its implications, with the issuance of the decision providing the "news peg" for attention to the affirmative action issue. On the other hand, given its role as an advocacy press, the black press should dedicate its coverage to interpreting the implications of the ruling from a black perspective. Thus, we expected the black press to allocate significantly more coverage to a discussion of the implications of the decision rather than to the ruling itself.

Our expectations for the black press are supported by the data. Sixty-two percent of the articles in black newspapers focused on the implications of the Court's decision, while 38% emphasized the ruling itself. This tendency toward addressing a ruling's implications for African Americans was also confirmed in interviews we conducted with black journalists concerning their coverage of the University of Michigan affirmative action cases (Towner, Clawson, and Waltenburg 2006). For example, Sharon Egiebor of the *Dallas Examiner* noted: "Our paper is an African American centered newspaper. . . . And we know that the issues we were reporting on, were (1) very important, period. And (2) it was very important to the people who were making decisions about how this would affect our community. In that sense, it influenced our reporting because we know who can make changes and we want to make sure that they have all the information in which to make the changes" (quoted in Towner, Clawson, and Waltenburg 2006, 125).

Somewhat surprisingly, the mainstream press split its attention almost evenly between the decision (53%) and the implications of that decision (47%). In the aftermath of the ruling, President Clinton ordered a review of federal affirmative action programs, and several articles in the mainstream press discussed the impact of the Court ruling on that review. The black press paid attention to the federal review of programs but also focused on the general Court trend against affirmative action and the impact of this conservative turn on African Americans.

As a general rule, the mainstream newspapers were much more likely than the black press to mention Supreme Court justices in their articles. This reflects the tendency of the mainstream press both to rely on authoritative, official sources (Gans 1979) and to portray the Court as an apolitical interpreter of the Constitution (Caldeira 1986; Gibson, Caldeira, and Baird 1998; Spill and Oxley 2003). Justice O'Connor, the author of the majority opinion, was mentioned (and often quoted) in 59% of the articles in the mainstream press, whereas only 28% of the stories in the black press devoted any coverage to her. This was the pattern for all of the justices except Clarence Thomas (Table 4.1). By concentrating on legalistic terms such as "strict scrutiny," "compelling governmental interests," and the "Constitution's guarantee of equal protection," the mainstream press reinforced the myth that the Court is above politics. Quoting the justices' written opinions has a similar effect. As Gibson, Caldeira, and Baird (1998) point out, the justices take great pains in their opinions to promulgate the view that their rulings are the product of objective "law," not personal values: "When ordinary people hear the judges of the nation's highest court frame their decision in this fashion, they believe the justices' account of why they made the decision" (345).

TABLE 4.1   REFERENCES TO SUPREME COURT JUSTICES
(IN PERCENTAGES)

	Majority				
	O'Connor	Thomas	Scalia	Rehnquist	Kennedy
Mainstream press (*n* = 32 articles)	59	34	34	28	22
Black press (*n* = 47 articles)	28	40	21	19	17

	Minority			
	Ginsburg	Stevens	Souter	Breyer
Mainstream press (*n* = 32 articles)	28	25	22	19
Black press (*n* = 47 articles)	15	15	13	13

Note: Table entries are the percentage of stories that contained at least one reference to a particular Supreme Court Justice.

Not surprisingly, Justice Thomas was a notable exception to this general trend. He was mentioned more often and *extensively criticized* in the black press. A significant number of the stories contained headlines that mentioned Thomas, whereas none of the mainstream articles featured him prominently. Some noteworthy examples: "Justice Thomas Does It to Us Again";[8] "Cong. Owens Calls Clarence Thomas a Danger to African-Americans";[9] "What a Fool Believes: Clarence Thomas and Affirmative Action";[10] "Thomas, An Embarrassment."[11] In the body of the articles, Thomas's actions on the Court were condemned, and black leaders were quoted denouncing him as a sellout and a fool. Here is an example from the *Cleveland Call & Post*:

Thomas has clearly failed to recognize that his Black skin color and affirmative action have played a major role in his life, from his admission to Yale law school, to his appointment to head the EEOC, then on to the U.S. Court of Appeals and the Supreme Court, and that is a disgrace. In a few short years, he has already gained the inside track to go down in history as the man who single handedly derailed Black Americans in their quest for equal employment and economic opportunity.[12]

And an excerpt from the *Sun Reporter*:

> While I realize that ad hominem attacks on people say as much about the source as the target, I find it hard to use anything but four-letter words to describe the Clarence Thomas commentary in Adarand v. Pena. Perhaps it is unseemly to call an Associate Justice of the Supreme Court a fool. Maybe I should call him Justice Fool. Or perhaps, because the man is so exalted and elevated, a simple four-letter, one syllable word does not capture my sense of his nonsense. Does Justice Buffoon strike a more responsive chord? It is a syllable longer, but no less disrespectful than fool. What about Justice Dolt, or Justice Imbecile? I hesitate to call anyone, even Justice Uncle Thomas, a moron, because that buys into the IQ theories that need to be debunked. But a reading of the Thomas words on Adarand suggest that Clarence may be reading a Playboy Magazine that is short a centerfold.[13]

In contrast, when the mainstream press focused on Justice Thomas, it was primarily in the context of his concurring opinion. For example, the *New York Times* explained that Justices Scalia and Thomas wrote opinions calling for the end of affirmative action altogether, and several articles quoted from Thomas's concurring opinion:

> With Thomas casting the fifth and deciding vote on Monday, the court reversed course and took a giant step toward wiping away preferential policies based on race. In a concurring opinion, Thomas denounced affirmative action in the strongest terms. It is a form of "racial paternalism," he wrote, whose "unintended consequences can be as poisonous and pernicious as any other form of discrimination."[14]

The mainstream media rarely made reference to Thomas's race; critics of the ruling focused on the policy, not on the person. The mainstream press primarily considered Justice Thomas newsworthy because of his concurring opinion, not because he was a black justice ruling against the interests of minorities.

Again this tendency is consistent with interview responses from journalists concerning their coverage of the Michigan affirmative action cases, *Gratz* and *Grutter*.[15] For example, Jodi Cohen of the *Chicago Tribune* told us that Thomas was quoted because he wrote an opinion. "He [Thomas] wrote a dissenting opinion if I remember, and I'm pretty sure that I quoted his opinion. I think that we tried to get a quote from every judge [sic] in the story . . . at least every judge that wrote an opinion. . . . We were trying to get all their views across." Sharon Egiebor, editor of the African American *Dallas Examiner,* on the other hand, told us: "We want to know what he [Thomas] thought, how he weighed in on the decision and what his opinion was. *As a black press, it was extremely important to point out Justice Thomas's opinion*" (quoted in Towner, Clawson, and Waltenburg 2006, 126 [emphasis added]).

We also examined which individuals and groups were mentioned in these stories beyond the Supreme Court justices. Here too there are systematic differences between the mainstream and black press. First, mainstream journalists were more likely to balance the use of pro– and anti–affirmative action sources, consistent with the mainstream press's goal of "objectivity," defined as providing two sides to an issue (Bennett 1988; Gans 1979). Sixty-nine percent of the articles that contained a pro–affirmative action voice also contained an anti–affirmative action counterbalance. In other words, the mainstream press tried to provide neutral coverage of the decision by balancing the competing interests. The black press was much more likely to present the pro–affirmative action side, and only 31% of the stories that provided a supportive view also included a less favorable one. This illustrates the priority the black press places on advocacy and presenting the news from a "black angle" rather than emphasizing objectivity as defined by the mainstream media.

Second, the mainstream media and the black press also differed in terms of *which* groups and individuals were considered newsworthy. In the mainstream press, a narrow range of pro–affirmative action sources were cited. President Clinton was mentioned several times, and Jesse Jackson and the NAACP were presented as the minority spokespersons for affirmative action. The black press, on the other hand, mentioned a much wider range of pro–affirmative action sources: Clinton, Jackson, and spokespersons for the NAACP, but also black officials in the Clinton administration, such as Labor Secretary Alexis Herman and Assistant Attorney General for Civil Rights Deval Patrick, and black members of Congress, including Maxine Waters, Donald Payne, Alcee Hastings, Bobby Rush, Major Owens, Carrie Meek, and Kweisi Mfume. The perspectives of a variety of black interest groups, ranging from the Rainbow Coalition to business groups to Colorado contractors, were also presented in our sample of black newspapers.

This emphasis on black sources carried over to the anti–affirmative action side of the argument as well. For example, Congressman J. C. Watts and a conservative black interest group, Project 21, were quoted in the black press. When drawing on white anti–affirmative action sources, however, the black press did not blaze new trails. California Governor Pete Wilson, Senator Bob Dole, and Randy Pech and his lawyers appeared in both black and mainstream stories.

Frames

Turning to a discussion of the frames used by the mainstream and the black press, we borrow from Gamson and Modigliani's (1987) work on affirmative action. They make a distinction between a "No Preferential Treatment" frame (NPT) and a "Remedial Action" frame (RA). The NPT frame presents affirmative action as a policy that provides unfair and undeserved advantages to minorities. From the NPT perspective, "the consideration of race or ethnicity, however benignly motivated, is not the American way" (Gamson and Modigliani 1987, 145).

The RA frame, on the other hand, focuses on affirmative action as a policy that is necessary "to redress the continuing effects of a history of racial discrimination" (Gamson and Modigliani 1987, 148). This frame is constructed around the argument that government is obligated to take steps to help minorities because of the legacy of racism in this country. A basic premise is that "to overcome racism, one must first consider race" (148). Gamson and Modigliani demonstrate that the RA frame was popular during the late 1970s.

After an initial reading of the stories, we determined that many of the articles were framed as a "Dramatic Setback" (DS) to the remedial efforts that had been taking place. This frame presented the Court ruling as a blow to affirmative action. In its most strident forms, it asserted that the decision sounded the death knell for affirmative action policies—and social justice more generally. Implicit, and often explicit, in this frame was the continued need for remedial action. We argue that the DS frame evolved from the RA frame Gamson found during an earlier period: the RA frame justifies affirmative action policies, while the DS frame decries the end of such programs.

In addition to the NPT and DS frames, we identified two other frames that structured stories on the Court ruling. First, several articles presented the argument that even though the Supreme Court had ruled against racial set-asides in this particular case, it had not undermined the basic principle of affirmative action: the "Affirmative Action Is Not Dead" frame (ND). From this perspective, affirmative action programs are still very much alive, and the argument that *Adarand* signals the end of affirmative action should be met with strong resistance. Finally, we identified a "Policy Implementation" (PI) frame that focused on the role of politicians in interpreting and reacting to the Court ruling. This storyline emphasized government efforts to apply the decision to current and future affirmative action programs.[16]

In the analysis that follows, we separate the articles that focused primarily on the ruling itself from those that concentrated on the implications of the ruling, since there are systematic differences in how those stories are framed. We turn first to an examination of stories about the Court's decision.

TABLE 4.2   FRAMES: ARTICLES FOCUSING ON
THE SUPREME COURT RULING (IN PERCENTAGES)

	No Preferential Treatment	Dramatic Setback	Policy Implementation	Affirmative Action Is Not Dead
Mainstream press (*n* = 17 articles)	65	24	6	6
Black press (*n* = 18 articles)	22	67	0	11

Note: Table entries are the percentage of stories representing each frame.

Because of its general role as an advocate, we hypothesized that the black press would focus more on the DS frame and much less on the NPT frame than the mainstream media. Our content analysis provides support for that hypothesis (Table 4.2). Sixty-five percent of the mainstream articles that focused on the Supreme Court ruling relied on the NPT frame, whereas only 22% of the black press used it. Also consistent with our expectations, the black press framed the decision in DS terms in 67% of its articles, compared with 24% of the mainstream stories (almost all of which were editorials or opinion pieces).

As for articles that focused on the implications of the decision, 87% of the mainstream stories concentrated on the PI frame (see Table 4.3), centering primarily on the Clinton administration's review of federal affirmative action programs. In contrast, there was much more variety among the articles in the black press. The DS

TABLE 4.3   FRAMES: ARTICLES FOCUSING ON THE IMPLICATIONS
OF THE SUPREME COURT RULING (IN PERCENTAGES)

	No Preferential Treatment	Dramatic Setback	Policy Implementation	Affirmative Action Is Not Dead
Mainstream press (*n* = 15 articles)	0	7	87	7
Black press (*n* = 29 articles)	0	38	21	41

Note: Table entries are the percentage of stories representing each frame.

frame was present (38%), along with some attention to the PI story-line (21%). Forty-one percent of the stories in the black press put forth the ND argument. These articles asserted two general themes: all is not lost, and the civil rights community must aggressively defend affirmative action. Proponents cannot roll over; they need to go out and make the case for the continuation of race-conscious policies (see Table 4.4 for examples of framing).

Conclusion

It is clear that the mainstream press and the black press covered the *Adarand v. Pena* decision in significantly different ways. As an advo-cate for black interests, the black press focused on the implications of the ruling for minorities, criticized Justice Thomas, and empha-sized pro–affirmative action sources. In addition, by relying on a Dramatic Setback frame, the black press stressed the detrimental effects of the ruling on black citizens. It also devoted significant attention to arguing that the Court's decision *was* consistent with the basic principle of affirmative action, and therefore affirmative action was still the law of the land. It seems possible that the black press used both of these frames—Dramatic Setback and Affirmative Action Is Not Dead—in an effort to "rally the troops" to defend affirmative action and prevent the Clinton administration from abandoning race-conscious policies. As Owens argues (1996), black newspapers are "weapons of the African American elite in the war of cultural symbols and politics" (97).

On the other hand, the mainstream press's use of legalistic and constitutional concepts reinforces the image of the Supreme Court as an apolitical institution. And this extends to its discussion of indi-vidual justices. Thus, where the black press was openly critical of Justice Thomas's ruling, the mainstream press presented it largely without comment, choosing merely to quote from his concurring opinion. And even though mainstream media coverage of black candidates often focuses on their race (Jeffries 2000; Reeves 1997), the mainstream papers did not emphasize Thomas's race. Campaigns are obviously political activities, and the racial identification of a

TABLE 4.4   EXAMPLES OF FRAMES

No Preferential Treatment

"The Constitution protects persons, not groups," wrote Justice Sandra Day O'Connor for the court. "Whenever the government treats any person unequally because of his or her race, that person has suffered an injury that falls squarely with the language and spirit of the Constitution's guarantee of equal protection," she said.

David G. Savage, "High Court Deals Severe Blow to Federal Affirmative Action Rights: Justices Hold That Race-Based Preferential Treatment Is Almost Always Unconstitutional. But An Opening Is Left for Narrow, Specific Bias Remedies," *Los Angeles Times,* June 13, 1995, sec. A.

Dramatic Setback

A dark shadow was cast this week across long standing efforts to overcome at least some of the effects of centuries of discrimination and segregation practiced against African-Americans when the U.S. Supreme Court handed down rulings, in two landmark racial cases. The first, and potentially the most damaging was the 5–4 decision in the Adarand Constructors v. Pena case, which hinged on whether the federal government could legally conceive and implement a program offering inducements to major contractors to employ minority and female subcontractors on federally funded projects. The rationale was that such a program would provide contracting opportunities for those segments of the society—meaning African-Americans, other minorities and women—who had previously been excluded from such opportunities.

"The Court and Affirmative Action," *Baltimore Afro-American,* June 17, 1995, sec. A.

Policy Implementation

A Justice Department analysis of the recent Supreme Court ruling on affirmative action concludes that the government will have a hard time defending its many programs that steer contracts to racial and ethnic minorities. Officials must "have some particularized evidence" of prior discrimination against these groups in particular industries, said Assistant Atty. Gen. Walter Dellinger in a report distributed to top government lawyers.

David G. Savage and Ronald J. Ostrow, "Ruling Will Hurt U.S. Anti-Bias Programs, Report Says," *Los Angeles Times,* June 29, 1995, sec. A.

Affirmative Action Not Dead

Amidst the apparent onslaught on affirmative action, Patrick, the nation's top civil rights official, expressed confidence that the programs will remain intact. "I think people who say Adarand is sounding the death knell of affirmative action haven't read Adarand, because that's not what Adarand said," Patrick commented in an interview with the Banner.

Yawu Miller, "Affirmative Action Is Still On," *Bay State Banner,* June 29, 1995.

black candidate is therefore considered relevant by the mainstream press. In contrast, a racial focus would not square with the mainstream newspapers' approach to covering the Court. To maintain the myth that the Supreme Court is the apolitical guardian of the Constitution, mainstream papers must ignore the role that race plays in judicial decision-making.

The mainstream press also largely relied on the Policy Implementation frame when examining the implications of the ruling, and this is consistent with the tendency for its coverage to be event-oriented. *Adarand* gave new energy and timeliness to the Clinton administration's review of federal affirmative action programs, and the mainstream press simply followed this story. Finally, although the mainstream press balanced pro– and anti–affirmative action sources, it framed the Court's decision in terms of reverse discrimination—a frame that has clear implications for public support for affirmative action (Kinder and Sanders 1996; Nelson and Kinder 1996). The mainstream press does not bill itself as an advocacy press (as the black press does); nevertheless, its framing of this Supreme Court decision was no more neutral or impartial than that of the black press. This raises important questions concerning the Court's legitimizing capacity.

As we documented in Chapter 3, the Court has a relatively greater capacity than other political institutions to throw the cloak of legitimacy over a policy—among both black and white citizens. But does the differential framing of the Court's policy pronouncements affect this legitimizing ability? If so, then the greater tendency of the black press to frame *Adarand* as a setback to racial equality could have profound effects on black support for the ruling. Similarly, the much greater emphasis on affirmative action as reverse discrimination in the mainstream press may explain white opposition to the policy.[17] In the next chapter, we present the results of an experiment that explores these hypotheses.

5

Media Framing and the Supreme Court's Legitimizing Capacity

As Chapter 2 makes clear, when it comes to black Americans' political and legal interests, no institution in American government has bored with a larger auger than the Supreme Court. It was instrumental in black Americans' full realization of their right to vote. Its decisions in the 1950s and 1960s razed state-sanctioned apartheid. And its chamber has been the battleground on which fierce contests over civil rights and affirmative action policies have been waged. Yet despite its substantial impact on racial matters, the Court is in a remarkably weak position when it comes to constructing or "framing" the way in which the public understands its articulation of policy. Where other policy makers use speeches, debates, press conferences, and the media to shape public opinion, the Court does no such thing. It is the Teddy Roosevelt of policy-making institutions—speaking softly and carrying a very big stick.

This does not mean that the Court's policies go unframed. Rather, its silence leaves the articulation of its policy vulnerable to the framing of others. And here the media play an especially influential role because they are the main sources of public knowledge about the Court and its policy pronouncements (Caldeira 1986; Franklin and Kosaki 1995). Consequently, the media's construction of the Court and its decisions may well shape public opinion about the institution's policies. In Chapter 4 we found systematic differences in the mainstream and black presses' coverage of a Supreme Court decision on affirmative action, and this is a significant phenomenon indeed. Using the National Black Politics Study (NBPS), Dawson (2001) reports high rates of exposure to black media sources among African Americans. Better than 50% of the NBPS respondents are weekly readers of a black newspaper, and over three-quarters of them listen to black news programs on the radio. With the black and mainstream presses framing the Court's articulation of a policy so differently, it is possible that the Court's legitimizing capacity is affected. It is that prospect on which we focus our attention in this chapter. More specifically: do differences in media framing affect public support for a Supreme Court ruling?

To answer that question, we conducted an experiment, using as our stimulus the different frames associated with the Court's *Adarand v. Pena*[1] decision that we identified in Chapter 4. Our results are compelling. The different media constructions of the decision had clear consequences for the levels of support for the Court's policy pronouncement, but those consequences are not uniform for whites and blacks. White subjects evinced the most marked media framing effects. Specifically, when the decision was framed as an instance of rejecting affirmative action because it is inconsistent with basic constitutional principles of equality before the law, white subjects had significantly greater levels of support for the anti–affirmative action ruling. But when the framing emphasized the practical political consequences of the decision, calling attention to the harm the ruling would cause to black attempts to gain equality, whites had less support for it. Black subjects' attitudes are more resistant to media framing effects; instead, individual predispositions, attitudes, and characteristics are the driving forces. This is not to say, however, that press constructions had no effect on black subjects. The different depictions of Justice Clarence Thomas in the black and mainstream presses had a substantial impact on blacks' evaluation of the Court's ruling.

In the next section, we review the different frames in the black and mainstream press coverage of the 1995 *Adarand* decision as well as the specific hypotheses concerning the Court's legitimizing capacity growing out of those different frames. Then we discuss our experimental design and present our results in detail. We conclude this chapter with some general comments and observations on the possible effects of media frames on support for the Court's decisions.

Adarand v. Pena: Frames and Hypotheses

The content analysis we performed in the previous chapter uncovered two principal frames for the issue, as well as appreciable differences in the presses' treatment of Justice Thomas. To structure its coverage of the *Adarand* ruling, the mainstream press typically used an anti–affirmative action "No Preferential Treatment" (NPT) frame, which described affirmative action as reverse discrimination. In contrast, the black press invoked a "Dramatic Setback" (DS) frame, which decried the Court's attack on race-conscious programs. The two presses were no less different in their treatment of Justice Thomas. The mainstream press paid attention to his concurring opinion, not his status as a black justice who voted against black interests. The black press, on the other hand, both focused on Thomas as a black justice and mentioned him far more often than any of his colleagues on the Court. Moreover, this attention was not at all flattering. Many references to Thomas were ad hominem attacks, and story after story criticized his role in undermining the cause of social justice.

We suspected that these differences in coverage would have an effect on public opinion.[2] Existing research on the presentation of racial topics and racial images in the media demonstrates the power of the media to affect public attitudes in this arena (Davis and Davenport 1997; Gilliam and Iyengar 2000; Peffley, Shields, and Williams 1996). This media effect, in turn, likely has consequences for the Court's ability to legitimize a policy. Stoker's (1998) analysis shows quite convincingly that the manner in which an affirmative action policy is described has an impact on both the level of support for the policy and which factors drive that support. Essentially, the mainstream and black press provide two very different descriptions and justifications for race-conscious policies, which led us to expect that citizens would react differently to these media frames.

The mainstream press's use of the NPT frame, with its characterization of affirmative action as an instance of reverse discrimination, emphasizes aspects of the issue that make it difficult to support such a program. This construction of the Court's decision as moving the nation closer to a color-blind Constitution is appealing to a lot of citizens. Moreover, the mainstream press's tendency to portray the Court as the apolitical guardian of the Constitution (Caldeira 1986) might well amplify these attitudes. Racial equality and social justice defenses of affirmative action might be enervated by the Court's declaration, cast as an apolitical pronouncement, that all governmentally designed racial classifications are suspect (see Mondak 1990 for the effects of source credibility).

The black press's open criticism of the *Adarand* decision and Justice Thomas, however, should cut directly into our subjects' levels of specific support—transient feelings concerning the Court's rulings (see Caldeira and Gibson 1992). The essence of specific support is whether a person is or is not satisfied with the outputs of an institution. Thus, when those outputs are openly and roundly criticized, we would expect their support to drop (Zaller 1992). Moreover, we suspected that the particular frame used by the black press would amplify this effect. In this case, the black press's DS frame might equip our subjects with arguments invoking racial justice and equality to counter the Court's policy (again see Mondak 1990).

Our expectations concerning the effects of these frames stemmed from our understanding of how citizens process political information. When people form opinions on political issues, they attend to unique information presented in a particular political context *and* they rely on longstanding predispositions (Marcus et al. 1995; Zaller 1992). For example, when citizens are exposed to media coverage of a Supreme Court ruling, they draw upon media frames to help them make sense of the Court's often complex decisions. The media frames establish which aspects of a political issue are most important when evaluating the Supreme Court's ruling, cutting to the heart of the matter and defining the essence of the decision. At the same time, citizens are not simply sponges passively absorbing the media's construction; longstanding attitudes, group-based sentiments, ideology, and values shape their political judgments. Media frames, however, also play a role in determining which existing predispositions seem most relevant to the situation at hand (Nelson, Clawson, and Oxley 1997). As Nelson and Kinder argue, "frames alter the *weight* or *importance* attributed to certain considerations (such as group attitudes) while making other, equally accessible ideas seem less consequential" (1996, 1073 [emphasis in original]).

Therefore, we hypothesized that citizens would have more support for the Court's policy pronouncement and be inclined to implement that policy more quickly when the Court's decision was given the NPT frame, which emphasizes apolitical, legalistic language, rather than the more political DS frame, with its emphasis on the negative practical consequences of the ruling. In addition, we expected that articles including criticisms of Justice Thomas would lower public support for the ruling and dampen enthusiasm for its speedy implementation. In other words, we thought that the mainstream press's coverage of the decision would increase support for the Court's ruling, while the black press's coverage would inhibit it.

In addition to the media frames' effect on the level of support for the Court's ruling, we also investigated whether the framing influenced the ingredients of public opinion (Kinder and Sanders 1996; Nelson, Clawson, and Oxley 1997; Nelson, Oxley, and Clawson 1997; Stoker 1998). Because of the NPT frame's emphasis on individual over group rights, we hypothesized that endorsement of economic individualism—that is, the belief that those who get ahead work harder than those who do not—would have a stronger effect on support for the Court ruling when it was framed in this manner. Indeed, Kinder and Sanders (1996) found that individualism is a stronger predictor of affirmative action opinion when the policy is framed as reverse discrimination against whites rather than as giving blacks unfair advantages.

When the ruling was framed as a Dramatic Setback, we expected racial resentment to be the driving force behind citizens' opinions.

Kinder and Sanders (1996, 106) argue that racial resentment is based on the belief that "blacks do not try hard enough to overcome the difficulties they face and that they take what they have not earned." By concentrating on the detrimental effects of the ruling on the black community and highlighting the ways in which this ruling undermines the longstanding struggles of the civil rights movement, this frame puts the focus squarely on black citizens. Thus, it encourages citizens to put more weight on their resentment of blacks (or lack thereof) as they form their opinion on the Supreme Court ruling.

We also had to consider whether blacks and whites would react similarly to these media frames. On the one hand, it was quite possible that blacks would not be moved by the different media constructions of the ruling. Many blacks care deeply about affirmative action and attach great importance to it. Consequently, they are likely to have a great deal of accurate information about the topic, allowing them to counterargue effectively when presented with the NPT frame (Boninger, Krosnick, and Berent 1995). Media framing, therefore, may not appreciably affect black attitudes toward the Supreme Court's ruling against affirmative action. Indeed, Gilliam and Iyengar's (2000) research on the impact of racialized crime stories on public opinion indicates that blacks, unlike whites, are not influenced by such media coverage. On the other hand, research by Davis and Davenport (1997) suggests that certain provocative images and themes in the media have the capacity to transform political attitudes and behavior. Specifically, they found that blacks became more racially conscious and concerned about race relations after viewing the film *Malcolm X* and a related CBS documentary.

As for the effect on black attitudes of the attack on Justice Thomas, we must take into account intra-group variation. Although blacks are often discussed as a monolithic group, there are certainly important within-group differences. For example, Davis and Davenport (1997) found that younger African Americans were particularly influenced by media coverage of *Malcolm X*. In the case of our analysis, we thought that it was likely that black ideology would be an important factor shaping public reaction to attacks on Justice Thomas in the media. Thomas stands out, particularly among the black elite, because of his conservative views and his willingness to complain about mistreatment at the hands of other (liberal) members of the black elite. As Zaller (1992) argues, people tend to reject messages that are inconsistent with their predispositions, assuming that they recognize the inconsistency. Thomas (and the criticism of him) is a powerful cue that helps blacks sort out how they should respond to the Supreme Court ruling. Thus, while the attack on Thomas might reinforce and amplify liberal blacks' opposition to the ruling against affirmative action, black conservatives might react quite differently. Black conservatives are aware that their views are out of step with much of the black community, and thus will be sensitive to criticism of one of their own. Dawson (2001), for example, argues that "black conservatives believe they pay a personal cost because their leaders are continually castigated by the rest of the black community" (295). Therefore, the attack on Thomas might only strengthen black conservatives' support for the anti–affirmative action Court decision.[3]

Research Design

In this study, we performed an experimental analysis on black and white subjects separately. From a theoretical standpoint, this makes sense, given the groups' often extensive differences of opinion, especially on race-related issues (Gilliam and Iyengar 2000; Kinder and Winter 2001). From a practical perspective, non-whites (including only a couple of black students) made up less than 8% of the students enrolled in the introductory American government classes from which we recruited our white subjects. Thus, we used a different method, discussed below, to find black subjects.

We recruited white students enrolled in introductory American government courses at Purdue University during the spring of 2001 to participate in our experiment ($N = 146$). The subjects were informed that we were conducting a study of how citizens gather information about politics from the news media. They were asked to read a "newspaper article" and then complete a questionnaire. The experimental manipulations were embedded in the newspaper article. We manipulated the media frame (NPT versus DS) and whether the article included an attack on Justice Clarence Thomas by a black member of Congress (Attack versus No Attack). Students were randomly assigned to one of the four conditions. The experimental stimuli are presented in Appendix C. The newspaper article was designed to look as if it had been cut out of the *New York Times* and copied for the subjects' perusal.

As we noted in Chapter 3, although it is quite easy to recruit white students for political science experiments simply by going into college classrooms, the small number of black students on campus makes it much more difficult to collect data on black attitudes in this way. Thus, we employed a recruitment strategy similar to the one we used in our legitimizing experiment. We advertised widely across campus, offering $10 to African American students for participation in a "study of political attitudes." Through advertising and word of mouth, we were able to recruit 137 black subjects for our experiment between November 26 and December 3, 2001. Subjects reported to the Department of Political Science lounge to read the newspaper article and complete the survey. As with the white sample, the black subjects were told that we were conducting a study of how citizens gather information about politics from the news media. The experimental stimulus was identical to the one used in the study conducted in the introductory American government classes (see Appendix C).[4] Upon completion of the survey, subjects were paid and asked to sign a log indicating that they had received the payment.

Although the use of an experimental research design gives us appreciable leverage for establishing causal relationships (see Chapter 3 as well as Aronson et al. 1990; Kinder and Palfrey 1993), we are mindful that this leverage comes with a price—the use of unrepresentative samples, with deleterious effect upon the generalizability of the results. Specifically, our experiments were conducted on convenience samples of college students, and therefore they are not representative of the nation as a whole. Neither, however, are they homogeneous (Sears 1986).

As we did in Chapter 3, we compare demographic and political characteristics of our participants with white respondents in the 2000

TABLE 5.1   DEMOGRAPHIC AND POLITICAL CHARACTERISTICS
OF PARTICIPANTS: MEDIA FRAMING STUDY

	2001 Black Participants (N = 137)	1996 NBES (N = 1,216)	2001 White Participants (N = 146)	2000 NES White Respondents (N = 1,393)
Sex				
Male	50%	36%	60%	44%
Female	50	64	40	56
Median age	20	37	21	46
Median income	$41,000–60,000	$25,000–30,000	$61,000–80,000	$50,000–64,999
Education				
Less than high school		13%		8%
High school		28		27
Some college	93%	39	99%	30
College graduate or more	7	21	1	34
Party identification				
1 = Strong Democrat	23%	49%	3%	16%
2	36	21	11	14
3	20	15	17	14
4 = Independent	17	7	20	12
5	2	4	20	14
6	2	2	20	15
7 = Strong Republican	1	2	9	15
Interest				
1 = Not interested	4%	24%	7%	14%
2	2		11	
3	10		15	25
4 = Somewhat interested	37	45	24	
5	31		23	38
6	10		15	
7 = Very interested	5	31	5	23

Note: The National Election Study (NES) and the National Black Election Study (NBES) use a branching and fully labeled measure of party identification. Our measure was a 7-point scale labeled at its midpoint and endpoints. The NES measures political interest on a fully labeled 4-point scale, while our interest item was a 7-point scale labeled at its midpoint and endpoints. The NBES does not include a general interest in politics question, but does contain an item measuring interest in political campaigns on a 3-point scale. Because of rounding, numbers may not sum to 100%.

National Election Study (NES) and black respondents in the 1996
National Black Election Study (NBES). Both samples differ from the
national populations in predictable ways: our participants are younger,
wealthier, and better educated (Table 5.1). There are more males in
our white sample than the national average, which is not surprising,

given the demographic makeup of undergraduates at Purdue University. Our white subjects are less likely to be Democrats and more likely to be Independent or Republican than the national sample, but in terms of political interest, the two groups are fairly similar. This is not the case for the black sample, who tend to be more interested in politics than the NBES sample. As is true of the general public, very few of our black subjects are Republicans, yet they are not as strongly committed to the Democratic party as a representative sample of black citizens. If we compare across the student samples, the median income of the black subjects is lower than that of their white counterparts, and there are more graduate students and first-year students in the black sample. Blacks are much more Democratic than whites and are more interested in politics—an even more striking difference given that the white students were enrolled in political science classes while the black students were drawn from across campus.

After reading the newspaper article, subjects completed a survey that included a variety of questions about their political attitudes. They were asked to indicate their specific support for the Supreme Court ruling by placing themselves on a 5-point scale ranging from "strongly disagree" to "strongly agree." Subjects also provided their opinion on how quickly the decision should be implemented, using a 4-point scale ranging from "very slowly" to "very quickly" (Appendix D).

Subjects were exposed to articles reflecting either the DS frame (0) or the NPT frame (1). Similarly, the articles either contained an attack on Justice Clarence Thomas (0) or did not include an attack on Thomas (1). The combination of these two conditions was represented by multiplying the individual items to create a Frame by Attack interaction term.

Other variables of interest include diffuse support, racial resentment, individualism, ideology, political interest, and sex. Diffuse support for the Supreme Court was measured using the five questions developed by Caldeira and Gibson (1992; see also Gibson and Caldeira 1992). The diffuse support scale was created by taking a mean of those items; a high number represents greater support for the Court.[5] Racial resentment was measured with four questions asking about "symbolic" predispositions toward blacks (Kinder and Sanders 1996; Kinder and Sears 1981). The racial resentment scale was created by taking a mean of those four items, with higher numbers indicating more racial resentment.[6] The individualism scale was constructed by taking a mean of three items that tap into respondents' endorsement of economic individualism—that is, the "pull yourself up by your own bootstraps" way of seeing the world (Feldman 1983; Kinder and Sanders 1996). A high number represents more individualistic thinking. To test whether the ingredients of opinion are affected by media frames, we created two interaction terms (Frame by Racial Resentment and Frame by Individualism) by multiplying the individual variables. Ideology was measured on a 7-point scale, with high scores indicating more conservative views. Each of these independent variables was recoded on a 0 to 1 scale. Finally, we also control for sex in our analysis: "female" is coded as a 0 and "male" as a 1. (See Appendix D for the wording of the questions.)

Research Findings: Blacks

Because of the nature of our dependent variables, we estimated our models with an ordered logit. Each model includes the two dummy variables representing the experimental manipulations and an interaction term of those dummy variables. In addition, we controlled for racial resentment, individualism, ideology, and sex. We begin our analysis by examining the impact of our experimental manipulations on specific support for the *Adarand* decision among black Americans. The results are displayed in the first column of Table 5.2. Here we see that neither the media frame nor the attack on Justice Thomas influences black Americans' opinion on the ruling; instead, black opinion is driven primarily by racial resentment and sex. That is, blacks who are more resentful toward their own race are more supportive of the ruling against affirmative action, as are black males. It appears, then, that media framing of a Court decision is not provocative enough to affect what are likely well-anchored black attitudes on such a salient issue. Instead, blacks fall back on what is in essence a standing decision when evaluating the Court's

TABLE 5.2 EXPLAINING BLACK SUPPORT FOR THE
SUPREME COURT RULING AGAINST AFFIRMATIVE ACTION

	Black Support for Supreme Court Ruling					
	Full Sample		Liberals		Moderates and Conservatives	
No Preferential Treatment frame	.08	(.44)	.10	(.72)	.07	(.57)
No attack on Justice Thomas	16	(.49)	1.21	(.82)	−.59	(.63)
Frame by Attack	−.16	(.65)	−1.54	(1.09)	.78	(.85)
Racial resentment	3.54***	(1.02)	5.80**	(1.82)	2.43*	(1.25)
Individualism	−.09	(1.14)	.60	(2.13)	−.54	(1.40)
Ideology	.13	(.94)	—		—	
Male	.81***	(.33)	.20	(.53)	1.40***	(.45)
N	137		55		82	
Log likelihood	−172.04		−64.51		−101.49	
χ²	12.01		16.99		15.86	
Pseudo *R*²	.06		.12		.07	
Cut 1	−.28	(.74)	.68	(1.13)	−.97	(.87)
Cut 2	2.24	(.77)	3.39	(1.23)	1.71	(.90)
Cut 3	3.44	(.80)	4.62	(1.30)	3.01	(.93)
Cut 4	5.78	(.97)	7.23	(1.66)	5.31	(1.15)

Note: Table entries are ordered logit regression coefficients with standard errors in parentheses. One-tailed significance tests: *p ≤ .05; **p ≤ .01; ***p ≤ .001.

policy pronouncement (see Franklin and Kosaki 1989; Hoekstra and Segal 1996).

This, however, is not the end of the story. Although the attack on Thomas does not have a uniform effect across our black subjects, this manipulation does have an effect on black support for the policy that varies with the subject's ideology (see columns 2 and 3 of Table 5.2). For liberal blacks, an attack on Thomas lowers support for the Court's anti–affirmative action ruling (although the coefficient just misses traditional levels of statistical significance).[7] It does not, however, influence the attitudes of moderate and conservative blacks.[8] Finally, we investigated whether the framing of the Court's decision influences the *ingredients* of black support for the ruling. We found no evidence that the different media frames altered the considerations blacks used to evaluate the ruling.[9]

In Table 5.3 we examine black attitudes toward the implementation of the Supreme Court ruling. To measure these attitudes, we asked how quickly the federal government should end programs that classify people by race. Again we see that the experimental effects are moderated by blacks' ideological leanings.[10] Among moderate and conservative blacks, the NPT frame leads citizens to be more supportive of the ruling against affirmative action. The mainstream press's portrayal of the Court's ruling as the edict of apolitical guardians of the Constitution appears to bolster support for quickly implementing

TABLE 5.3   EXPLAINING BLACK SUPPORT FOR THE
IMPLEMENTATION OF THE SUPREME COURT RULING

	Black Support for Implementation					
	Full Sample		Liberals		Moderates and Conservatives	
No Preferential Treatment frame	.41	(.44)	−.50	(.73)	.95*	(56)
No attack on Justice Thomas	−.40	(.48)	−1.18	(.78)	−.12	(.63)
Frame by Attack	−.73	(.66)	.91	(1.08)	−1.54*	(.87)
Racial resentment	3.24***	(1.03)	5.02**	(1.72)	2.62*	(1.31)
Individualism	−.71	(1.17)	−3.49	(2.21)	.42	(1.42)
Ideology	.72	(.95)	—		—	
Male	.13	(.32)	−.51	(.53)	.50	(.42)
N	137		55		82	
Log likelihood	−160.32		−61.03		−94.92	
χ^2	21.78		14.23		14.78	
Pseudo R^2	.06		.10		.07	
Cut 1	−.14	(1.15)	−1.95	(1.15)	.23	(.81)
Cut 2	1.95	(.75)	.31	(1.12)	2.33	(.85)
Cut 3	3.61	(.81)	1.65	(1.16)	4.26	(.96)

Note: Table entries are ordered logit regression coefficients with standard errors in parentheses. One-tailed significance tests: *$p \le .05$; **$p \le .01$; ***$p \le .001$.

its pronouncement, at least among moderates and conservatives. Even more importantly, there is a significant interaction between the NPT frame and the attack on Justice Thomas. Pulling this interaction term apart shows that black moderates and conservatives react to the attack, particularly in the NPT condition, by advocating *quick* implementation of the anti–affirmative action policy. The harsh criticism of Thomas, coupled with an apolitical portrayal of the Court, spurs moderate and conservative blacks' support for implementation of the decision. On the other hand, the framing manipulation and attack on Thomas do not influence liberal blacks' opinion on timing; instead, liberal blacks fall back on their longstanding views about race, as measured by racial resentment.

Research Findings: Whites

Turning to our white subjects, we estimated models containing the same set of forces as above, with one exception—for white subjects we included a measure of diffuse support (Tables 5.4, 5.5, and 5.6). As presented in Table 5.4, the affirmative action frame had both a substantial and a statistically significant effect on white support for the Court ruling. Exposure to the NPT frame results in greater support. In contrast, calling attention to the harm the ruling does to black attempts to gain equality, as the DS frame does, causes subjects to be less enamored with the ruling. Subjects in the condition that did *not* contain an attack on Justice Thomas were also more likely to favor the ruling. Thus, whites reacted to the attack as liberal blacks did: both groups' support for the anti–affirmative action policy declined.

There was also an interaction between the frame and the attack on Justice Thomas. The interaction term indicates that the combination of the DS frame and the attack leads subjects to be the least supportive of the Court decision. Racial resentment and ideology, two important and longstanding predispositions, also have an effect on agreement with the ruling: conservatives and those who demonstrate higher levels of racial antipathy are more likely to favor the Court

TABLE 5.4   EXPLAINING WHITE SUPPORT FOR THE
SUPREME COURT RULING AGAINST AFFIRMATIVE ACTION

	White Support for Supreme Court Ruling	
No Preferential Treatment frame	1.08*	(.46)
No attack on Justice Thomas	1.35**	(.49)
Frame by Attack	−1.37*	(.68)
Diffuse support for the Court	4.56***	(1.20)
Racial resentment	3.96***	(1.12)
Individualism	1.12	(1.23)
Ideology	1.97*	(.78)
Male	.21	(.35)
N	140	
Log likelihood	−150.34	
χ^2	69.77	
Pseudo R^2	.19	
Cut 1	3.40	(1.25)
Cut 2	5.37	(1.16)
Cut 3	6.72	(1.19)
Cut 4	9.09	(1.33)

Note: Table entries are ordered logit regression coefficients with standard errors in parentheses. One-tailed significance tests: *$p \leq .05$; **$p \leq .01$; ***$p \leq .001$.

opinion against affirmative action. Consistent with recent research (see Hoekstra 2000; Hoekstra and Segal 1996), diffuse support for the Court also leads to greater agreement with the decision.

We are also interested in whether the framing of the decision influences the ingredients of public opinion. In other words, do the media frames elicit particular values or attitudes in the subjects' minds that then shape opinion toward the Court's ruling? As discussed above, we hypothesized that individualism would be a prominent force driving agreement with the decision in the NPT condition. The NPT frame emphasizes that the consideration of race in the allocation of government resources is unconstitutional and in doing so implies that individual effort and hard work, not group membership, should lead to success. We test this proposition by examining the interaction of the framing condition and individualism on support for the Supreme Court ruling against affirmative action. As depicted in Table 5.5, the Frame by Individualism interaction term is statistically significant and substantively important. To illustrate the nature of this interaction effect, we present the analysis separately for each framing condition (see columns 2 and 3 of Table 5.5). In the NPT condition, individualism is a critical factor leading to agreement with the ruling. In sharp contrast, individualism is not related to support for the ruling when it is framed as a Dramatic Setback.

Does racial resentment have a greater effect in the DS condition than in the NPT condition? The interaction term reveals that the impact of subjects' racial animosities is magnified by the DS frame (see column 1 of Table 5.5). Putting the focus on the detrimental effect on blacks makes white citizens' symbolic predispositions about the group more important in their assessment of the ruling (columns 2 and 3). Thus, the media's framing of the Supreme Court's pronouncement influences the weight that citizens give to certain considerations as they form their evaluation of the Court's action. By influencing the mix of ingredients that shape public opinion, the media modify the "recipe" driving public reaction to the Court's rulings.

Finally, Table 5.6 displays the results of the analysis of media effects on the desired speed of policy implementation. We hypothesized that both the media frame and whether the article included an attack on Justice Thomas would influence white opinion concerning the appropriate speed at which the anti–affirmative action policy should be put into effect. Only the attack, however, dampened white enthusiasm for a quick end to federal affirmative action programs. This is directly counter to the finding among moderate and conservative blacks, for whom Thomas-bashing *spurred* support for rapid implementation. In the case of whites, it appears that the tough criticism of Thomas by a black member of Congress may have served as a signal (or perhaps even a wake-up call) that the justice's opinion was not shared by blacks in general, and that there was strong opposition to the Court ruling among blacks. This, in turn, probably raised

TABLE 5.5   EXPLAINING THE INGREDIENTS OF WHITE SUPPORT
FOR THE SUPREME COURT RULING AGAINST AFFIRMATIVE ACTION

	White Support for Supreme Court Ruling					
	Full Sample		No Preferential Treatment		Dramatic Setback	
No Preferential Treatment frame	−1.36	(1.38)	—		—	
No attack on Justice Thomas	1.40**	(.50)	−.01	(.49)	1.30**	(.50)
Frame by attack	−1.43*	(.69)	—		—	
Diffuse support for the Court	4.25***	(1.25)	4.64**	(1.87)	3.99*	(1.71)
Racial resentment	5.96***	(1.54)	1.44	(1.60)	5.71***	(1.57)
Individualism	−1.78	(1.56)	6.43**	(2.21)	−1.48	(1.52)
Ideology	2.13**	(.79)	3.00**	(1.14)	1.43	(1.14)
Male	.31	(.37)	.61	(.53)	−.07	(.52)
Frame by racial resentment	−4.24*	(2.11)	—		—	
Frame by individualism	7.63**	(2.59)	—		—	
N	140		72		68	
Log likelihood	−145.81		−65.48		−79.26	
χ^2	78.84		47.19		30.41	
Pseudo R^2	.21		.27		.16	
Cut 1	2.35	(1.41)	4.17	(1.95)	2.01	(1.70)
Cut 2	4.44	(1.32)	6.49	(1.78)	3.98	(1.61)
Cut 3	5.88	(1.35)	8.17	(1.88)	5.29	(1.64)
Cut 4	8.53	(1.47)	10.94	(2.13)	7.57	(1.80)

Note: Table entries are ordered logit regression coefficients with standard errors in parentheses. One-tailed significance tests: *$p \leqslant .05$; **$p \leqslant .01$; ***$p \leqslant .001$.

doubts about the optimal pace for ending race-conscious programs. Racial resentment and ideology also influenced opinion on implementation, with more resentful and conservative subjects indicating support for quickly eliminating affirmative action programs. Neither the frames nor the manipulation involving Thomas affected the ingredients of attitudes toward implementation.[11]

TABLE 5.6   EXPLAINING WHITE SUPPORT FOR THE
IMPLEMENTATION OF THE SUPREME COURT RULING

	White Support for Implementation	
No Preferential Treatment frame	.37	(.46)
No attack on Justice Thomas	.89*	(.48)
Frame by Attack	−.39	(.67)
Diffuse support for the Court	.41	(1.12)
Racial resentment	3.28***	(1.06)
Individualism	−1.25	(1.20)
Ideology	2.29***	(.78)
Male	.54	(.36)
N	140	
Log likelihood	−135.34	
χ^2	36.59	
Pseudo R^2	.12	
Cut 1	−1.39	(1.22)
Cut 2	2.46	(1.04)
Cut 3	5.05	(1.12)

Note: Table entries are ordered logit regression coefficients with standard errors in parentheses. One-tailed significance tests: $*p \leq .05$; $**p \leq .01$; $***p \leq .001$.

Discussion and Conclusions

Several of our findings deserve additional comment. First, how the press frames a policy clearly has a profound impact on the level of support for that policy. The mainstream press's NPT construction, with its apolitical and legalistic presentation, led to greater levels of support, whereas the black press's open criticism of the ruling reduced support among white subjects. This would be a rather intuitive finding, except for the fact that the effect of the media frame is present even when the policy in question is articulated by a source with the credibility of the Supreme Court. Mondak (1990) has demonstrated that the high levels of credibility enjoyed by the Court contribute substantially to its ability to confer legitimacy on a policy. Our results indicate, however, that this conclusion should be partially modified: the effect of the Court's credibility on support for its policy outputs is moderated by the manner in which those outputs are constructed. Stoutenborough, Haider-Markel, and Allen (2006) draw a similar conclusion in their analysis of public opinion in the wake of the Court's *Lawrence v. Texas* decision.[12] They write that *Lawrence* had a negative effect on public opinion toward homosexual relations "because media coverage of the decision turned negative and provided mixed signals about the Court's position by highlighting Justice Scalia's dissenting opinion" (2006, 431).

This result, in turn, whets our appetite for further examination of the effect of source credibility and media framing on policy legitimation. Here we did not vary the source of the policy. That we found a framing effect is all the more impressive because of the Court's high level of credibility. It may well be that the effect of the media's framing varies with different policy sources, growing as the credibility of the source of the policy declines. Along these same lines, source credibility may also vary with the prestige or type of media outlet constructing the policy maker's actions. In our analysis we attributed all the news stories to the *New York Times,* a media source widely perceived among the white mass public as highly authoritative and prestigious. And our experimental manipulations produced effects. But would white subjects react in the same way to media frames had we attributed the coverage to less well known mainstream or obviously African American papers? As Druckman's (2001) compelling analysis shows, a source must be credible to frame an issue effectively. Perhaps if we had attributed our stories to the *New York Amsterdam News,* rather than the *New York Times,* black subjects would have been more susceptible to media framing effects. Indeed, Dawson (2001) points out that black public opinion is shaped by "non-elite sources (particularly 'nonwhite' or 'nonmainstream' sources) of information" (70). Perhaps media framing effects on support for Court policies are not so different between blacks and whites once the proper media are considered.

To a large extent, the different constructions of the Court's *Adarand* decision are a function of the different missions of the mainstream and black presses. The mainstream press's goal is to be objective and neutral (Bennett 1988; Gans 1979), whereas the black press strives to act as a corrective for the inaccuracies and omissions in mainstream coverage (Owens 1996; Wolseley 1990). Although the mainstream press's goal may be neutrality, its effect is certainly not "neutral."[13] Indeed, its framing of the Court and the decision had a significant effect on white opinion. The mainstream press did ignore (intentionally or not) the strident, even vitriolic, reaction of black Americans to the ruling and to Justice Thomas. White Americans are often ignorant of black opinion and therefore shocked when black opinion and white opinion diverge sharply (reactions to the O. J. Simpson verdict and the 2000 Florida election contests are two prime examples). Blacks, on the other hand, are rarely surprised when their opinions differ from whites'. Our results suggest one explanation for this phenomenon. Whites are very rarely exposed to black media sources, while many blacks are exposed to both mainstream and black media outlets (McClerking and White 1999; Wolseley 1990). Thus, given the nature and focus of the mainstream media's coverage, it is little wonder that whites are taken aback when controversial issues boil to the surface.

That the black and mainstream presses may engender appreciable divergence between black and white opinion raises an intriguing question. Does the different manner in which the black and mainstream presses treat the Court affect the level of diffuse support for that institution? Some of the findings of the research literature suggest that the answer is yes. First, studies have consistently shown that most Americans are very supportive of the Court and perceive it as a highly legitimate institution (Caldeira and Gibson 1992; Gibson, Caldeira, and Spence 2003b; Mondak and Smithey 1997). Second, although the black and white mass publics are generally quite supportive of the Court, there are appreciable differences between their levels of diffuse support, with the black public being decidedly less positive (Gibson and Caldeira 1992; Gibson, Caldeira, and Spence 2003b). Third, knowledge of the Court is strongly correlated with positive attitudes toward it, and this relationship seems to derive from the way in which the Court is portrayed by the media (Gibson, Caldeira, and Baird 1998). Finally, as we document in this chapter, the black press does not necessarily focus on the same legitimizing symbols in its coverage of the Court. Consequently, African Americans, with their high rates of exposure to black media sources (Dawson 2001), are much less likely than the general mass public to experience "the slow accretion of positive messages" about the Court and the law that "leads to legitimacy" (Gibson, Caldeira, and Baird 1998, 345). Thus, we would expect African Americans who are exposed to black media sources more often to have lower levels of diffuse support for the Court.

Although the experimental data we have presented in this chapter do not bear on this subject, we can put the relationship we just sketched out to a preliminary test using data collected in the Blacks and the U.S. Supreme Court Survey (BSCS). These data include measures of diffuse support for the Court, exposure to black media sources, and several of the forces Caldeira and Gibson (1992) used to model the origins of the Court's institutional support (see also Gibson, Caldeira, and Spence 2003b). Using these data, our dependent variable is the individual's level of diffuse support for the Court, while our independent variable is the individual's level of exposure to black media sources. Given the work of Caldeira and Gibson (1992; see also Gibson, Caldeira, and Spence 2003b), however, we are mindful that a variety of forces have been shown to affect levels of diffuse support. Accordingly, to adequately test the effect of exposure to black media sources, we included indicators of knowledge about the Court, interest in politics, support for the norms of democracy, commitment to social order, attention to the Court's outputs, partisan identification, ideology, and a host of conventional demographic variables in our model specification. Finally, because of the positive messages on the Court from the mainstream media, we also included a measure of exposure to mainstream media sources.[14] The results of estimating this model are displayed in Table 5.7.

Although the model explains only 12% of the variation in diffuse support, it does provide rudimentary confirmation of our hypothesis that exposure to black media sources is negatively related to levels of institutional commitment to the Court. Based on the model's estimates, the predicted diffuse support score for African Americans with

TABLE 5.7   MEDIA EXPOSURE AND DIFFUSE SUPPORT FOR THE
SUPREME COURT: BLACKS AND THE U.S. SUPREME COURT SURVEY

Variable	Coefficient		Standardized Coefficient
Ideology	−.01	(.03)	−.03
Education	.04	(.03)	.09
Knowledge of the Court	.55*	(.23)	.16
Attention to affirmative action	.04	(.05)	.05
Party identification	−.02	(.03)	−.04
Norms of democracy	.09	(.07)	.08
Commitment to social order	−.11	(.07)	−.11
Gender	−.07	(.10)	−.04
Trust in government	.00	(.09)	.00
Exposure to black media	−.09**	(.03)	−.18
Exposure to white media	.02	(.03)	.05
Intercept	2.60**	(.47)	
N		257	
Adjusted R^2		.12	

Note: Table entries are multiple regression coefficients with standard errors in parentheses. The dependent variable is diffuse support for the Supreme Court measured after the University of Michigan affirmative action decisions were announced. Significance tests: $*p \le .01$; $**p \le .001$.

the highest incidence of exposure to black media sources is nearly two-thirds of a unit less than the predicted score for their counterparts with the lowest exposure to black media sources. This is not an insignificant difference in a 4-unit scale. Finally, it also bears mention that in the fully specified model, exposure to black media sources has the largest effect on an individual's diffuse support for the Court (as demonstrated by the β coefficient of −.18; see Table 5.7).

As we return to the results of our experiment, our findings demonstrate that the black press's attack on Justice Thomas was quite potent for blacks as they evaluated the Court's decisions. Thomas is a flashpoint dividing liberal and conservative blacks, and that is reflected in our data. An attack on him stimulates opposition to the Court's ruling among liberal blacks, but it may drive more moderate and conservative blacks into Thomas's camp. This pattern of results provides further evidence of the influence of both longstanding predispositions and contemporary information presented in the media as citizens make political judgments.

Finally, our analysis to this point suggests a nuanced role for the Court's legitimizing capacity for both the black and the white public. To be sure, the Court's pronouncements on controversial policies affect the shape of black and white opinion toward those policies, but this effect is moderated by a collection of other forces. In Chapter 3, we establish the moderating effect of group-centrism on the Court's capacity to legitimize. Here, we show that the way in which the Court's pronouncements are communicated to the mass public affects its ability to shape attitudes, particularly for the white public. We find that when an anti–affirmative action decision is framed as injurious to black political and legal equality, whites are less supportive of the Court's policy. Black attitudes on affirmative action, on the other hand, appear to be too well anchored to be susceptible to the Court's decision, regardless of the way in which it is framed. This is not to say, however, that black opinion on affirmative action is uninfluenced by the Court and media framing. Whether they agree with the ruling or not, for moderate and conservative blacks, framing it as apolitical and guided by the Constitution increases their support for rapid implementation. This is the essence of Legitimacy Theory.

The Supreme Court's Legitimizing Capacity among African Americans

Support for Capital Punishment and Affirmative Action

Through experimental analyses we have demonstrated the Court's capacity to shape the public opinion of African Americans. Specifically, the experiments we conducted in Chapter 3 pointed to the Court's greater legitimizing ability (relative to the federal bureaucracy) among both African Americans and whites. Thus, it seems that the Court, because of its relatively higher levels of institutional credibility, can convince important segments of the American electorate to accept or at least tolerate policies it articulates.

Before we pronounce this question settled, however, we must acknowledge two key points. First, the legitimizing effect we have found for the Court is in relation to the bureaucracy, an institution with far less credibility. Recall that in our experiments, policies attributed to the Court enjoyed greater support among black and white subjects than the same policies attributed to a bureaucratic agency. Thus, our experiments showed only the *relatively* greater effect of the Court on public opinion, not the Court's absolute capacity to affect public opinion per se. To be sure, our experiments showed the Court's ability to legitimize, but whether this effect is present only when it stands in relation to another institution's more meager level of attachment with the public is uncertain. Second, we must acknowledge that the findings we reported in Chapter 3 are based upon data derived from an experimental design. Critics of this type of research design point out that the concomitant results are not generalizable beyond the rarified atmosphere of the laboratory. Although we took steps to ensure that our experiments were high in "mundane realism" (Aronson et al. 1990, 70), and we are convinced that the effect we found is genuine, the fact remains that our experimental data limit our ability to draw more general conclusions about the magnitude of the Court's effect on the black mass public.

Here our aim is to address each of these points. First, we examine the Court's ability to shape attitudes toward public policies. Specifically, we analyze whether citizens with higher levels of diffuse support for the Court are more likely to agree with its policy pronouncements. Second, our results are based on data drawn from national, representative samples of black Americans' attitudes toward two issues on which the Court has left deep footprints—capital punishment and affirmative action.

We believe these issues are particularly rich targets for our purposes. First, few other policies are as salient in the black public's mind, or focus as brilliant a light upon the Court's actions. And second, perhaps with the exception of abortion, no other policies pronounced by the Court are as likely to trigger group-centric attitudes—in this case race consciousness, given the racial disparity in the implementation of the death penalty and the identity of the subgroup most closely associated with affirmative action. Using data from the 1987 General Social Survey (GSS) and the 1996 National Black Election Study (NBES), we ask: Do group-centric attitudes and diffuse support for the Court among black Americans influence their acceptance of the Court's capital punishment and affirmative action policies? And does group-centrism condition the impact of diffuse support for the Court?

We begin this chapter with a brief review of the Court's legitimizing capacity, after which we take up the effect of group-centric attitudes on public opinion, the black public's perception of the death penalty and affirmative action, and the Court's role in establishing the basic law of the land on both policies. Next we present and discuss our hypotheses, paying particular attention to the causal order of the primary relationship we are attempting to model. Then we describe our data, specify the models, and present the results of our statistical analyses. In the chapter's penultimate section, we present the results of several tests of the causal order of the relationship between diffuse support for the Court and individual attitudes toward a policy articulated by it. Our theoretical perspective suggests that an individual's level of diffuse support affects his or her opinion of the Court's policy outputs, and not the other way around. This causal order, however, is difficult to fix, and we spend some time here (and in Chapter 7) conducting specification tests. Finally, we conclude with some general observations on the complex relationship between public opinion toward the Court and public opinion toward its outputs, as well as the influence of the Court and group-centric attitudes on black opinion regarding social policies.

The Court's Legitimizing Capacity

One of the major themes undergirding the Court's capacity to legitimize policies is the notion that the public reaction to its decisions hinges on the Court's credibility as a source of policy (Caldeira and Gibson 1992; Casey 1974; Gibson 1989). We have established already that the Court fares quite well in this regard. Public approval is relatively high and constant, and as a result it enjoys a deep reservoir of political capital. In Chapter 3 we demonstrated that these public evaluations enhance the Court's ability to legitimize its controversial policies, thereby increasing the likelihood that a substantial proportion of the public will support or at least accept its position.

But what attribute, characteristic, or combination of forces explains this heightened legitimizing capacity? In Chapter 1 we speculated that the potent characteristic was diffuse support, which Legitimacy Theorists point to as necessary for an institution's legitimizing capacity. The Court's high level of diffuse support endows its articulation of policy with a sense among its constituents that its pronouncements must and ought to be obeyed.

It is likely, however, that the Court's legitimizing effect is neither simple nor unqualified. Evidence shows that even the Court's legitimacy-conferring capacity is not unmitigated. Examining public responses to *Roe v. Wade*,[1] for example, Franklin and Kosaki (1989) demonstrated that reactions to the Court's decisions are dependent upon the individual's political context. They concluded that the Court appears not to bring citizens into basic agreement on a controversial policy. Rather, its effect is conditional—hardening preexisting issue preferences within groups and exacerbating between-group differences. Extending Franklin and Kosaki's (1989) study to the Court's decisions on capital punishment, Johnson and Martin (1998) add further evidence supporting the conclusion that the Court's effect is conditional (see also Stoutenborough, Haider-Markel, and Allen 2006). They too showed that the Court's decisions polarized preexisting views. Their study went on to indicate that the Court's effect on public opinion is significant only when it is speaking on an issue for the first time: "when the Court speaks more than once, its effect is minimal in later cases" (Johnson and Martin 1998, 306). Finally, other research literature indicates that the Court's persuasive effect is contingent upon the characteristics of the individuals exposed to its message—for example, whether the issue at hand was especially proximate to the individual's daily life, the degree to which an individual possessed strongly held preexisting views, the level of the individual's diffuse support for the Court, or the type of media coverage of the Court to which the individual was exposed (Hoekstra 1995, 2000; Hoekstra and Segal 1996; Mondak 1990, 1992; and see Chapter 5 above).

These findings, along with the analysis we present in Chapter 3, suggest that group-centric forces might bear on public reaction to Supreme Court policies. This is not at all surprising. Decades of research have shown that social groups are central to the way citizens think about politics, and in particular how they structure opinion on matters of social policy (see, for example, Conover 1988; Conover and Feldman 1981; Converse 1964; Dawson 1994; Kinder and

Sanders 1996; Nelson and Kinder 1996; Tate 1994). Since many public policies disproportionately affect members of certain social groups, opinion on these policies turns in large measure on citizens' attitudes toward and identification with the groups involved. Indeed, as we showed in Chapter 3, strong and credible source though it is, the Court's shaping effect on public opinion is moderated by citizens' sentiments toward the social group they see as the principal beneficiary or victim of its policies (see also Clawson, Kegler, and Waltenburg 2001).

Group-Centrism, Policy Opinion, and the Court

Many important and controversial public policies directly implicate identifiable social groups, and, not surprisingly, attitudes toward the groups involved form the foundation of support or opposition to those policies. Indeed, a wealth of public opinion research shows that citizens' identification with and antipathy toward social groups have a large impact on their policy attitudes. This is the "group-centric" nature of public opinion (Nelson and Kinder 1996). And it appears to be no less present for policies attributed to the Supreme Court, as indicated by the results of the experiments that we present in Chapter 3. Accordingly, we take into account group-centric effects as we examine the impact of diffuse support for the Court on attitudes toward its policy outputs.

We accomplish this by examining black support for two controversial and highly salient public policies—capital punishment and affirmative action—that have clear group overtones and feature a prominent role for the Supreme Court. First, although capital punishment is a purportedly race-neutral policy, it has a disproportionate effect on black citizens, a point recognized by the Supreme Court. In a memo written three months before arguments in *McCleskey v. Kemp*[2] were heard, Justice Scalia wrote that racial discrimination in the death penalty is "real [and] acknowledged in the decisions of this Court" (quoted in Baldus 1995, 1040). Fifteen years earlier, while deciding *Furman v. Georgia,*[3] Justice Stewart expressed concern that racial bias might operate in the application of the death penalty so as to render it "wantonly and . . . freakishly imposed" (408 U.S. 238, 310). Moreover, a fair body of statistical evidence seems to give this concern a solid foundation. Black Americans account for only 13% of the U.S. population, and yet since the death penalty was reinstated in 1976, over one-third of those executed have been black. Today blacks make up almost 42% of the nation's death row inmates.[4] In short, whether judged by executions or those waiting to be executed, black Americans are appreciably overrepresented And then there is the *McCleskey* case itself. At stake there was whether statistical studies showing that blacks who killed whites were more likely to be sentenced to death than whites who killed blacks rendered the death penalty unconstitutional. In a 5–4 decision, the Court said no.

Because of these pronounced and well-documented racial disparities, it is not surprising that blacks and whites have significantly different attitudes toward the death penalty. Using GSS data from 1974 through 1988, Tate demonstrates that "whites, by a margin of 30 percent, are more likely to favor capital punishment" (1994, 38). And in repeated polls, black respondents perceive the imposition of the death penalty as racially loaded. A few examples should suffice.[5] In 1994, a *Los Angeles Times* survey of 1,515 adults found that 71% of blacks believed that non-whites were more likely to face death sentences than whites, whereas only 34% of whites believed this.[6] A 1997 Princeton Survey Research Associates/*Newsweek* poll of 751 adults found that 82% of blacks (versus 44% of whites) felt that black defendants were more prone to be sentenced to death.[7] Finally, a 1999 Gallup Poll showed that the distributions had not changed much over the years: 71% of blacks agreed with the statement: "a black person is more likely than a white person to receive the death penalty for the same crime," whereas only 47% of whites did so.[8]

A similar story unfolds for affirmative action. The conventional perception is that this public policy is designed to advantage blacks and other minorities, largely at the expense of whites. This perception, in turn, fuels substantial differences in black and white support for the policy. For instance, a 1997 CBS News/*New York Times* survey of 1,258 adults found that 80% of black respondents believed that affirmative action was necessary in order to prevent discriminatory practices, while only 37% of white respondents believed this.[9] In the same poll, 62% of blacks believed that the policy should be continued if its abolition would mean fewer black professionals, while a mere 29% of whites held this view.[10] Simply asking whether or not a respondent favored affirmative action, regardless of its intention or consequences, produces nearly identical results. A 1995 NBC/*Wall Street Journal* poll of 1,465 adults found that black support for affirmative action was more than two times greater than white support.[11]

In terms of political and legal history, both capital punishment and affirmative action are issues in which the Supreme Court has been an active policy participant. In the case of capital punishment, the Court has essentially determined for the states the procedures required for carrying out the death penalty. In its 1972 *Furman* decision, it invalidated the death penalty because of its unpredictable and capricious use, thereby prompting the legislatures of 35 states to tighten the laws under which the death penalty could be meted out.

Four years after *Furman,* the Court used three cases to evaluate the states' responses and clarify the procedures necessary for death penalty convictions to satisfy constitutional requirements.[12] Even with these clarifications, however, questions about the application of the death penalty continue to be raised. Whether rape is punishable by death, the use of expert testimony, whether a trial judge may override a jury's recommendation of life imprisonment and impose the death penalty, whether an insane person may be put to death, whether an accomplice to felony murder may be executed, and whether statistical data suggesting racial discrimination in the death penalty's use may be presented to demonstrate the punishment's unconstitutionality are all issues brought to the bar of the Supreme Court over the last quarter-century.[13] There can be little doubt, therefore, that the Court has had a great deal of influence over the contours of this policy. Indeed, it is not too great a stretch to claim that, effectively, the nation's death penalty statutes have been indirectly written by the Court.

In the case of affirmative action, the Court has been the ground on which acrimonious constitutional and statutory battles have been waged for over three decades. As we discuss in Chapter 2, at the advent of the 1960s the federal government took the lead in efforts to end racial discrimination in housing, employment, and education. In doing so, it promoted the use of affirmative action programs to overcome the effects of past and present discrimination. By urging the use of racial preferences, however, the federal government presented the nation with an explosive issue—one that the Court could not avoid and that it has revisited on a basis nearly as regular as the changing of the seasons.

Although the ideals underlying race-based remedies are not particularly controversial, the specific measures aimed at achieving those ideals are. Defining the permissibility of those measures is the task to which the Court has bent itself. In this endeavor it has not charted a constant course. During the Burger Court era, the justices were sharply divided over affirmative action policies and claims of racial discrimination, narrowly dividing to uphold most programs. By the Rehnquist Court era, however, conservative Reagan appointees had made their mark, and the Court had substantially shifted in its analysis of, and approach to, race-based measures. Accordingly, throughout the 1990s, affirmative action programs met an increasingly chilly reception at the high bench; and although the Court did not extirpate them in its 2003 University of Michigan rulings,[14] it did curtail their more expansive incarnations (see Chapter 2).

Obviously the Court has had a large role in the formation of both capital punishment and affirmative action policies. Consequently, we argue that the attitudes of blacks toward both can be thought of as attitudes toward *the Court's policies*. Although it is received wisdom that few people are interested in or informed about the Court, some recent research on public awareness of decisions about which people might reasonably be expected to hear indicates that knowledge of the Court's decisions is broader than is generally understood (see Franklin and Kosaki 1995; Franklin, Kosaki, and Kritzer 1993). Capital punishment and affirmative action are especially salient in the lives of black Americans, who are therefore likely to be particularly attuned to the Court's pronouncements in these areas. Indeed, research on attitudes demonstrates that the more important an issue is to an individual, the more attention and energy the individual will give to that issue and its implications for his or her life (see Fiske and Taylor 1991; Hoekstra 2000; Krosnick et al. 1993). Further, as Hoekstra (2000) points out, perceived importance need not result solely from having individual material interests at stake. Rather, there is a subjective sense of importance, the sources of which include identification with the people or group involved most closely with the issue (see also Boninger, Krosnick, and Berent 1995). Finally, Hoekstra (2000) notes that the work of Franklin and Kosaki (1995) demonstrates that case-specific factors affect the level of attention individuals may give to Court actions. As she puts it, "Catholics should pay more attention to abortion decisions, and African Americans should pay more attention to discrimination cases" (Hoekstra 2000, 94).

But if these dispositions of African Americans toward awareness of and attention to the Court's capital punishment and affirmative action pronouncements are not enough, there is the mass media and its role as information source. The media certainly connect these policies to the Court. A search of the Television News Archive at Vanderbilt University shows that 23% of news stories that mentioned the death penalty between 1980 and 2001 also mentioned the Supreme Court. A search of Ethnic Newswatch, which archives African American newspapers, for stories that mention the death penalty written between 1990 (the year in which the archive service began) and 2001 likewise demonstrates that just under 23% of the stories in the black press that mentioned the death penalty also made reference to the Court. Similarly, from 1980 to 2001 the network news linked affirmative action and the Court in 38% of their stories, while African American newspapers connected the two in 21% of their articles between 1990 and 2001. These percentages are quite high when you consider all of the possible ways these two public policies might be covered in the media.

Accordingly, then, we suspect that black Americans' diffuse support for the Court will have a significant impact on their opinion of capital punishment and affirmative action, policies identified with the Court. Our theoretical perspective defines diffuse support for the Court as a reservoir of good will that encourages citizens to accept its decisions, even when those decisions cut against their best interests. The opposition among blacks, at least in the aggregate, to the Court's current position on capital punishment and the relatively great weight African Americans place on the utility and validity of race-based affirmative action, therefore, provide particularly severe tests of the legitimizing effect of diffuse support for the Court. It is to those tests that we now turn.

Hypotheses

In the absence of an experimental design, examining public reaction to Supreme Court decisions is a tricky business. Uncertainties abound—not the least of which, as just noted, is whether the mass public is even sufficiently aware of the decision for the Court to affect their opinion (Adamany and Grossman 1983; Jaros and Roper 1980; Murphy and Tanenhaus 1968). Then there are questions concerning the direction of any relationship. Is the Court reacting to the landscape of public opinion, or is the mass public responding to the Court? And these difficulties only scratch the surface. Adding to the overall complexity are the possible effects of diffuse support and group-centric forces. Each of these figures into how citizens position themselves in light of a Supreme Court ruling—the former by providing the necessary political capital to purchase support for the ruling, the latter by shaping citizens' reactions according to their attitudes toward the group perceived as most directly affected by the decision. To begin, then, we hypothesize that black citizens' opinions on the Supreme Court's death penalty and affirmative action policies are affected by their levels of diffuse support for the Court itself. Given that diffuse support generates acceptance of a policy *even in the face of attitudes and characteristics that militate for the policy's rejection,* we expect that, all things being equal, those blacks with higher levels of diffuse support for the Court are more apt to fall in line with its policy pronouncement.

This hypothesis begs the question of the causal order of the relationship we are positing, an important point that deserves extended treatment here. (We take up this question even more directly and in greater detail in the next chapter.) We are proposing that deeply held attitudes toward the Court affect support for the policies it articulates; yet it is not unreasonable to suggest that the causal arrow points in the opposite direction—support for the policies affects attitudes toward the Court. So, how exactly is approval for the Court related to public opinion on a policy articulated by it? The causal relationship we are proposing is predicated on Legitimacy Theory (see Easton 1965). It emphasizes diffuse support and conceptualizes it as a reservoir of favorable attitudes that allows an institution to articulate policies that are generally unpopular, and yet be confident that a majority will accept them. As we discuss in Chapter 1, this reservoir is enduring and not contingent upon the satisfaction of an institution's constituents with its specific policy outputs. To state the causal relationship concretely, we hypothesize that an individual's attitudes toward the Court as an institution affect his or her attitudes toward its rulings.

The alternative causal stream states that attitudes toward specific Court outputs affect the public's attitude toward the Court as an institution. This understanding of causality is also present in the research literature. Mondak (1992), for instance, concludes that the Court's institutional credibility is not immune to public reaction to its outputs. Through specific rulings, debits and credits are made to the Court's bank of political capital—its diffuse support (see also Mondak and Smithey 1997). Similarly, Grosskopf and Mondak (1998) find that the Court's institutional credibility is dynamic, affected in no small measure by evaluations of specific decisions; consequently, its diffuse support may decay in the light of unpopular decisions. Finally, Hoekstra (2000) shows that a portion of support for the Court is explained by prior support, but this support is not immune to the effect of current decisions. As she puts it, "satisfaction with [Court] decisions influences subsequent evaluations of the Court" (97).

To be sure, the relationship between institutional support for the Court and specific support for its outputs is a dynamic one, characterized by some degree of feedback. Just the same, however, there is good reason to believe that the causal order we propose—namely, support for the Court as an institution affects support for its policies—has the greatest currency.[15]

Theoretically, there appears to be a temporal order to the two kinds of support, with institutional or diffuse support for the Court antedating its specific counterpart. Easton (1965) contends that diffuse support is effectively defined by its durability, source, and fundamental basis. Thus, whereas specific support for the Court waxes and wanes with its outputs and composition at any point in time, diffuse support is much more stable and is not merely a function of short-run evaluations of the Court's performance. As Easton puts it, "Except in the long run, diffuse support is independent of the effects of daily outputs. It consists of a reserve of support that enables a system to weather the many storms when outputs cannot be balanced off against inputs of demands" (1965, 273). Using the most valid sounding of diffuse support for the Court available, Gibson, Caldiera, and Spence (2003b) confirm this conceptual argument. Examining levels of diffuse support for the Court in the wake of the *Bush v. Gore*[16] decision, they conclude that its basic legitimacy was unaffected by the justices' involvement in the election controversy. And conducting a two-stage least squares analysis to explore causality, they find "institutional loyalty [for the Court] influences judgements of the fairness of the decision in *Bush v. Gore,* but not vice versa" (Gibson, Caldiera, and Spence 2003b, 551).

Rather than bending with the winds of day-to-day evaluations, then, diffuse support has a more secure foundation in political socialization. Easton and Dennis, for example, show that by eighth grade, children see the Court as a powerful, knowledgeable, and important body that rarely makes mistakes; further, children hold the Court in higher esteem than other institutions, including the president, police, and senators (Easton and Dennis 1969, ch. 13; see also Caldeira and Gibson 1992). Thus, the attitudes giving rise to diffuse support are acquired relatively early in life and are not prone to dramatic, rapid change (Easton and Dennis 1969; Caldeira and Gibson 1992). In the end, diffuse support is an analytically distinct concept from its more immediate and time-sensitive counterpart, a point that Caldeira and Gibson (1992; see also Gibson, Caldeira, and Spence 2003b) systematically verify.

Empirically, extant studies (Caldeira and Gibson 1992; Gibson and Caldeira 1992; Gibson, Caldeira, and Spence 2003b; Hoekstra 2000; Mondak and Smithey 1997) demonstrate that prior attitudes toward the Court do affect individual assessments of the institution, even after hearing about specific decisions (see also Bartels 2003). For instance, in a series of experiments, Hoekstra (2000) shows that a substantial portion of support for the Court is explained by prior support: "Prior attitudes do spill over into current evaluations" (97). And we have already recounted the Gibson and Caldeira (1992) findings that associate different levels of diffuse support for the Court among black cohorts with the political era during which they came of age. Finally, from a statistical standpoint, we address the issue of causal order for the data analysis presented in this chapter by conducting sensitivity tests (discussed below), while in Chapter 7 we bring more definitive statistical tests to bear. There, using panel survey data of a national representative sample of the black mass public, we estimate a two-wave model with synchronous effects. To briefly anticipate the model's results, we find clear evidence that diffuse support for the Court affects an individual's attitudes toward a Court policy, but that attitudes toward the Court's outputs have meager and insignificant effects on the individual's level of institutional loyalty for the Court.

Returning, then, to our specification of models explaining levels of black support for capital punishment and affirmative action, we readily note that diffuse support is not the end of the story. A wealth of evidence documents the importance of group-centrism in shaping the politics of black citizens. In terms of candidate preference, political participation, and policy opinion, race consciousness is a fundamental factor guiding black political behavior (see, for example, Allen, Dawson, and Brown 1989; Dawson 1994; Gurin, Hatchett, and Jackson 1989; Kinder and Sanders 1996; Miller et al. 1981; Shingles 1981; Tate 1994).[17] Thus, race consciousness enters the mix as something of a standing decision, and this has two basic consequences. First, and most directly, those blacks who have greater affective and cognitive attachment to their own racial group will be less supportive of the death penalty and more supportive of affirmative action, all things being equal. After all, as we noted above, the death penalty is broadly perceived as discriminatory and applied in a racially conscious way, while affirmative action is understood as a race-based remedy to past and present racial discrimination. Second, black group-centrism should condition the influence of diffuse support. Group-centric attitudes are a primary ingredient in public opinion, and as such they will effectively anchor attitudes toward the death penalty and affirmative action. Accordingly, we expect that those blacks with lower levels of racial consciousness will be appreciably influenced by diffuse support for the Court, whereas blacks with higher levels of group attachments will be much more resistant to its institutional influence.[18]

Group-centric sentiments and levels of diffuse support are but two of the forces that may affect public reaction more generally to either of the Court's policies. Prior research points to a variety of other factors that shape public response to both issues, including political predispositions, religiosity, and demographics. And then there is a special issue associated with measuring attitudes about the Supreme Court and its outputs—the degree to which support for the Court is something apart from support for the general political system in the public's mind. All these must be considered before we can accurately assess the effects of our key forces of interest.

Much research has shown that political predispositions have an appreciable bearing on levels of support for the death penalty. Specifically, Republicans and conservatives are *more* supportive than Democrats and liberals are (Barkan and Cohn 1994; Fox, Radelet, and Bonsteel 1990–91; Peffley and Hurwitz 2002; Sandys and McGarrell 1995). Thus, we expect that blacks who identify themselves as Republicans or as conservatives will be more supportive of capital punishment.

In terms of affirmative action, although there is evidence that white Democrats are more likely to support such policies (Sears et al. 1997), Tate's (1994) research using 1984 data shows that party identification and ideology are not significant predictors of black attitudes on affirmative action. Given the general importance of party identification and ideology in studies of public opinion, however, we include these variables as controls.

Young's analysis (1992) of support for the death penalty illustrates the importance of religiosity. He found that even in the midst of multivariate controls, individuals with greater levels of religiosity were more opposed to capital punishment. We hypothesize, therefore, that individuals who exhibit greater religious devotion will tend to oppose capital sentences; yet affirmative action policy lacks the clear religious overtones and implications of the death penalty. Finally, slightly different collections of demographic forces have been shown to affect opinion on both of these policies, including gender, region, education, income, marital status, whether or not the respondent has children, and suburban residence (Barkan and Cohn 1994; Fox, Radelet, and Bonsteel 1990–91; Sandys and McGarrell 1995; Tate 1994; Tyler and Weber 1982; Young 1992). Therefore, we include them as controls when appropriate for each policy.

Finally, it is quite possible that citizens see the three branches of the federal government as monolithic, a single governing coalition. As such, their support for the Court—and that support's possible effect on attitudes regarding Court policies—is not distinct from support for the political system writ large (but see Caldeira and Gibson 1992). Consequently, to ensure that the effect of diffuse support for the Court is not conflated with that of support for the general political system, we include a measure of support for the federal government in our models.

Data, Model Specification, and Analyses

Capital Punishment

To test our propositions concerning black reaction to the Court's death penalty policy, we draw on data from the 1987 GSS. The

1987 GSS is particularly useful for our purposes (Davis and Smith 1972–1998). First, that year it oversampled blacks.[19] Second, the survey was put in the field during the time period in which *McCleskeyKemp* was heard and decided, a case that turned on racial disparities in death penalty convictions and was the most watched Supreme Court case that year (Simon 1996). Thus, the question of racial bias in the death penalty was likely quite close to the surface for the black public. And, finally, the 1987 survey instrument includes the questions that constitute the Caldeira and Gibson (1992) measure of diffuse support for the Court. Consequently, we have the most direct and valid sounding available on public attitudes toward the U.S. Supreme Court as an institution.

Our dependent variable is whether or not the respondent favors or opposes the death penalty for convicted murderers, coded 1 if in favor, 0 otherwise. Almost 48% of blacks support the death penalty, while roughly 52% oppose it. Our measure of black group-centric forces is the factor score of four items tapping race consciousness: opposition to laws banning interracial marriage, opposition to neighborhood segregation, support for a hypothetical open housing law, and endorsement of the statement that blacks have too little influence in American politics.[20] Higher scores indicate greater race consciousness.[21] As noted above, our indicator of diffuse support for the Court is the Caldeira and Gibson (1992) diffuse support measure, a factor score composed of five separate items gauging the willingness of the respondent to countenance profound and drastic changes to the Court as an institution.[22] Higher scores indicate greater support for the Court.[23]

The GSS also includes an array of variables that allows us to account for the collection of forces that prior research has shown to bear upon public opinion regarding capital punishment. These independent variables include gender, partisanship, ideology, the frequency of church attendance, suburban residence, and whether or not the respondent has children. Finally, to control for the possible confounding effects of trust in the overall political system, we include measures of trust for the federal government in our model.[24]

With these measures, then, we specify the probability model of any given person (i.e., the ith individual) supporting the death penalty as follows:

$x1i$ = the Caldeira and Gibson (1992) measure of *diffuse support* for the Court: higher scores indicate greater levels of support

$x2i$ = *black group-centrism*: higher scores indicate greater levels of race consciousness

$x3i$ = the interaction of *diffuse support* and *black group-centrism*

$x4i$ = 1 if the ith respondent is *female,* 0 otherwise

$x5i$ = the ith respondent's *partisanship*: higher scores are Republican

$x6i$ = the ith respondent's *ideology*: higher scores are conservative

$x7i$ = 1 if the ith respondent has *children,* 0 otherwise

$x8i$ = 1 if the ith respondent lives in a *suburb,* 0 otherwise

$x9i$ = the frequency of the ith respondent's *church attendance*

$x10i$ = the ith respondent's *trust in the federal government*: higher scores indicate greater levels of trust

We estimated the model through a maximum likelihood logit procedure. The results are displayed in Table 6.1.

In general, the model performs reasonably well. The χ^2 statistic is significant; the fit is satisfactory; and many of the coefficients have the expected sign and attain or approach statistical security. Overall, respondents with children and, to a lesser degree, women respondents[25] are more likely to support capital punishment (13% and 11%, respectively), whereas black respondents who attend church more frequently are 10% less likely to favor death sentences.[26] Of greater importance and interest, though, is that our results underscore the effect of group-centric attitudes and diffuse support on reaction to policies articulated by the Supreme Court.

TABLE 6.1   EFFECT OF GROUP-CENTRIC FORCES AND
DIFFUSE SUPPORT ON BLACK ACCEPTANCE OF THE COURT'S
PRO–DEATH PENALTY POLICY (WEIGHTED DATA)

Variable	Coefficient	T-Statistic
Constant	.17	.22
Diffuse support for the Court	.37***	3.00
Black group-centrism	−.18	−1.08
Diffuse support by black group-centrism	−.37**	−2.39
Female	.45*	1.88
Partisanship	.17	.58
Ideology	−.01	−.04
Children	.57**	2.13
Suburb	−.33	−1.11
Church attendance	−.09*	−1.74
Trust in the federal government	.21	1.24

Notes: Table entries are logit coefficients. Dependent variable = support for death penalty (1 = yes).
N = 328. Log likelihood = −212.4. χ^2 = 27.8. $p > \chi^2$ = 0.00. Percent correctly predicted = 62.2.
MLE Improvement = 17.8%. Two-tailed significance tests: *$p < .1$; **$p < .05$; ***$p < .01$.

Consistent with our expectations, blacks with higher levels of group attachment are less likely to support capital punishment, although this main effect does not approach traditional levels of statistical significance ($b = -.18$; $t = -1.08$). There is a strong main effect of diffuse support for the Court on black opinion regarding the death penalty ($b = .37$; $t = 3.00$), such that blacks who possess higher levels of support for the Supreme Court are 19% more likely to favor capital punishment—a position that is in line with the Court's policy pronouncement but contrary to black group interests. Moreover, this effect is strong even though we have controlled for trust in the federal government. Thus, the statistical evidence indicates that black support for capital punishment is affected more by support for the Supreme Court as an institution than by a general sense of confidence in the government and its actions.

Most importantly, the interaction between diffuse support for the Court and black group-centric attitudes is statistically significant

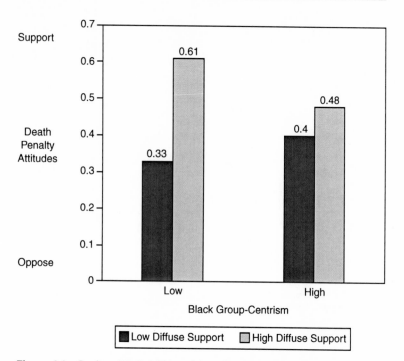

Figure 6.1 Predicted Probabilities of the Effect of Diffuse Support for the Court on Supporting the Death Penalty at High and Low Levels of Black Group-Centrism

$(b = -.37; t = -2.39)$. To unpack this interaction, we computed predicted probabilities for the effect of diffuse support at high and low values of black group-centrism.[27] The results are displayed in Figure 6.1. The bars are the predicted probability of black support for capital punishment at high and low levels of diffuse support for the Court and black group-centrism. For example, the likelihood of a black citizen supporting capital punishment if he or she has a low level of diffuse support and high group-centrism is .4. Examination of the figure reveals a complex, yet predictable, relationship between diffuse support for the Court and approval of its capital punishment policy. As we expected, group-centric attitudes condition the influence of support for the Court. For those individuals with lower levels of black group-centrism, diffuse support for the

Court affects their attitudes toward its capital punishment policy, increasing their likelihood of supporting the death penalty by 85%.[28] Institutional support for the Court, however, has far less sway over those individuals with high levels of group-centric attitudes, increasing their level of support by 20%. It appears, then, that their more intense race consciousness results in opinions on the death penalty that are too securely anchored to be moved by any measure of institutional support for the Court. To put it more clearly, a high level of race consciousness acts as a standing decision that stabilizes black opinion against the effects of diffuse support for the Court.

Affirmative Action

The analysis to this point provides evidence that black reaction to the Court's social policies is a function of both the Court's credibility as an institution and black group-centric attitudes. However, it may be that these results are unique to the Court's death penalty policy. To explore further the general effect of diffuse support and group-centric attitudes on black reaction to the Court's articulation of social policies, we now turn to an examination of black opinion on the Court's affirmative action policy.

Here, we draw on data from the 1996 NBES, a full-coverage, stratified random sample of the national black electorate (Tate 1996).[29] It includes information on an array of basic political, social, and demographic forces. Using data from a large national sample of blacks, we are able to conduct a full analysis of black opinion.

Our dependent variable is support for affirmative action, coded 1 if the respondent strongly supports minorities' being given special considerations in hiring decisions, 2 if the respondent supports such considerations, 3 if the respondent opposes such considerations, and 4 if the respondent strongly opposes them. Twenty-seven percent of blacks strongly support and another 31% support race-conscious hiring, whereas 24% oppose and 18% strongly oppose such practices.

To operationalize group-centrism, we use a general measure of racial sentiment: a black feeling thermometer. We recoded this measure on a 0 to 1 scale, with higher scores representing greater black-centrism. Since the NBES contains a variety of items designed to tap group attitudes, we also include measures of linked fate (Dawson 1994) and black nationalism (Gurin, Hatchett, and Jackson 1989; Tate 1994). Both were recoded on a 0 to 1 scale, with higher scores indicating a belief that one's fate is tied to blacks as a group and an endorsement of black nationalist sentiments. Unfortunately, the NBES does not include measures of the attitudes that make up the Caldeira and Gibson diffuse support scale (1992). Consequently, we use a feeling thermometer to measure diffuse support for the Court. Certainly, that measure is not free of aspects of specific support (see Caldeira and Gibson 1992; Gibson, Caldeira, and Spence 2003a). It does, however, measure "highly general attitudes toward the institution, which include some elements of loyalty" (Gibson, Caldeira, and Spence 2003a, 363). Moreover, it is the best available measure in our data set.

The NBES, like the GSS, includes an array of variables that allows us to specify a model that controls for some of the other forces shown to bear upon public opinion regarding affirmative action. These additional exogenous forces include gender, partisanship, ideology, income, and educational level. Finally, we again include a measure of trust in the general political system to ensure that the effect of diffuse support for the Court is not conflated with support for the broader federal government.[30]

To conduct our multivariate analysis, we specify the probability of the ith individual supporting affirmative action as follows:

$x1i$ = *diffuse support* for the Court: higher scores represent greater support

$x2i$ = *black group-centrism*: higher scores represent greater levels of affinity

$x3i$ = the interaction of *diffuse support* and *black group-centrism*

$x4i$ = 1 if the ith respondent is *female,* 0 otherwise

$x5i$ = the ith respondent's *partisanship*: higher scores are stronger Democrat

$x6i$ = the ith respondent's *ideology*: higher scores are more conservative

$x7i$ = the ith respondent's annual *income*

$x8i$ = the ith respondent's level of *education*

$x9i$ = the degree to which the ith respondent believes his or her fate is linked to that of other African Americans: higher scores indicate a great sense of *linked fate*

$x10i$ = the degree to which the ith respondent endorses *black nationalism*: higher scores represent greater nationalism

$x11i$ = the ith respondent's *trust in the federal government*: higher scores indicate greater trust

Because of the ordinal nature of our dependent variable, we estimated this model through a maximum likelihood ordered logit procedure. The results are displayed in Table 6.2.

Generally, the model performs as well as the probability model examining the structure of black opinion on the death penalty. Again, the χ^2 statistic indicates that the model is highly significant; its fit is reasonably strong; and most of the coefficients are correctly signed and bump up against conventional levels of statistical significance. Blacks with higher incomes are 15.3% less likely to support affirmative action, while blacks with higher levels of education are more likely to support it (16.6%).[31] And finally, black nationalists and Democratic identifiers are particularly supportive.

As in the case of black opinion on the death penalty, the effect of diffuse support for the Court survives the introduction of multivariate controls. There is a significant main effect of diffuse support on black attitudes toward affirmative action. Blacks with higher levels of diffuse support are more opposed to affirmative action ($b = 2.92$; $t = 2.76$)—a position that is consistent with the general drift of Supreme Court decisions at the time of this survey but inconsistent with conventional black interests. In this model, the main effect of black group-centrism fails to even approach statistical significance. This does not mean, however, that group-centric attitudes do not affect black opinion regarding affirmative action. Indeed, the effect of black group-centrism is captured by the interaction term.

TABLE 6.2   EFFECT OF GROUP-CENTRIC FORCES AND
DIFFUSE SUPPORT ON THE BLACK PUBLIC'S ATTITUDES TOWARD
THE COURT'S ANTI–AFFIRMATIVE ACTION POLICY

Variable	Coefficient	T-Statistic
Diffuse support for the Court	2.92**	2.76
Black group-centrism	.78	1.06
Diffuse support by black group-centrism	−3.38***	−2.69
Female	.23	1.45
Partisanship	−.68**	−2.04
Ideology	.13	.54
Income	.54*	1.70
Education	−.86**	−2.16
Linked fate	−.07	−.31
Black nationalism	−2.75***	−6.42
Trust in the federal government	−.39	−.96
N	611	
Log likelihood	−793.38	
χ^2	73.7	
Cut 1	−1.97 (.73)	
Cut 2	−.56 (.73)	
Cut 3	.83 (.73)	

Notes: Table entries are ordered logit regression coefficients. Percent correctly predicted = 36.
MLE Improvement = 7%. Two-tailed significance tests: *$p < .1$; **$p < .05$; ***$p < .01$.

The interaction between black group-centrism and diffuse support is highly significant in this model ($b = -3.38$; $t = -2.69$). We explored this interaction by the same method we used in the capital punishment model.[32] The predicted probabilities are displayed in Figure 6.2. Once again the bars represent the likelihood of a black respondent's supporting the Court's policy output at high and low levels of diffuse support and group-centrism. As was the case for black attitudes regarding capital punishment, group-centrism conditions the influence of support for the Court. For blacks with lower levels of in-group affinity, diffuse support for the Court

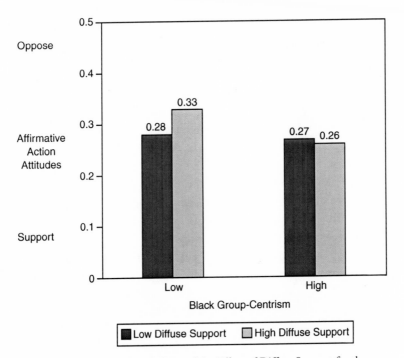

Figure 6.2   Predicted Probabilities of the Effect of Diffuse Support for the Court on Opposition to Affirmative Action at High and Low Levels of Black Group-Centrism

draws their opinion in the direction of the Court's policy, increasing their opposition to affirmative action by 18%. Institutional support for the Court, however, fails to exert any meaningful influence on the opinion of blacks with high levels of group-centrism. Again, it seems that group-centrism anchors attitudes.

Tests of Causal Direction

Before closing the book on our analysis in this chapter, we must return to the problem of causal order. Ideally, of course, we would have conducted instrumental variable analyses when putting our model specifications to the test, thereby purging our measure of diffuse support for the Court of endogenous effects. As is often the case, however, the real world manages to frustrate idealism because the data sets we used to test the effect of diffuse support did not include sets of variables that were efficiently and highly correlated with our measures of diffuse support, while at the same time being themselves genuinely exogenous. This difficulty is not at all unusual. For instance, Johnston (1972) writes of instrumental variable analysis that "the real difficulty in practice of course is actually finding variables to play the role of instruments" (280).

Since we are unable to purge potential endogeneity biases with the GSS and NBES data at hand, we conducted sensitivity checks on the capital punishment and affirmative action models to corroborate the causal order we posited above. For each model, we used simultaneous equation modeling to explore how robust the effects of diffuse support on policy attitudes are when a particular amount of "feedback" is introduced. As noted above, we have good theoretical reasons to expect only a modest amount of feedback; diffuse support for the Court is likely to be causally prior to issue preferences. It is reassuring to note, however, that our measure of diffuse support continues to have a significant impact on capital punishment beliefs even when we assume that there is an equal amount of feedback running from policy attitudes to diffuse support. In the affirmative action model, the effect of diffuse support remains significant even if we posit a feedback coefficient approximately 40% as large. These sensitivity checks suggest that a substantial amount of endogeneity would have to be present before our basic argument would be undermined, a theoretically unlikely condition. Thus, we have confidence in our finding that diffuse support influences opinion on capital punishment and affirmative action, not vice versa.[33]

Conclusions

In Chapter 1 we quote Easton's (1965) definition of diffuse support as "a reservoir of favorable attitudes or good will that helps members to accept or tolerate outputs to which they are opposed or the effects of which they see as damaging to their wants" (273). Over the course of the past two or three decades, the Supreme Court has articulated capital punishment and affirmative action policies that black Americans perceive as "damaging to their wants." And yet some black Americans accept these policies. Why? The answer seems to lie, at least in part, in their diffuse support for the Court. For those blacks with higher levels of diffuse support, the Court's stature and credibility appear to allow it to legitimize policy. At the same time, even diffuse support for the Court has its limits. Blacks with the highest levels of group consciousness are less likely to be drawn in the direction of the Court's policy. Simply put, even the Court's relatively strong legitimizing capacity is not unaffected by group-centrism.

For blacks who feel a strong sense of racial solidarity, their in-group identification trumps their diffuse support for the Court, further evidence of the importance of group attitudes in American politics. Indeed, perhaps the best characterization of race consciousness as it pertains to individual attitudes toward a public policy is that it is a standing decision. Policies are evaluated in terms of group attachments, and the more firmly rooted the group attachment, the less effect other forces will have in the evaluation of those policies—even for a force as credible as the Court. Franklin and Kosaki (1989) offer some evidence that at least partially confirms this argument. Examining the response of Catholics to *Roe,* they found that those Catholics most solidly rooted in their religious community were the most affected by Catholic-group norms and, therefore, most resistant to the persuasive effect of the Court.[34]

Finally, this chapter offers clear evidence that the Court can encourage public support for controversial policies. In simplest terms, its institutional prestige purchases public acceptance. This finding, in turn, both speaks to the Court's role in effecting broader social change and might shed light on the litigation decisions of interest groups and social reform activists. In a leading analysis of the Court's ability to produce broad-gauge social reform, Rosenberg (1991) concludes that the "U.S. courts [including the Supreme Court] can *almost never* be effective producers of significant social reform" (338 [emphasis in original]). Consequently, he avers that interest groups and social activists squander their resources when they decide to locate their energies in the judiciary in pursuit of their policy goals. Upon closer inspection, however, there may be a method to these litigants' apparent madness. Perhaps they are more sophisticated than Rosenberg's understanding admits, and they recognize that part of bringing about social change is marshaling public opinion. Thus, as one element in a more general strategy to achieve change, they engage the Court—not necessarily to effect the social reform itself, but to help engender conditions that are conducive to the reform.

7

The Causal Relationship between Public Opinion toward the Court and Its Policies

The University of Michigan Affirmative Action Cases

In the preceding chapters we have demonstrated that the U.S. Supreme Court is more capable than other political institutions of dressing controversial policies in the cloak of legitimacy (see also Gibson 1989; Hoekstra 1995; Hoekstra and Segal 1996; Mondak 1990, 1991, 1992). Moreover, as the empirical results presented in Chapter 6 indicate, the basis of this signal legitimizing capacity—this power to affect public opinion—is the public's opinion of the Court itself. There is nothing particularly novel here. Indeed, it is a hoary practice in studies of public opinion and the Supreme Court to quote Alexander Hamilton's maxim that the judiciary is the "least dangerous branch," and to observe that, invested with neither the purse nor the sword, the Court is ultimately dependent upon the good will of the public for the effectuation of its policies. Thus, the logic continues, the Court must be ever mindful of this precious asset and carefully husband its institutional credibility with the mass public. Yet this symbiotic relationship between public opinion toward the Court itself, on the one hand, and public opinion toward the Court's outputs, on the other, raises a methodological issue to which we must attend—namely, what is the proper specification of this relationship? More specifically we ask: Does the Court's institutional credibility affect public opinion toward its outputs, or do public attitudes toward the Court's outputs affect the public's evaluation of the Court?

Correctly understanding and mapping the causal pathways of this relationship is of no small theoretical consequence, for it has a direct bearing on the substantive place of the Court in the political system. To put the matter bluntly, if the latter specification is correct, the Court is much less able to play the democratic role that Legitimacy Theory suggests for it (see Chapter 1). In Chapter 6 we recognized the ambiguity inherent in the relationship between public opinion regarding the Court's outputs and public opinion regarding the Court. Unfortunately, the data we used to test our models of the Court's effect on black attitudes toward capital punishment and affirmative action allowed us only to build a circumstantial case that the causal arrows point from the Court's institutional credibility to black opinion. Given the gravity of this conceptual issue, a more definitive answer is in order. It is to that end that we now turn our attention.

In simplest terms, this chapter is a specification test of the relationship between public opinion toward the Court and public opinion toward the Court's policies. As indicated above, the causal directions composing that relationship are complex and murky. Charting them is no simple chore. Compelling cases can be made for the causal arrows running in either direction, and analysts have been bedeviled by their reliance on cross-sectional data.[1] We, however, have a unique data set to use to sort out the causal relationship. Specifically, we draw on panel data on the University of Michigan affirmative action cases to examine the causality between black Americans' diffuse support for the Court and their attitudes toward affirmative action.

In the following section we briefly set the context for, and the political stakes surrounding, the University of Michigan cases. We then describe our data. One common criticism of using public opinion data to analyze the relationship between the mass public and the Supreme Court is that most people have little interest in the Court and therefore are not particularly well informed about it or its actions. We present evidence that puts this criticism to rest. We show that an appreciable share of the black public was attentive to the Court and its decisions and, thus, able to formulate meaningful opinions. Next we specify the model that we use to examine the causality between diffuse support for the Court and black attitudes toward affirmative action, and we discuss our statistical results. We conclude by taking stock of our findings and discussing their implications for the Court's role in our political system.

The University of Michigan Affirmative Action Cases

On December 2, 2002, the Supreme Court agreed to revisit the issue of the use of racial preferences in higher education by granting petitions for writs of *certiorari* in *Gratz et al. v. Bollinger et al.* and *Grutter v. Bollinger et al.*—the University of Michigan affirmative action cases.[2] When it decided to hear *Gratz* and *Grutter,* the Court placed itself in the middle of an emotionally charged and highly controversial issue with well-entrenched camps. Few issues in modern American politics are more likely to polarize the public than affirmative action. Moreover, the Court's inattention to the use of affirmative action by educational institutions had allowed the public's views to harden. It had not spoken to the use of racial preferences in higher education since its seminal *Bakke* decision,[3] nearly a quarter-century earlier, and over those intervening years an affirmative action system had accreted. Now the continuation of that system was jeopardized, and its proponents were well aware of the danger embedded in the Court's action; likewise, the system's antagonists were aware of the opportunity with which they were being presented.

Given the stakes involved, the cases commanded tremendous attention among both the general and special interest publics. A record number of *amicus* briefs were filed, eclipsing the previous mark by better than 100% (Thornton 2003). NBC alone devoted an hour of its prime time television schedule to the cases and the social and political issues surrounding them, while ABC, CBS, and CNN dedicated a combined three hours of evening news and special programming to the cases' acceptance, reactions to the Bush administration's brief, oral arguments, and the decisions themselves. Black Entertainment Television (BET), indicative of the intense interest of the African American community, gave over five hours of coverage to *Gratz* and *Grutter* during the span of the Court's deliberations. On the day of the decision, ABC and CNN interrupted their normal programming to announce the rulings and discuss their implications for higher education. Newspapers across the nation carried the rulings as their lead headline, along with related reports or "sidebars" placed above the fold.

The University of Michigan affirmative action cases, of course, did not take place in a "news vacuum." There were other major political developments competing for the media's and the public's attention during this same time period. For example, both the Texas sodomy case[4] and congressional action on the bill outlawing partial birth abortion occurred while the Court adjudicated *Gratz* and *Grutter* or shortly thereafter. Yet they were merely also-rans in the race to be noticed. The media devoted less than one hour of evening news and special programming to these two issues combined. Rarely does the business of the Court so capture the public eye.

The Blacks and the
U.S. Supreme Court Survey

The heightened attention given to the affirmative action cases, coupled with the certainty that the Court would act, presented us with a remarkable opportunity. Substantial portions of the public, particularly the black public, would be well informed about the issue before the bar and therefore would be able to formulate meaningful opinions regarding the Court's outputs. And because of the time lag between the Court's acceptance of a case and its ruling on it, we would be able to measure both the effect of the Court's decision on black opinion toward affirmative action *and* the effect of the Court's decision on black opinion toward the Court. To avoid missing this opportunity, it was essential that we place in the field, before the Court handed down its decisions, a panel instrument that would measure both pre- and post-ruling attitudes toward the Court and affirmative action policy among black Americans. The Blacks and the U.S. Supreme Court Survey (BSCS) is just such an instrument (Clawson, Tate, and Waltenburg 2003).

The BSCS was conducted during the summer of 2003.[5] For the pre-ruling survey, telephone interviewing began May 1, 2003, and ended June 22. The decisions were announced on June 23. Four hundred twenty-five interviews were completed with voting-eligible blacks. The post-ruling interviews began on June 26, shortly after the rulings, and continued through August 10. Reinterviews were conducted with 286 black respondents. The pre-ruling survey lasted approximately 35 minutes; the post-ruling survey was roughly 7 minutes long.

The 2003 BSCS is a random digit dial telephone survey that targeted telephone exchanges with a 15% or greater black population density. Such a sample yields an incidence of black households of 35% and covers 74% of all black households nationally. Unfortunately, this sampling methodology resulted in blacks living in predominantly white neighborhoods being automatically excluded from the sample. Members of telephone households were eligible to participate in the study if they were at least 18 years old and a citizen of the United States. Within telephone households, respondents were selected using the most "recent birthday method," with no substitutions. Specifically, interviewers asked, "Before I can begin this survey, I need to ask about the people who live at this residence so we can identify the correct person to interview. May I please speak with an adult who is a citizen of the United States and who celebrated the most recent birthday?" Because birthdays are randomly distributed, this method ensures that chance alone determines which person in a household is interviewed.

For the pre-ruling survey, seven callbacks were made in an attempt to complete the interviews. This persistence resulted in 425 completed interviews with voting-eligible blacks, resulting in an effective incidence rate of 50.6%.[6] For the post-ruling survey, three attempts were made to complete each reinterview, a strategy that yielded reinterviews of 67% of the original 425 respondents. Overall, our typical pre- and post-sample respondent is an employed woman with at least some college education and a family income of $20,000 or greater (see Appendix E, Table E.1).

In terms of sample methodology, the greatest concern with panel data such as these is that the respondents who were reinterviewed systematically differ from the respondents who participated only in the first panel, so that in effect the panel methodology results in selection on the dependent variable (see King, Keohane, and Verba 1994 for the pernicious consequences of selection effects). To test for systematic differences across the panels, we included a variety of attitudinal and demographic forces in a logit equation where the dependent variable equals 1 if the respondent took part in both panels, and 0 otherwise. The resulting estimate yielded only one significant correlate—age: older respondents were more likely to participate in both panels. Bivariate tests of the relationship between age and the dependent variables of substantive interest (support for affirmative action and diffuse support for the Court), however, failed to produce statistically secure relationships between the variables (see Appendix E, Table E.2, for the results of these tests).

Black Attentiveness to the Cases and Opinions on Affirmative Action and the Court

Before turning to an analysis of the causal relationship between black Americans' diffuse support for the Court and their attitudes toward its affirmative action rulings, it is important to lay a foundation by establishing the salience of the cases to black Americans and describing the nature of black opinion on the policy articulated by the Court as well as the Court itself.

As we noted above, the Court's actions on these cases commanded tremendous public attention generally. There were substantial opportunities for the mass public, white and black alike, to become informed of the Court's business in *Gratz* and *Grutter*. But we suspected that blacks would be especially attentive to the Court's actions. First, recent research on the level of attention individuals devote to an issue before the Court finds that it varies systematically with their sense of

TABLE 7.1   IMPORTANCE OF THE SUPREME COURT RULINGS
TO BLACK AMERICANS

	Question: How important is this issue to you? Would you say it is extremely important, very important, somewhat important, not too important, or not important at all?
Extremely important (5)	27.9%
Very important (4)	38.2
Somewhat important (3)	27.9
Not too important (2)	4.2
Not important at all (1)	1.8
Mean (sd)	3.86 (.93)
N	283

the issue's importance in their lives (see Fiske and Taylor 1991; Hoekstra 2000; Krosnick et al. 1993). Adding to this is the notion that an issue's perceived importance to an individual is not based only on material interests. Research by Boninger, Krosnick, and Berent (1995; see also Hoekstra 2000) indicates that perceived importance also stems from a sense of identification with the people or group most closely associated with the issue. On these dimensions we would expect few issues to be more important to black Americans than affirmative action, making them especially attentive to the University of Michigan affirmative action rulings. Our survey results do not disappoint. Almost two-thirds of our respondents reported that the affirmative action ruling was either an extremely or a very important issue to them (see Table 7.1), while the data displayed in Table 7.2 verify that the majority of our respondents were attentive to the Court's actions. Roughly 56% of our respondents reported that they paid quite a lot or some attention to the Court rulings, while only 13.3% said they paid no attention at all.

Given the issue's importance to black Americans and their concomitant attention to the Court's actions, black Americans were certainly able to formulate an opinion concerning the Court's outputs. How then did they respond to the rulings? The Court was confronted with two different affirmative action programs. It upheld one as facilitating a diverse student body (the law school program) but knocked down the other (the undergraduate program) on the

TABLE 7.2   BLACK ATTENTION TO THE SUPREME COURT RULINGS

	Question: We understand that not everyone has the time or interest to follow everything that occurs in the news. However, we are interested in how much attention you've paid to the recent Supreme Court rulings on affirmative action—would you say you've paid quite a lot, some, just a little, or none at all?
Quite a lot (4)	21.8%
Some (3)	34.4
Just a little (2)	30.5
None at all (1)	13.3
Mean (sd)	2.65 (.97)
N	285

grounds that it did not treat prospective students as individuals. To measure black opinion on the decisions, we carefully designed a survey item that would convey the complexity of the Court's rulings in a succinct and fairly simple way. The results are displayed in Table 7.3. Overall, blacks are quite supportive of the Court's nuanced affirmative action policy. Two-thirds of our respondents agreed with the Court that race could be used as one among many factors in college admissions, but not in a way that would militate against individual-by-individual decisions. Interestingly, roughly half of those who disagreed with the Court ruling did so on the grounds that *more* weight should be given to race in the process (see the bottom of Table 7.3).

How did the Court's decisions in the University of Michigan cases affect black support for affirmative action policies in general (in contrast to opinions on the specific Court rulings)? To address that question, we examined black support for affirmative action policies before and after the Court's decisions were handed down. Given the findings of Johnson and Martin (1998) as well as those of Stoutenborough, Haider-Markel, and Allen (2006), we would expect *Gratz* and *Grutter* to produce little aggregate change in opinion, since they were not the first time the Court spoke on the use of racial preferences in higher education, nor did they fundamentally overrule the *Bakke* precedent. Our survey results bore this expectation out. Before

TABLE 7.3   BLACK SUPPORT FOR THE SUPREME COURT RULINGS

	Question: The Supreme Court has ruled that having a diverse student body is important and therefore race may be considered as one among many factors in college admissions, but that a point system benefiting minorities cannot be used in college admissions because it treats students as group members rather than individuals. Would you say you agree or disagree with the Supreme Court on this issue? (IF AGREE/DISAGREE:) Do you strongly (agree/disagree) or only somewhat (agree/disagree)?
Strongly agree (4)	30.3%
Somewhat agree (3)	35.6
Somewhat disagree (2)	15.9
Strongly disagree (2)	18.2
Mean (sd)	2.78 (1.07)
N	264
	Question: Do you disagree with the Court ruling because you think that race should be given more weight in college admissions decisions or because you think that race shouldn't be considered at all in college admissions?
More weight	51.7%
Not considered at all	48.3
N	87

the ruling, over 60% of blacks indicated that they strongly favor preferential policies, and an additional 10.8% said that they favor such policies. After the ruling, there is a roughly 5% increase on the supportive side of the continuum. Thus, overall there is striking aggregate-level stability (see Table 7.4), further evidence that "when the Court speaks more than once, its effect is minimal in later cases" (Johnson and Martin 1998, 306).

Finally, we also examined black support for affirmative action in employment before and after the Court's rulings. In the pre-ruling data, approximately two-thirds of blacks either somewhat or strongly agreed that minorities should be given special consideration when hiring decisions are made. The post-ruling picture is similar, although agreement with affirmative action in employment was less intense (see Table 7.5).

TABLE 7.4   BLACK SUPPORT FOR AFFIRMATIVE ACTION
IN EDUCATION: PRE- AND POST-RULING

Question: Some people say that preferences in college admissions should be given to qualified blacks to ensure diversity on college campuses. Others say preferential admissions policies are wrong because they discriminate against equally qualified whites. What about your opinion— are you for or against preferential college admissions policies for blacks?

(IF FOR/AGAINST:) Do you (favor/oppose) preferential college admissions policies strongly or not strongly?

	Pre-Ruling	Post-Ruling
Strongly favor (4)	61.3%	62.8%
Favor (3)	10.8	14.5
Oppose (2)	7.9	7.1
Strongly oppose (1)	20.0	15.6
Mean (sd)	3.13 (1.22)	3.25 (1.13)
N	380	269

TABLE 7.5   BLACK SUPPORT FOR AFFIRMATIVE ACTION
IN EMPLOYMENT: PRE- AND POST-RULING

Question: Please tell me whether you agree or disagree with the following statement: Because of past discrimination, minorities should be given special consideration when decisions are made about hiring applicants for jobs.

(IF AGREE/DISAGREE:) Do you (agree/disagree) strongly or somewhat?

	Pre-Ruling	Post-Ruling
Strongly agree (4)	45.0%	38.4%
Somewhat agree (3)	20.4	26.5
Somewhat disagree (2)	20.6	21.1
Strongly disagree (1)	14.1	14.0
Mean (sd)	2.96 (1.10)	2.89 (1.07)
N	398	279

To examine support for the Court (Table 7.6), we created a diffuse support index by taking a mean of four items measuring support for the Court as an institution (Table 7.7).[7] Using a 4-point scale, citizens were asked to indicate whether the Supreme Court should engage in judicial review, whether the Court should exist if

TABLE 7.6   BLACK DIFFUSE SUPPORT FOR THE COURT:
PRE- AND POST-RULING

	Pre-Ruling Diffuse Support	Post-Ruling Diffuse Support
Mean (sd)	2.83 (.78)	2.80 (.81)
N	421	283

Note: The diffuse support index was constructed by taking the mean of four items measuring support for the Court as an institution. The index ranges from 1 (low diffuse support) to 4 (high diffuse support).

TABLE 7.7   MEASUREMENT MODEL FOR DIFFUSE SUPPORT
AND AFFIRMATIVE ACTION

	Pre-Ruling Standardized Coefficients	Post-Ruling Standardized Coefficients
Diffuse support		
Eliminate Judicial Review: The power of the Supreme Court to declare acts of Congress unconstitutional should be eliminated.	.49	.56
Eliminate Court: If the Supreme Court continually makes decisions that the people disagree with, it might be better to do away with the Court altogether.	.51	.68
Rewrite Constitution: It would not make much difference to me if the U.S. Constitution were rewritten so as to reduce the powers of the Supreme Court.	.46	.49
Reduce Court's Jurisdiction: The right of the Supreme Court to decide certain types of controversial issues should be limited by the Congress.	.34	.48
Affirmative action		
Preferential college admissions	.54	.71
Special considerations when hiring	.55	.50

Note: Table entries are standardized regression coefficients. All coefficients are statistically significant at .001.

it makes decisions the public opposes, whether the Constitution should be revised to reduce the Court's power, and whether Congress should be able to limit that power. In Table 7.6 we report the average level of diffuse support for the Court before and after it spoke on the subject of affirmative action. In the aggregate, opinion

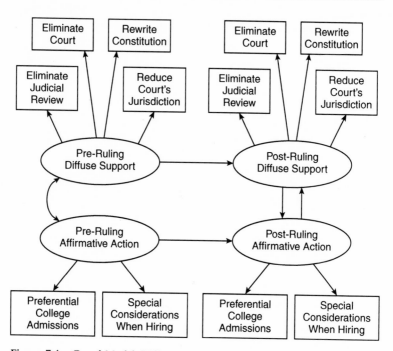

Figure 7.1 Causal Model: Diffuse Support and Attitudes toward Affirmative Action

is fairly supportive of the Court and remarkably stable across time, with blacks scoring 2.83 out of 4 prior to the rulings and 2.80 following them. It appears that blacks maintain a reservoir of support for the Court, but that reservoir is not extremely deep.[8]

Modeling Causality

In the wake of the Court's actions on the University of Michigan cases, blacks were clearly receptive to the Court's affirmative action policy and at least moderately committed to the Court itself. But what is the nature of the relationship between these two opinions? Figure 7.1 depicts our proposed causal model.[9] Simply put, we hypothesize that affirmative action attitudes after the Supreme Court rulings are a function of both affirmative action opinion before the

TABLE 7.8   STRUCTURAL MODEL FOR DIFFUSE SUPPORT
AND AFFIRMATIVE ACTION

	Standardized Coefficients
Diffuse Support$_1$ → Diffuse Support$_2$	.88*
Affirmative Action$_1$ → Affirmative Action$_2$	.79*
Diffuse Support$_2$ → Affirmative Action$_2$	.29*
Affirmative Action$_2$ → Diffuse Support$_2$	.16
	$\chi^2 = 88.995$
	$df = 48$
	$p = .00$
	$\chi^2/df = 1.854$
	RMSEA $= .045$
	$N = 425$

Note: Table entries are standardized regression coefficients. *$p < .05$.

decisions *and* diffuse support for the Court after the rulings. Similarly, we model diffuse support after the Supreme Court rulings as a function of both diffuse support before the rulings and attitudes toward affirmative action after the rulings. Our expectation is that post–ruling diffuse support will have a strong, positive effect on post–ruling affirmative action attitudes; however, there will be a much smaller, probably insignificant, feedback loop from affirmative action to diffuse support. We use structural equation modeling to test these expectations.[10] The results are displayed in Tables 7.7 and 7.8.

To begin, we note that our theoretical model enjoys a fairly tight fit to the data (see the bottom of Table 7.8). Although the χ^2 is statistically significant, which suggests that the model does not fit particularly well, that statistic is sensitive to minor differences within a large sample. Thus, we also report two commonly used fit statistics for structural equation modeling: the χ^2 to degrees of freedom ratio and the root mean square error of approximation (RMSEA). The χ^2/df ratio is under 2 at 1.854, which is considered a good fit. In addition, the RMSEA is .045, which suggests that our model fits the data fairly well (Browne and Cudek 1993).

Turning next to the results of the estimation, both diffuse support for the Court and attitudes on affirmative action are latent variables in our model. Thus, we begin by describing the results for the measurement model. In both the pre-ruling and post-ruling surveys, the four items measuring support for the Court as an institution are available to use as indicators of the latent variable diffuse support for the Court. During both time periods, these items load nicely on the underlying variables, as demonstrated by the standardized coefficients presented in Table 7.7. The coefficients range from .34 to .51 for the pre-ruling data and from .48 to .68 for the post-ruling data, and in all cases are statistically significant at .001. Thus, the underlying belief in the institutional legitimacy of the Court leads citizens to think that the Court should be protected from the whims of Congress and the public, including those who might tinker with the Constitution to diminish the Court's powers.

We have two items to specify attitudes on affirmative action: preferences in college admissions and special considerations when hiring. Here too the items load well on the affirmative action constructs (see Table 7.7), and the coefficients are statistically significant at .001. Therefore, latent support for affirmative action drives black agreement with such policies in the realm of education and employment. Interestingly, the post-ruling coefficient for preferential college admissions is the highest at .71, which probably reflects the prominence of the issue in citizens' minds in the wake of the Michigan rulings.

The results from the estimation of the structural model are presented in Table 7.8. Turning to it, we see, not surprisingly, that diffuse support before the Court ruling predicts diffuse support after the Court's pronouncement, with a standardized regression coefficient of .88. In other words, citizens who bestowed institutional legitimacy on the Court prior to the ruling were likely to do the same after the decisions were handed down. Likewise, pre-ruling affirmative action attitudes have a significant impact on post-ruling support for affirmative action, with a standardized coefficient of .79. Both coefficients are significant at .05 and indicate a substantial amount of stability across time.

Even more interesting for our purposes is the statistically significant effect of post-ruling diffuse support on post-ruling attitudes toward affirmative action. The standardized coefficient is .29 and is statistically significant at .05. Thus, greater diffuse support for the Court leads citizens to be more favorable toward affirmative action policies. The feedback from affirmative action to diffuse support, however, is not significant (see Table 7.8). Hence, the Court's institutional legitimacy allows it to influence attitudes toward the specific issues on which it rules. Here, the Court is able to wrap its cloak of legitimacy around affirmative action and thereby strengthen black support for the policy. But the reverse does not occur: changes in affirmative action attitudes do not cause a significant shift in diffuse support for the Court. This finding is consistent both with Caldeira and Gibson's (1992) original conceptualization of diffuse support as a remarkably stable force that is not readily moved by specific Court outputs and with Gibson, Caldeira, and Spence's (2003b) finding that the controversial *Bush v. Gore*[11] decision did not significantly depress the Court's institutional credibility. Moreover, it permits us to place greater store in the empirical results presented in Chapter 6. The Court's institutional prestige allows it to legitimize controversial policies, but the Court's policies do not appear to substantially affect its institutional prestige (at least not in the short run).

Finally, given the empirical results presented in Chapters 3 and 6, we are interested in whether race consciousness moderates the causal relationship between diffuse support for the Court and affirmative action attitudes. The cross-sectional data analysis presented in earlier chapters indicates that greater diffuse support for the Court pulled blacks with low levels of race consciousness toward the Court's anti–affirmative action position. In contrast, the Court was unable to budge blacks with high race consciousness. It was unclear whether the same pattern would hold here, however, since overall the Court rulings favored affirmative action. We suspected that in this instance diffuse support for the Court might bolster support for affirmative action among blacks regardless of race consciousness. To examine this proposition, we conducted a multigroup analysis.

High- and low-race-consciousness groups were formed by dividing the sample at the mean of a race identity scale. The race identity scale was created by taking a mean of two items. In the pre-ruling survey, respondents were asked whether what happens to black people in this country affects their life and whether the movement for black rights has affected them personally. Both questions were on a 4-point scale, and the mean was 2.58, with a standard deviation of 1.06. Fifty-four percent of the respondents fell into the low-race-consciousness group, and 46% fell into the high-race-consciousness group. The multigroup analysis showed that for blacks with low *and* high levels of race consciousness, diffuse support for the Court after the ruling causes greater support for affirmative action policies. Moreover, there was no significant feedback from affirmative action attitudes to diffuse support. Thus, the causal relationship we described above for blacks in general (and presented in Table 7.8) holds across levels of race consciousness.[12]

Conclusions

A number of fundamental empirical findings deserve emphasis here. First, our survey results indicate that black Americans are highly supportive of race-conscious programs in both education and employment. Indeed, of the minimal disagreement voiced with the Court's generally pro–affirmative action rulings, roughly half of it was born of the sense that race should count as more of a factor than the Court was willing to countenance.

Second, despite its demonstrated effect on black political attitudes (see Allen, Dawson, and Brown 1989; Dawson 1994; Tate 1994), in the case of the causal connection between support for the Supreme Court and attitudes regarding affirmative action, racial identification does not appear to moderate the relationship. Why this is so is an intriguing and important question that we intend to take up in subsequent research.

Third, our data confirm Johnson and Martin's (1998) findings that the Court's largest impact on mass public opinion occurs when it speaks on an issue for the first time. In subsequent rulings, its effect on public opinion is minimal. Our survey results indicate that the University of Michigan decisions moved aggregate black opinion on affirmative action hardly at all.

Fourth, our data show that black Americans were quite stable in their levels of diffuse support for the Court. This comports neatly with the findings of Gibson, Caldeira, and Spence (2003b). Thus, across multiple years, samples, and surveys, we have evidence confirming the enduring nature of the concept of diffuse support (see Caldeira and Gibson 1992).

But certainly our most important finding stems from our effort to sort out the dynamic nature of the causal relationship between institutional support for the Court and support for a Court output. Here again our findings echo the conclusions of Gibson, Caldeira, and Spence (2003b)—attitudes toward the Court affect attitudes toward a policy it has articulated, but not vice versa. To put it in somewhat more concrete terms, black Americans with higher levels of diffuse support for the Court were moved to follow the Court and become more intense in their support for affirmative action policy, but the Court's pro–affirmative action ruling did not produce greater individual levels of institutional support among black Americans. Finally, we should note that the panel nature of our data permits us to place greater confidence in our conclusions concerning the lack of an effect on diffuse support from the Court's outputs than is possible in studies relying solely on a cross-sectional design.

In the final analysis, it appears that the Court can play a crucial role in encouraging public support for controversial policies. Its institutional prestige can purchase public acceptance. As important, its performance of this role does not appear to detract appreciably from that bank of prestige that is so indispensable to its legitimizing capacity.

8

Conclusion

A basic question has motivated this analysis: is the Supreme Court able to legitimize policies among African Americans? Based upon the evidence presented in the foregoing chapters, the simple answer is yes. Within that pithy declaration, however, resides a complex mix of antecedent conditions, relative effects, and moderating forces.

That black Americans enjoy a special historical relationship with the Supreme Court is well established. In Chapter 2 we reviewed that historical legacy, specifically those actions of the Court that reshaped race relations in the United States. From the inception of the NAACP in 1909, black leaders pursued a strategy of appealing to the judiciary in the pursuit of political and legal equality. This strategy began to pay off when the Court took a progressive turn in 1937. From knocking down the white primary to pulling the plug on racial covenants to declaring segregated schools unconstitutional to upholding affirmative action programs, the Court emerged as the most important institution defending black political and legal rights. We argue that this legacy left many black Americans with a deep reservoir of diffuse support for the Supreme Court.

This history suggests that black Americans have reason to invest the Court with greater institutional credibility relative to other policy makers in the political system. And this in turn makes the Court comparatively more capable of legitimizing policies among African Americans than these other institutions—a point we empirically demonstrated in Chapter 3.

Using an innovative experimental design, in Chapter 3 we examined whether the Court was better able to pull citizens in the direction of its policy pronouncements than the federal bureaucracy. After exposure to a mock newspaper article that discussed either a Supreme Court ruling or an Education Department ruling in favor of a quota-based affirmative action policy, black subjects were significantly more supportive of the policy when it was attributed to the Supreme Court. Although black support for affirmative action is not especially startling, that the policy established a quota makes it a much stronger test of the Court's legitimizing capacity.

Our experimental results also demonstrated the Court's legitimizing ability for white citizens on racial issues. That the Court was able to pull whites in the direction of a pro–affirmative action policy indicates that it bores with a considerable auger when it comes to conferring legitimacy. This is especially noteworthy given the highly controversial status of quotas for public school admissions, and it has important implications for the pluralist nature of the American political system. Few public policy issues in American politics are as heated and divisive as quota-based affirmative action programs. By their nature, these policies create winners and losers and concomitant frustrations. That the Court can legitimize these policies across racial groups indicates that it is an important force for tolerance of the political system's outputs.

The Court's legitimacy-conferring effect, however, is not unmoderated. Forces both internal and external to the individuals exposed to its outputs affect the degree to which the Court's articulation of a policy shapes attitudes toward that policy. Not surprisingly, given that groups are fundamental to the practice of politics in the United States, we found in Chapter 3 that attitudes toward groups have both direct and moderating effects on policy opinions. For both black and white subjects, feeling more positive toward black Americans and less positive toward white Americans led to greater support for the pro–affirmative action ruling. In addition, for white subjects the effect of the Supreme Court condition was moderated by attitudes toward blacks. That is, whites who felt coldest toward blacks were not swayed by the Court ruling, whereas whites who had warmer feelings toward blacks were more likely to support the policy when it was attributed to the Court.

Another force that affects the degree to which the Court's policy pronouncements shape individual attitudes is the level of institutional support for the Court. In Chapter 6 we examined black attitudes toward capital punishment and affirmative action in relation to levels of diffuse support for the Court. We found that black Americans with greater levels of diffuse support were more likely to favor policies articulated by the Court even though those policies ran contrary to the a priori interests of black Americans. Recall that the empirical results presented in Chapter 6 are based on public opinion data drawn from national, representative samples. This gives us greater confidence in the generalizability of the Court's capacity to legitimize controversial policies.

In Chapter 6 we again found the moderating effects of group identification. In this case, we showed that group attitudes conditioned the effect of diffuse support for the Court. The most race-conscious blacks were anchored in their opposition to capital punishment, whereas blacks with lower levels of race consciousness were pulled along by their institutional support for the Court to be more supportive of the death penalty. We found a similar pattern of results for affirmative action, with diffuse support for the Court having a direct and moderating effect on attitudes toward a race-conscious employment policy. The nature of the moderating effect was as follows: high race consciousness kept blacks supportive of affirmative action regardless of their level of diffuse support, whereas diffuse support for the Court encouraged blacks with low race consciousness to lean toward the Court's anti–affirmative action position.

The mass media play a critical role in American politics, particularly with respect to the Court. Since the Supreme Court actively engages neither the press nor the public, the media become a power-ful entity shaping the judicial news received by citizens. In Chapter 4, we analyzed the coverage of the Court's ruling in a well-publicized 1995 affirmative action case, *Adarand v. Pena,* which limited (but did not end) race-conscious federal contracting programs. Black news-papers acted as an advocacy press, focusing on the implications of the ruling for minorities, highlighting sources supportive of affirmative action, and roundly criticizing Justice Clarence Thomas, even calling him a fool and a danger to African Americans. In contrast, the white, mainstream papers balanced pro– and anti–affirmative action sources and typically mentioned Justice Thomas in the context of concurring opinions without focusing on his race. Furthermore, the mainstream press emphasized legal and constitutional terminology, seeming to perpetuate the myth of the Supreme Court as an apolitical institution. These results are consistent with the different missions of the two presses: the black press serves as an advocate, while the mainstream press proclaims its role as an objective reporter.

Investigating the different frames used by the mainstream and black presses, we noted that the black press primarily presented the ruling as a dramatic setback for civil rights, whereas the mainstream news-papers organized their stories within a frame we labeled "No Preferen-tial Treatment." The Dramatic Setback frame emphasized the harm-ful effects of the ruling on black Americans and lamented that the ruling would undermine the pursuit of racial justice. The No Prefer-ential Treatment frame suggested that affirmative action is a form of reverse discrimination, which is inimical to the Constitution.

What effect did this differential media coverage have on public support for the Court's ruling? We answered that question in Chap-ter 5 by conducting an experiment, again using both black and white subjects. Recall that our experiment included two manipulations that mirrored the differences between the mainstream and black presses. The first manipulation used a (fictitious yet highly realistic) *New York Times* article to give the *Adarand* decision either a Dra-matic Setback or a No Preferential Treatment frame. The second manipulation concerned the coverage of Justice Clarence Thomas: in one condition, the article included a paragraph that quoted a black member of Congress strongly attacking Thomas; this paragraph was absent in the other condition. Interestingly, we found that our black subjects were not influenced by the media framing or by the attack on Justice Thomas—with two exceptions. First, black liberals were less supportive of the Court's anti–affirmative action ruling when exposed to the attack on Thomas. And, second, black moderates and conservatives were more supportive of the policy's implementation when they were exposed to *both* the No Preferential Treatment frame and the attack on Thomas. Thus, ideology clearly influenced how blacks reacted to the stimuli. We should also mention that black opinion was primarily driven by longstanding predispositions on race. On the whole, this evidence suggests that the mainstream media have a limited yet noteworthy effect on black public opinion about the Court's rulings.

In contrast, whites were more reactive to the differential media coverage. They were more supportive of the Court's anti–affirmative action policy when exposed to the No Preferential Treatment frame, which suggests that while mainstream media coverage of the Court's rulings may be balanced and objective, it is anything but neutral. Whites were also sensitive to the attack on Justice Thomas, becoming less opposed to affirmative action in that condition. Furthermore, the combination of the Dramatic Setback frame and the attack on Thomas led white subjects to be least sympathetic to the Court's stand against affirmative action.

Media framing also influenced the ingredients of white support for the Court's pronouncement. Whites' endorsement of the value of individualism was a strong predictor of anti–affirmative action sentiment in the No Preferential Treatment framing condition. This is not surprising, given the frame's emphasis on individual achievement rather than group-based rewards. In the Dramatic Setback condition, white subjects' hostility toward blacks became an important factor shaping attitudes toward the Court's policy. Again, this makes sense because the Dramatic Setback frame drew attention to the harmful effects of this decision on black Americans, which made predispositions about the group more prominent in white citizens' evaluation of the Court's ruling. Thus, by affecting the weight of the ingredients, the media influence the recipe for white public opinion about Court policies.

Finally, our analysis is predicated on Legitimacy Theory, a fundamental underpinning of which is the level of diffuse support enjoyed by the political system's institutions. Conceptually, diffuse support has two aspects that are of particular importance. First, institutions with diffuse support are able to wash controversial policies in the waters of legitimacy. And, second, diffuse support is stable, enduring, and (except in the long run) unaffected by outputs. We empirically demonstrated the first of these aspects in Chapter 6, where, however, we could only offer circumstantial evidence for the stability of the Court's diffuse support. In Chapter 7 we directly tackled the causal relationship between levels of diffuse support for the Court and attitudes toward its policies. The 2003 Blacks and the U.S. Supreme Court Survey was a unique study designed to sort out the causal relationship between black Americans' diffuse support for the Court and their attitudes on affirmative action. A panel study, the BSCS allowed us to examine black attitudes toward the Court and affirmative action before *and* after the Court ruled in the 2003 University of Michigan affirmative action cases. We found that blacks with higher levels of diffuse support followed the Court's lead and became more supportive of affirmative action, but that the Court's pro–affirmative action stance did not lead to higher levels of diffuse support for the institution.

Returning, then, to the motivating question of our analysis: is the Supreme Court able to legitimize policies among African Americans? The answer is better stated as a more nuanced yes. First, the Court legitimizes policies among black Americans—policies that *both* cut against and are congruent with their interests as conventionally defined. But that is not all. The Court's ability to legitimize policies is not unique to black Americans. Its legitimizing reach extends to white Americans as well. Next, we must recognize that the Court does not operate in a vacuum, and that a number of forces condition the receipt of its message. Consistent with Legitimacy Theory, an individual's level of diffuse support for the Court affects the extent to which he or she will be moved in the direction of the

Court's articulation of policy. Simply put, individuals with greater levels of diffuse support are more susceptible to the Court's legitimizing effect, all other things being equal. Rarely, however, are other things truly equal. And, not surprisingly, group attitudes and media frames—two forces in particular that have been shown to shape the formation of attitudes in the American political system—affect the impact of the Court. As would be expected given the centrality of groups in American politics, we found that group attitudes act as standing decisions moderating the influence of the Court's outputs for both black and white Americans. Finally, media frames determine how the Court's outputs are interpreted and received. There are a variety of media outlets in the United States, and we found that these media frame the Court's articulation of policy differently. Of more significant consequence, we showed that the different frames have an appreciable effect on the nature and impact of the Court's rulings on public opinion.

Broader Implications

In the final analysis, then, what does our research say about the broader effects of the U.S. Supreme Court, the role of the mass media in a democratic society, and the centrality of group attitudes in American politics? On the subject of the Court, perhaps the poet Ralph Ellison said it best. In a letter to a friend upon learning of the *Brown* decision—a letter we quote in part in Chapter 1—Ellison wrote: "The court has found in our favor and recognized our human psychological complexity and citizenship and another battle of the Civil War has been won. . . . *What a wonderful world of possibilities is unfolded for the children*" (quoted in Patterson 2001, xiv [Patterson's emphasis]). Ellison was careful to note that the eventuality of full political and legal equality for black Americans was ultimately up to blacks themselves, but he intimates a belief that the Court's decision had opened the door to a much brighter future. To no small degree, his belief has been borne out. One need only look at polling places, hotels, restaurants, and integrated classrooms throughout the nation for empirical verification that blacks enjoy greater political and legal guarantees today than they did prior to the 1950s.[1]

Of course, the Court did not effectuate this outcome single-handedly. As Robert Dahl notes, "By itself the court is almost powerless to affect the course of national policy" (1957, 293). Gerald Rosenberg puts it even more starkly: "U.S. courts can *almost never* be effective producers of significant social reform" (1991, 338 [emphasis in original]; see also O'Brien 1996, 359). What the Court did manage to do was dress the idea of black Americans' political and legal equality in the cloak of its constitutional authority. And this, in turn, paid at least three interrelated dividends.

First, the Court's imprimatur invested remedial policies and initiatives aimed at overcoming decades of racial discrimination with legitimacy. This provided those policies with invaluable political cover and contributed mightily to (perhaps even brought about) their creation (see Chapter 2 for a more complete discussion). In turn, these policies have dramatically expanded the opportunities available to black Americans.

Second, the Court's decisions dealing with racial apartheid had something of a catalytic effect on both governmental and nongovernmental action. Had the Court not pulled the trigger in the 1940s and 1950s, the nation's elected officials (let alone their state counterparts) might never have mustered the political will to address black constitutional rights and guarantees. (One need only consider the painfully slow pace of *Brown*'s implementation for evidence of the general reluctance of political authorities to deal with the issue, about which we have more to say below.) Meanwhile, these same decisions lent the civil rights movement energy and moral authority. With both, the civil rights community mobilized and then mounted public demonstrations to achieve the rights the Court's decisions promised (see Lee 2002 for a persuasive analysis of how the civil rights movement activated public opinion, leading to elite change).

Furthermore, the success of the civil rights movement in getting the Supreme Court to accede to its demands "provided a model and inspiration for a wide array of new social movements and political organizations" (Schudson 1998, 255). Schudson argues that many groups, including women, the poor, people with disabilities, workers, students, and patients followed the lead of the civil rights activists and pressed the Court for protection of their rights. The "rights revolution" linked the very notion of citizenship to the rights of individuals. "The new model citizenship added the courtroom to the voting booth as a locus of civic participation" (Schudson 1998, 250).

Some observers have criticized this emphasis on rights (e.g., Glendon 1991; see Schudson 1998 for a review of these critiques), arguing that the focus on individual rights takes away from the pursuit of the public good. In this view, defining citizenship in terms of rights makes individuals more central to politics than communities. The emphasis on rights also expands the power of the federal government and lawyers, since a federal bureaucracy must be in place to ensure that rights are upheld, and lawyers must be available to pursue rights violations in the court system. Furthermore, pursuing rights in the judicial system means that one party will win and another will lose—in contrast to a legislative battle, in which compromise usually carries the day.

Ultimately Schudson (1998) argues that these critiques go too far. The civil rights activists who pursued cases in the judicial system were not solely, perhaps not even primarily, concerned with their own narrow individual rights; instead, they were very much concerned with ensuring that their whole community could engage in the political process. Furthermore, the bureaucracy that developed in response to rights litigation dealt with, and continues to deal with, important political problems. It may be cumbersome at times, but the bureaucracy was put into place to ensure that all citizens could participate in our democratic society—a critical goal indeed. In short, Schudson argues, "We have to recognize that the claiming of rights, though it should not be the end of a citizen's political consciousness, is an invaluable beginning to it" (1998, 309).

Finally, the Court's destruction of the legal underpinnings of a racial caste system had the effect of educating the nation's white majority that denying blacks their full and equal citizenship was simply wrong. To be sure, the Court's desegregation decisions were met with strident white resistance (see Rodgers and Bullock 1972), and racial animus has not been magically excised from the nation's psyche. But the Court has acted as something of a "republican schoolmaster" in this issue area. That is, "through its explication of the law and its high moral standing, [the Court gave] the populace an example of the way good republicans should behave" (Franklin and Kosaki 1989, 752). In the case of black Americans, its decisions have certainly conferred legitimacy on their claims for equal rights, thereby increasing the white majority's support for this outcome. This may be the Court's greatest legacy. The Court has not resolved the "American dilemma," but it has brought the majority to a recognition and acceptance that legalized racial discrimination cannot be permitted.

Could the president or Congress have achieved this or a similar result? This hypothetical case is impossible to verify, but it seems very unlikely. As we point out in preceding chapters, neither the presidency nor Congress commands the level of public approbation (and the concomitant legitimizing capacity) of the Court. Consequently, neither can rely on the willing compliance of the public to effectuate their policies. Rather, they must enact and implement them, and the historical record indicates that their ability to do so is quite weak. To be sure, FDR and Truman took steps to arrest racial discrimination on the part of the federal government. Roosevelt, for instance, issued an executive order prohibiting racial discrimination in defense industries contracting with the national government, while Truman used his executive order power to integrate the nation's armed forces. (See Chapter 2 for more detailed discussions of both presidents' efforts on behalf of black political and legal rights.) The executive branch's ability to expand or at least protect black Americans' rights, however, was severely circumscribed by the opponents of black equality in Congress. By dint of the seniority system, southern senators and representatives chaired many of Congress's most powerful committees. The segregationists' power was especially pronounced in the Senate, where, despite minority status, Senate rules provided them with an influence far beyond their numerical presence. As a result, supporters of continued racial apartheid in Congress had an effective veto over the executive branch's actions.

If a bloc in Congress could scuttle efforts to advance black political and legal interests emanating from the executive branch, that same bloc might also be capable of sinking similar initiatives originating in the legislature. It seems that this is just what occurred. Indeed, it was not until the passage of the Civil Rights Act of 1957 that proponents of black political and legal rights mounted a successful legislative action—several years into the Court's expansion of civil rights protections.

At the dawn of the twenty-first century, the special historical relationship between black Americans and the Supreme Court may be wearing thin. As we pointed out in Chapter 2, the Court today is significantly more conservative than it was at the height of the civil rights revolution, and far less sympathetic to black Americans' calls for political and legal equality. On issues ranging from capital punishment to school desegregation, the Court has handed down a lengthening string of decisions that at best seem to have arrested black Americans' movement toward full and equal citizenship, and at worst have set it back. Take, for example, the school desegregation cases decided in 2007.[2] In a 5–4 ruling, the Court rejected the constitutionality of the use of race as a factor in student assignments to voluntarily address racial segregation in school districts. Inherent in this ruling is the danger that the omission of race as a consideration in school assignments may well result in residential patterns effecting segregated schools—in other words, a return to de facto segregation in schools countenanced, even encouraged, by the Supreme Court.

According to Legitimacy Theory, individual decisions should have little effect on black Americans' support for the Court in the short run. *In the long run, however, their effect may be more pernicious.* Diffuse support for an institution can decay over time if it is not replenished by the occasional output that is broadly and deeply accepted. As we have mentioned, black Americans who came of age during the height of the Warren Court's civil rights decisions have especially deep and largely immutable reservoirs of institutional loyalty to the Court (Gibson and Caldeira 1992). This cohort forms the bedrock of black support for the high bench. Black Americans who came of age during the Republican Court era, however, are both far less supportive of the Court and far more likely to see their already weak attachments to it fray in the face of outputs that run counter to their interests. As natural generational replacement reduces the presence of the Warren Court cohort in the black public, the firm bedrock of loyalty to the Court among blacks becomes thinner.

Exacerbating this trend is another development that might well challenge the Court's capacity to legitimize controversial policies among black Americans. Over the long run, Clarence Thomas's appointment may have undermined black support for the Court. Whereas Thurgood Marshall's presence on the bench encouraged a feeling of inclusion in the legal process and constitutional politics among black Americans (see Chapter 1), his replacement by Thomas has undone this sense. Strongly criticized by the black press (see Chapter 4), Thomas is portrayed and quite likely perceived by large elements of the black community as a racial turncoat. No longer does the Court include a figure in whom black Americans can lodge their hopes and expectations. Quite the opposite—the "black seat" on the present Court is a nearly constant source of frustration and constitutional hopes dashed.

We should note, however, that Justice Thomas is perceived favorably by some black citizens and thus may encourage faith in the Court among those with conservative leanings. Conservatives are relatively rare among blacks as a group, but Luks and Elms (2005) demonstrate a small yet significant increase in Republican party identification among the youngest generation of blacks. Blacks who were socialized after the civil rights movement are more likely to identify with the Republican party than their elders, and Thomas may serve as a rallying figure for these young black Republicans. To be sure, our experiment in Chapter 5 demonstrated that an attack on Thomas by a black member of Congress (coupled with the No Preferential Treatment frame) pushed moderate and conservative blacks closer to Thomas's conservative position on affirmative action.

Our research also has implications for the role of the media in a democratic society. Our study illustrates the high premium mainstream journalists place on objective reporting, by which they mean presenting both sides of a debate. There are many criticisms of that approach, including the fact that many issues have more than two sides. In American politics, presenting both sides is most often defined as providing both the Republican and the Democratic perspectives, but of course there are many other ways to present issues besides simply looking through the lens of one major party or the other. Another criticism is that on some issues there is only one correct side. Take global warming, for example. By trying to balance the argument that global warming is due to human behavior with arguments against that view, misinformation is communicated to the public (Boykoff and Boykoff 2004).

Our book highlights yet another criticism of the journalistic norm of objectivity: objective reporting is *not* neutral. Mainstream media coverage of Supreme Court rulings has an impact on public opinion. To be precise, mainstream media framing molds citizens' attitudes toward the Court's policy pronouncements. Mainstream journalists, of course, would not consider themselves advocates, but our findings clearly show the effect of their coverage on opinion, especially white public opinion. This raises the question of how different the advocacy press is from the mainstream press, and leads us to ask a provocative question: should objectivity be a journalistic norm, or would we be better off if journalists put aside the norm of objectivity and more openly presented their views? If all media were advocacy-oriented, then citizens would be aware of the perspective held by a particular outlet and would be able to filter the message accordingly, as the black subjects in our media experiment seemed to do. As the reader will recall, blacks were less influenced by the message from the mainstream media than whites were. We speculated that blacks are probably less trusting of mainstream media sources and therefore better able to guard against messages that do not square with their preexisting attitudes and values. Perhaps an advocacy-oriented media environment would better assist citizens in judging which policies and which candidates serve their personal interests and further their fundamental values.

A media environment dominated by advocacy-oriented outlets could result in citizens who are rarely exposed to information contrary to their views. If they sought news from several different advocacy presses, thereby exposing themselves to a wide marketplace of ideas, they would be well prepared to participate in enlightened democratic debate. But it is much more likely that, lacking either time or inclination, they would seek out news from a limited number of outlets. Thus, a reliance on an advocacy press could exacerbate citizens' existing partisan and ideological predispositions and perpetuate narrow, parochial understandings of issues. Although the mainstream media present only two sides, that is one more side than citizens would get from a democracy populated exclusively by advocacy media.

Our research also leads us to speculate on the impact of changing media technology. The rise of the "new media" might well be undermining blacks' diffuse support for the Court. In Chapter 5 we presented empirical results showing that greater exposure to the black media was related to lower levels of diffuse support for the Court. We suggested that this relationship was due to the absence of legitimizing symbols in the black press's coverage of the Court—symbols that the mainstream media regularly present and that help to build a foundation of institutional loyalty. Like the black press, new media outlets, such as cable channels that target narrow audiences, comedy programs that focus on politics, and Internet blogs, are more likely to be cause-oriented. These media are polarized and polarizing, and far more likely than the traditional media to present the Court and its outputs in political terms. Rather than focusing on symbols of judicial objectivity and impartiality, the new media tend to emphasize ideological winners and losers and thus will cast the Court's decisions in those terms. The danger for the Court is that as citizens increase their exposure to new media outlets, the positive messages about the Court will be reduced to a mere trickle, replaced by a series of messages presenting the Court as an ideological, perhaps even racially biased, player with a dog in the political fights of the day. As a result, one of the few remaining national institutions in which citizens still have appreciable confidence will see that confidence decay, and with it the Court's capacity to legitimize.

Finally, we turn to the importance of group attitudes in American politics. Since de Tocqueville, at least, observers of the American political system have recognized the importance of groups in our democracy. Here, we focus not on group membership, but on attitudes toward key groups in our society and how those attitudes influence opinion toward public policies. Our findings reaffirm the centrality of groups in public opinion formation and show that public opinion is not simply an elite-driven phenomenon. Instead, citizens bring a whole host of attitudes and experiences to the table. In the case of race, many citizens' attitudes stem from their experiences with mass-based political movements, especially the civil rights movement (Lee 2002). Not surprisingly, then, despite the Court's success at eliminating racial apartheid, racial attitudes still appreciably affect public opinion toward a wide range of public policies. From capital punishment to education to employment to where one lives to a whole host of other issues, racial identification and animosity influence citizens' beliefs, opinions, and choices. In a nation that prides itself on being a melting pot, a place where racial classification is not supposed to matter, it is fascinating the degree to which group attitudes still influence public opinion.

Future Directions

Using a multi-method approach, we have painted a fairly clear portrait of the Court's legitimizing capacity among African Americans and whites, albeit one moderated by the influences of the media and attitudes toward groups. Nevertheless, it would be a serious omission *not* to recognize that the Court speaks on a range of issues of salience to many other groups in American society. Indeed, the Court has protected the rights of a variety of racial, ethnic, and religious minorities: the Chinese,[3] Jews,[4] and Arabs,[5] for example. The Court addresses women's rights with some frequency,[6] and the rights of homosexuals were taken up in *Lawrence v. Texas*,[7] a case that garnered a decent amount of media attention when it was decided in 2003. Latinos are of growing importance in the American political system, and the Court has addressed,[8] and will continue to address, issues relevant to them.

Is the Court able to legitimize policies for these groups? Obviously, this is not an unimportant question. In a pluralist system such as ours, one hamstrung by separation of powers and checks and balances, it is unlikely that policy demands from identifiable groups are ever rapidly or fully met, thereby setting a context for mounting group frustrations. Latinos, for example, are a large and growing presence in the political system, as of 2006 the largest minority group in the nation. And as their numbers continue to grow, they will become an ever more powerful force, placing policy demands on the political process. Here the Court's legitimizing capacity among Latinos will be especially consequential. Doubtless the Court will be the arbiter on a wide range of issues of particular significance to them, from immigration policy to border and national security to English-only requirements to the refusal of businesses to serve non-English-speaking customers. How the Court rules and, even more importantly, how Latinos respond to the Court's rulings will affect the legitimacy of those policies and the continued stability of the American political system.

Just as we were somewhat myopic in our consideration of groups, it should also be noted that the range of controversial issues heard by the Court is not exhausted by capital punishment and affirmative action. To be sure, these are issues of great salience to African Americans, and, to a significant degree, they have taken on something of a racial cast in the eyes of the American populace. Cases concerning discrimination in housing and public accommodations, voting rights, legislative districting, criminal justice issues, and segregation in public schools continue to turn up in the federal courts. Considering the effects of the Supreme Court on public opinion with respect to these issues would make our research far more generalizable.

It also bears mentioning that our study documents the differences between mainstream and black newspapers and demonstrates the effect of those differences on public opinion, leading us to conclude that the mass media play an important role in communicating judicial news to American citizens. Our focus on newspapers, however, is somewhat narrow, especially given the large variety of media outlets that exist today. Mainstream papers like the *New York Times,* the *Washington Post,* and the *Los Angeles Times* are clearly traditional forms of media. Likewise, many of the black newspapers we examined are longstanding fixtures of the black community. The *New York Amsterdam News,* for example, has been published since 1909. Questions remain, then, about how nontraditional media outlets cover the Supreme Court and what effect that coverage has on public opinion.

We can turn on the television and see political issues discussed on *Oprah* and *The View.* Young Americans in particular receive their political news from outlets like *The Daily Show* and *The Colbert Report.* And of course many citizens turn to the internet for their news of the day, with some just glancing over Yahoo headlines and others spending hours blogging. Much more research needs to be conducted to gain an understanding of how these nontraditional media cover the Supreme Court, especially when it comes to issues of special concern to black Americans.

That the Supreme Court is consequential to the American experiment is beyond doubt. The exact contours of its consequence, however, remain to be fully determined. We have shown that the Court has the capacity to legitimize policies among a discrete and politically potent group in the political system, but we acknowledge that there are other important groups as well. We have shown that the Court, through its rulings, is able to shape public opinion on capital punishment and affirmative action—two politically salient issues, to be sure. But there are other issues that have left deep footprints on our political landscape and that the Court regularly considers. Does it mold opinion on these issues too? We have shown that media accounts moderate the public's reaction to a Court decision, but, as we noted, we examined only conventional types of media. Yet more and more of the American public gets political information from alternative media sources. Do these types of media moderate the effect of the Court? Obviously, this is a rich vein of scholarly inquiry. Significant questions remain and deserve to be answered. It is a vein not nearly played out, and in the future we intend to mine it.

Postscript

In response to the Supreme Court ruling upholding the University of Michigan Law School's affirmative action program, an initiative banning affirmative action was placed on the Michigan ballot in 2006. The ballot initiative—which declared affirmative action in public education, contracting, and employment unconstitutional—passed with support from 58% of Michigan voters. Given our argument concerning the legitimizing capacity of the U.S. Supreme Court (see Chapter 7), how is it that three short years after the Court ruled in favor of the law school's affirmative action program, a majority of voters in that state voiced their disagreement with affirmative action policies? We argue that the proponents of affirmative action did not chart the correct course in their campaign advertisements. One United Michigan, a coalition of groups supporting race-conscious policies, primarily focused on convincing voters that women would be harmed by ending affirmative action programs. Trisha Stein, the campaign manager for One United Michigan, was quoted as saying, "If this is a campaign about gender, the proposal [to ban affirmative action] will not pass, but if it's a campaign about race, it will likely pass."[9]

Instead of framing affirmative action as a women's issue, we believe that the supporters of the policy should have wrapped themselves in the robes of a particular woman—Lady Justice. In other words, the backers of affirmative action should have focused on the Supreme Court ruling in their favor and used constitutional and legal language justifying the policy. Through rhetoric and visual images, the supporters should have linked themselves as closely as possible to the majesty of the Supreme Court, allowing its legitimacy to spill over onto affirmative action policies. Our study certainly implies that this would have been an effective campaign strategy.

APPENDIX A

Stimulus for

Legitimacy Experiment

The first story was the stimulus in the Supreme Court condition; the second story was the stimulus in the Department of Education condition.

Supreme Court Rules for Affirmative Action

WASHINGTON, D.C. — The Supreme Court ruled in favor of affirmative action earlier this week in a case involving a 15-year-old white female student. Sarah Wessman claimed she was illegally denied admission to Boston Latin, a merit based public high school, in favor of less qualified minority students.

Boston Latin is one of four public schools in Boston that admits the first 50 percent of its students solely on exam scores and grades, while the remaining 50 percent are weighted by race. For example, if 15 percent of the remaining applicants are black, 15 percent of those admitted must be black. The Supreme Court supported this policy in their ruling.

Justice Sandra Day O'Connor spoke for the Court in the majority opinion, "School admission committees like that at Boston Latin have a compelling interest in promoting diversity within public merit-based educational programs."

Kweisi Mfume, the President of the NAACP, praised the ruling as a victory. Mfume said, "The ruling allows minorities a better chance at admittance to esteemed schools throughout the United States."

The Supreme Court decision will force Wessman and other students like her to attend other public schools.

The case was *Wessman, et al. v. Boston Municipal Board of Education*, No. 99-1723.

Education Department Rules for Affirmative Action

WASHINGTON, D.C. — The Department of Education approved a new rule favoring affirmative action earlier this week. The ruling affects a case involving a 15-year-old white female student. Sarah Wessman claimed she was illegally denied admission to Boston Latin, a merit based public high school, in favor of less qualified minority students.

Boston Latin is one of four public schools in Boston that admits the first 50 percent of its students solely on exam scores and grades, while the remaining 50 percent are weighted by race. For example, if 15 percent of the remaining applicants are black, 15 percent of those admitted must be black. The Department of Education's ruling supported this policy.

Education Secretary Richard Riley said that, "School admission committees like that at Boston Latin have a compelling interest in promoting diversity within public merit-based educational programs."

Kweisi Mfume, the President of the NAACP, praised the Department of Education's new rule as a victory. Mfume said, "The ruling allows minorities a better chance at admittance to esteemed schools throughout the United States."

The Education Department's rule will force Wessman and other students like her to attend other public schools.

APPENDIX B

List of Black Newspapers

Our sample included 22 black newspapers:

Baltimore Afro-American
Bay State Banner (Boston, MA)
Chicago Weekend
Cincinnati Call & Post
Cleveland Call & Post
Columbus Times (GA)
Los Angeles Sentinel
Miami Times
Michigan Chronicle
Michigan Citizen
Network Journal (NY)

New Pittsburgh Courier
New York Amsterdam News
New York Beacon
Philadelphia Tribune
Portland Skanner (OR)
Precinct Reporter (San Bernadino, CA)
Sacramento Observer
Sun Reporter (San Francisco, CA)
Tri-State Defender (Memphis, TN)
Washington Afro-American
Washington Informer

APPENDIX C

Stimulus for
Media Framing Experiment

The first story below represents the No Preferential Treatment frame; the second article illustrates the Dramatic Setback frame. In each story, the manipulation involving Justice Clarence Thomas is presented in boldface.

Supreme Court Deals Blow to Programs that Give Preferences Based on Race

By ELIZABETH NORTON

WASHINGTON, June 12 — The Supreme Court jeopardized a broad range of federal affirmative action programs Monday in a landmark case, ruling that preferential treatment based on race is almost always unconstitutional.

Federal programs that classify people by race, even for an ostensibly benign purpose such as expanding opportunities for members of minorities, are presumed unconstitutional, the Court said in a 5-to-4 opinion. Writing for the majority, Justice Sandra Day O'Connor said such programs must be subject to the most searching constitutional inquiry and can survive only if they are "narrowly tailored" to accomplish a "compelling governmental interest."

The affirmative action case arose when a white road builder from Colorado complained that he lost a federal contract for a guard rail repair to a Hispanic businessman, even though the white businessman had submitted a slightly lower bid.

The Hispanic businessman had benefited from a 1987 law that requires the Department of Transportation to steer at least 10% of its funds to firms owned by racial minorities or women.

A federal district court and the Tenth Circuit Court of Appeals rejected the white contractor's claim on the grounds that the Supreme Court had twice before upheld affirmative action programs authorized by Congress.

But, since the Court last visited the issue in 1990, Justice Thurgood Marshall, the first black appointee to the Court and a leading liberal, had retired, and his seat was taken by Justice Clarence Thomas, a staunch black conservative.

With Thomas casting the fifth and deciding vote on Monday, the Court reversed course and took a giant step toward wiping away preferential policies based on race. In a concurring opinion, Thomas denounced affirmative action in the strongest terms. "Government cannot make us equal," Thomas said, "it can only recognize, respect and protect us as equal before the law. That these programs may have been motivated, in part, by good intentions cannot provide refuge from the principle that under our Constitution, the Government may not make distinctions on the basis of race."

[New York Congressman Major Owens, a Black representative from Brooklyn, called Thomas a danger to African Americans. "His voting record on critical issues facing the very survival of the Black community is deplorable. The judge believes that affirmative action is a form of paternalism and that minorities cannot compete with whites without their patronizing indulgence. Judge Thomas, although an African American, is definitely not acting in the best interests of the Black community."]

Thomas and O'Connor were joined in the majority by Chief Justice William H. Rehnquist and Justices Antonin Scalia and Anthony M. Kennedy.

Justice Ruth Bader Ginsburg led the dissent, joined by Justices John Paul Stevens, David H. Souter, and Stephen G. Breyer.

The case was *Adarand Constructors v. Pena*, No. 93-1841.

Supreme Court Deals Blow to Programs that Correct Past Discrimination

By ELIZABETH NORTON

WASHINGTON, June 12 — A dark shadow was cast this week across long standing efforts to overcome at least some of the effects of centuries of discrimination and segregation practiced against African Americans when the Supreme Court handed down its ruling Monday in a landmark case.

Federal programs that classify people by race, even for an ostensibly benign purpose such as expanding opportunities for members of minorities, are presumed unconstitutional, the Court said in a 5-to-4 opinion. Writing for the majority, Justice Sandra Day O'Connor said such programs must be subject to the most

searching constitutional inquiry and can survive only if they are "narrowly tailored" to accomplish a "compelling governmental interest."

The affirmative action case arose when a white road builder from Colorado complained that he lost a federal contract for a guard rail repair to a Hispanic businessman, even though the white businessman had submitted a slightly lower bid.

The Hispanic businessman had benefited from a 1987 law that requires the Department of Transportation to steer at least 10% of its funds to firms owned by racial minorities or women.

The law's rationale was that such a program would provide business opportunities for those segments of the society—meaning, African Americans, other minorities, and women—who had previously been denied such opportunities.

A federal district court and the Tenth Circuit Court of Appeals rejected the white contractor's claim on the grounds that the Supreme Court had twice before upheld affirmative action programs authorized by Congress.

But, since the Court last visited the issue in 1990, Justice Thurgood Marshall, the first black appointee to the Court and a leading liberal, had retired, and his seat was taken by Justice Clarence Thomas, a staunch black conservative.

With Thomas casting the fifth and deciding vote on Monday, the Court reversed course and took a giant step toward wiping away preferential policies based on race. In a concurring opinion, Thomas denounced affirmative action in the strongest terms. "Government cannot make us equal," Thomas said, "it can only recognize, respect and protect us as equal before the law. That these programs may have been motivated, in part, by good intentions cannot provide refuge from the principle that under our Constitution, the Government may not make distinctions on the basis of race."

[**New York Congressman Major Owens, a Black representative from Brooklyn, called Thomas a danger to African Americans. "His voting record on critical issues facing the very survival of the Black community is deplorable. The judge believes that affirmative action is a form of paternalism and that minorities cannot compete with whites without their patronizing indulgence. Judge Thomas, although an African American, is definitely not acting in the best interests of the Black community."**]

Thomas and O'Connor were joined in the majority by Chief Justice William H. Rehnquist and Justices Antonin Scalia and Anthony M. Kennedy.

Justice Ruth Bader Ginsburg led the dissent, joined by Justices John Paul Stevens, David H. Souter, and Stephen G. Breyer.

The case was *Adarand Constructors v. Pena,* No. 93-1841.

APPENDIX D

Question Wordings for
Media Framing Experiment

DEPENDENT VARIABLES

Opinion on Supreme Court Ruling
Subjects were asked to place themselves on a 5-point scale ranging from "strongly disagree" (1) to "strongly agree" (5): "Do you agree or disagree with the Supreme Court's ruling in this case?"

Opinion on Implementation of Supreme Court Ruling
Subjects were asked to place themselves on a 4-point scale ranging from "very slowly" (1) to "very quickly" (4): "Regardless of whether you agree or disagree with the Supreme Court's ruling on affirmative action, how quickly do you think the federal government should end programs that classify people by race?"

INDEPENDENT VARIABLES

No Preferential Treatment Frame
    Dramatic Setback (0)
    No Preferential Treatment (1)

No Attack on Justice Thomas
    Attack on Thomas (0)
    No Attack on Thomas (1)

Racial Resentment

Subjects were asked to place themselves on a 5-point scale ranging from "strongly agree" to "strongly disagree." Individual items were recoded as necessary, so the high number (5) indicates more racial resentment. The racial resentment scale was created by taking a mean of the following four items:

1. "Irish, Italians, Jewish and many other minorities overcame prejudice and worked their way up. Blacks should do the same without any special favors."
2. "Over the past few years, blacks have gotten less than they deserve."
3. "It's really a matter of some people not trying hard enough; if blacks would only try harder they could be just as well off as whites."
4. "Generations of slavery and discrimination have created conditions that make it difficult for blacks to work their way out of the lower class."

Individualism

Subjects were asked to place themselves on a 5-point scale ranging from "strongly agree" to "strongly disagree." Individual items were recoded as necessary, so the high number (5) indicates greater support for individualism. The individualism scale was created by taking a mean of the following three items:

1. "Most people who don't get ahead shouldn't blame the system; they have only themselves to blame."
2. "If people work hard they almost always get what they want."
3. "Most people who do not get ahead in life probably work as hard as people who do."

Ideology

Subjects were asked to place themselves on a 7-point scale ranging from "extremely liberal" (1) to "extremely conservative" (7): "Which point on this scale best describes your political views?"

Male

Female (0)
Male (1)

Frame by Attack Interaction

The AFFIRMATIVE ACTION FRAME BY ATTACK CLARENCE THOMAS interaction was created by multiplying the individual terms.

Frame by Racial Resentment Interaction

The AFFIRMATIVE ACTION FRAME BY RACIAL RESENTMENT interaction was created by multiplying the individual terms.

Frame by Individualism Interaction

The AFFIRMATIVE ACTION FRAME BY INDIVIDUALISM interaction was created by multiplying the individual terms.

Blacks and the
U.S. Supreme Court Survey

TABLE E.1   DEMOGRAPHIC CHARACTERISTICS
OF BSCS RESPONDENTS

	2003 BSCS: Pre (N = 425)	2003 BSCS: Post (N = 286)
Sex		
Male	39.3%	38.5%
Female	60.7	61.5
Age		
18–24	12.6%	9.5%
25–34	15.6	14.4
35–44	21.3	21.5
45–54	22.5	22.9
55–64	15.9	17.6
65+	12.1	14.1
Education		
Elementary	3.1%	3.6%
Some high school	10.2	10.6
High school graduate	28.1	25.4
Some college	30.9	32.8
College graduate	14.3	13.0
Some post-graduate+	13.3	14.8

(continued)

TABLE E.1 *Continued*

	2003 BSCS: Pre (N = 425)	2003 BSCS: Post (N = 286)
Family income		
Less than $10,000	14.0%	13.8%
$10,000–14,999	11.5	12.3
$15,000–19,999	11.5	11.9
$20,000–29,999	14.0	13.8
$30,000–49,999	20.8	19.3
$50,000–74,999	13.3	12.6
$75,000+	15.0	16.4
Marital status		
Married/separated	37.7%	36.3%
Never married	41.2	39.1
Widowed	7.1	8.5
Divorced	14.0	16.2
Labor force status		
Working full/part time	61.0%	58.9%
Unemployed/laid off	8.1	8.2
Not in labor force	30.9	33.0

TABLE E.2   LOGIT ESTIMATES OF WAVE 2 PARTICIPATION

Variable	Coefficient	Standard Error
Party identification	−.01	.07
Ideology	.03	.07
Member of black political organization	−.04	.26
Political interest	−.10	.13
Sex	.20	.24
Age	.02*	.01
Education	.02	.09
Marital status	−.21	.26
Employment status	−.42	.27
Income	.05	.08
Constant	−.02	.79

Note: Dependent variable is participation in reinterview (1 = yes); N = 368; Log-Likelihood = −227.62; Pseudo R^2 = .03. Two-tailed significance tests: *p < .05.

Notes

CHAPTER 1. LEGITIMACY AND AMERICAN DEMOCRACY

1. 347 U.S. 483 (1954).

2. The following discussion relies heavily on Easton (1965).

3. Not all legitimacy theorists accept the Eastonian framework's legitimizing role for diffuse support (see Craig 1993; Lowenberg 1971). Their criticism stems from the bright-line conceptual division between diffuse support (and its ability to cloak controversial policies with legitimacy) and specific support for a policy. Craig (1993) argues that Easton's conceptualization of diffuse versus specific support is untestable because the concepts and attitudes central to it defy measurement with any degree of validity or precision. According to him, by definition attitudes that tap diffuse support cannot covary with short-term forces, and any losses of popular affect that produce calls for systemic change cannot be the product of specific support. "Exceptions can be interpreted only as the product of inferior methodology" (1993, 9). A telling criticism, to be sure; yet it is not necessarily fatal to our theoretical perspective. "It is possible with careful conceptualization and measurement to keep the two [types of support] separate" (Caldeira and Gibson 1992, 637 n. 1). We studiously follow their counsel here.

4. 515 U.S. 200 (1995).

5. The overall response rate for the 1996 NBES is 65%.

6. *Gratz et al. v. Bollinger et al.* (539 U.S. 244 [2003]); *Grutter v. Bollinger et al.* (539 U.S. 306 [2003]).

CHAPTER 2. BLACKS, CIVIL RIGHTS,
AND THE SUPREME COURT

A version of this chapter, coauthored with Katherine Tate (University of California, Irvine), was presented at "America's Second Revolution: The Path to and from *Brown v. Board of Education*," a symposium sponsored by the Benjamin L. Hooks Institute for Social Change, University of Memphis, March 12–14, 2004.

1. *Dred Scott v. Sanford* (60 U.S. 393 [1857]) concerned the status of Dred Scott, a Missouri slave, who had resided for some time in Illinois, a free state. Writing for an extremely divided Court, Chief Justice Taney ruled against Scott's emancipation. In his opinion, Taney held that Scott had no standing to sue because he was not a citizen of the United States. But Taney did not stop there. He proceeded to declare that slaves were precluded from ever being endowed with national citizenship. Finally, Taney found the anti-slavery provisions of the Missouri Compromise unconstitutional. Taney's decision may have been an attempt to resolve the slavery controversy once and for all and preserve the Union. If so, it failed miserably. The decision helped to sharpen the sectional divisions that erupted four years later in the Civil War.

2. 83 U.S. 36 (1873).

3. 92 U.S. 542 (1876).

4. 109 U.S. 3 (1883).

5. The notion that the Fourteenth Amendment only protects private citizens from improper, discriminatory actions of the state.

6. 163 U.S. 537 (1896).

7. The NAACP used this strategy in an education case for the first time in *Missouri ex rel. Gaines v. Canada* (305 U.S. 337 [1938]). Lloyd Gaines, a black citizen of Missouri, was denied admission to the Missouri University Law School because of his race. Since the state did not have a black law school, it offered to pay out-of-state tuition for blacks seeking a legal education in one of the neighboring states. Gaines and the NAACP sued, arguing that Missouri had denied him his right to an equal, if separate, education in Missouri. The state's responsibility could not be obviated by shipping him to a neighboring state; nor could Missouri delay its responsibility to some future, indeterminate date when it would build and staff a substantially equal black institution. Gaines's rights, as defined by *Plessy,* could be met only by his immediate admission to Missouri's all-white law school.

The U.S. Supreme Court agreed. Writing for a 6–2 majority, Chief Justice Hughes emphasized the "equal" requirement of the "separate but equal" doctrine. "By the operation of the laws of Missouri a privilege has been created for white law students which is denied negroes by reason of their race. The white resident is afforded a legal education within the State; the negro resident having the same qualifications is refused it. . . . That is a denial of the equality of legal right" (305 U.S. 337, 349).

8. Much of the following discussion is based upon Kelly, Harbison, and Belz (1991, 581–83) and McAdam (1982, 73–116).

9. *Bailey v. Alabama* (219 U.S. 219 [1910]), *Guinn v. U.S.* (238 U.S. 347 [1915]), and *Buchanan v. Warley* (245 U.S. 60 [1917]).

10. The significance of the NAACP to the cause of black civil rights cannot be overstated, and we do not pretend to do justice either to its organizational history or to its role in the battle for equality here. Excellent and far more thorough treatments can be found in Kluger (1975), Patterson (2001), Tushnet (1987), and Vose (1967).

11. The so-called "switch-in-time" is well documented elsewhere (see, for example, Cushman 1994; Leuchtenburg 1995; McCloskey 1994; Pritchett 1948; Schwartz 1993), though the reason for it is unclear (it was probably not because the Court was cowed by FDR's threat to pack it: see Cushman 1994; Leuchtenburg 1995). Whether because of a change in the strength of the government's arguments or a change in the ideology of the entire legal community, the Court's transformation was complete by 1941. By then, FDR had appointed eight of the nine justices.

12. 323 U.S. 214 (1944).

13. This was a party primary election restricted to white voters. Proponents argued that white primaries did not run afoul of the Fourteenth and Fifteenth Amendments because the primary elections were not structured to exclude blacks under the color of state law. Rather, it was the state's Democratic party, a private organization, that passed a rule denying blacks the right to participate in the primary election. Initially, this interpretation was supported by the Supreme Court (*Grovey v. Townsend,* 295 U.S. 45 [1935]).

14. 321 U.S. 649 (1944).

15. *Grovey v. Townsend* (295 U.S. 45 [1935]).

16. 313 U.S. 299 (1941).

17. *Breedlove v. Suttles* (302 U.S. 277 [1937]).

18. Alabama, Arkansas, Mississippi, Texas, and Virginia.

19. 383 U.S. 663 (1966).

20. *Guinn v. U.S.* (248 U.S. 347 [1915]).

21. *Lassiter v. Northampton County Board of Elections* (360 U.S. 45 [1959]).

22. Moreover, alternative tests (e.g., "grandfather clauses," property qualifications) were prescribed so as not to disenfranchise illiterate whites.

23. Pritchett (1984, 342) cites the following figures: "in at least 129 counties in 10 Southern states, less than 10 percent of eligible blacks were registered. In 17 representative 'black belt' counties where blacks constituted a majority of the population, only about 3 percent were found to be registered."

24. For more on the origin and intent of the Citizenship Schools, see Morris (1984, 149–55).

25. Alabama, Georgia, Louisiana, Mississippi, South Carolina, and Virginia. The act did not apply to Arkansas, Florida, and Texas because they did not use literacy tests.

26. 383 U.S. 301 (1966).

27. 400 U.S. 12 (1970).

28. *Shelley v. Kraemer, McGhee v. Sipes* (334 U.S. 1 [1948]); *Hurd v. Hodge, Urciolo v. Hodge* (334 U.S. 24 [1948]). The former two cases dealt with restrictive covenants at the state level; the latter two, with restrictive covenants in the District of Columbia. Upon granting *certiorari,* the four cases were consolidated. *Shelley* is typically the titular case and therefore the best known. Accordingly, we briefly review its facts here. For the seminal treatment of the restrictive covenant cases per se, see Vose (1967).

29. *Buchanan v. Warley* (245 U.S. 60 [1917]).

30. 271 U.S. 323 (1926).

31. 334 U.S. 1 (1948).

32. 313 U.S. 80 (1941).

33. 339 U.S. 816 (1950).

34. "The issue before us . . . is whether the railroad's rules and practices cause passengers to be subjugated to undue or unreasonable prejudice or disadvantage in violation of §3(1) [of the Interstate Commerce Act]" (*Henderson v. U.S.,* 339 U.S. 816, 824 [1950]).

35. 339 U.S. 629 (1950).

36. 339 U.S. 637 (1950).

37. This notion was based on the NAACP's "sociological argument," which held simply that separate institutions based upon race necessarily confer a badge of inferiority on members of the minority race. The NAACP first used this argument in an *amicus* brief in 1946. In *Sweat* and *McLaurin* it reappeared alongside straightforward inequality arguments. The Court's increasing receptiveness to the argument is indicated by its mention of intangible aspects handicapping minority litigants in both opinions. By the time *Brown v. Board of Education of Topeka* (347 U.S. 483 [1954]) was briefed, the NAACP's argument was highly polished, and the Court accepted it wholesale.

38. 347 U.S. 483 (1954).

39. *Holmes v. City of Atlanta* (350 U.S. 879 [1955]), *Gayle v. Browder* (352 U.S. 903 [1956]), *Evers v. Dwyer* (358 U.S. 202 [1958]), *Johnson v. Virginia* (373 U.S. 61 [1963]).

40. "We, therefore, conclude that the action of the Congress in the adoption of the Act as applied here to a motel which concededly serves interstate travelers is within the power granted it by the Commerce Clause of the Constitution" (*Heart of Atlanta v. U.S.,* 379 U.S. 241, 261). Interestingly, in the debate surrounding the 1875 Civil Rights Act, Senator Matthew Carpenter suggested that the act's aim of prohibiting private discriminatory conduct might be better accomplished by basing it in Congress's commerce authority.

41. 379 U.S 241 (1964).

42. 379 U.S 294 (1964).

43. *Green v. New Kent County* (391 U.S. 430 [1968]), *Alexander v. Holmes* (396 U.S. 19 [1969]), and *Swann v. Charlotte-Mecklenburg School System* (402 U.S. 1 [1971]).

44. 401 U.S. 424 (1971).

45. *Swann v. Charlotte-Mecklenburg School System* (402 U.S. 1 [1971]).

46. *Keyes v. School District No. 1, Denver, Colorado* (413 U.S. 189 [1973]). Here the Court required the Denver school board to prove that it had not intentionally kept black children out of white schools. Since it could not, the city was constitutionally obligated to desegregate the entire system. In effect, the Court ordered Denver to institute citywide busing, the first time such an order was imposed on a city outside the South.

47. *Columbus Board of Education v. Penick* (443 U.S. 449 [1979]). "While the Columbus School System's dual black-white character was not mandated by state law as of 1954, the record certainly shows intentional segregation by the Columbus Board." And therefore: "The Board's continuing 'affirmative duty to disestablish the dual system' is . . . beyond question" (456, 460).

48. *Board of Education of City School District of New York v. Harris* (444 U.S. 130 [1979]).

49. *University of California Regents v. Bakke* (438 U.S. 265 [1978]).

50. *United Steelworkers v. Weber* (443 U.S. 193 [1979]).

51. *Fullilove v. Klutznick* (448 U.S. 448 [1980]). Congress established a 10% target for the participation of minority business enterprises.

52. 411 U.S. 1 (1973).

53. 418 U.S. 717 (1974).

54. Warren Burger in 1969, Harry Blackmun (1970), Lewis Powell and William Rehnquist (1971), and John Paul Stevens (1975).

55. The "misery index" is the annual sum of the nation's unemployment and inflation rates.

56. $t = -2.25$ (1960–1976); $t = -4.49$ (1982–present).

57. Sandra Day O'Connor (1981), Antonin Scalia (1986), Anthony Kennedy (1988). Rehnquist became Chief Justice in 1986.

58. 490 U.S. 228 (1989).

59. This was effectively the disparate impact theory of *Griggs v. Duke Power Company* (1971), discussed above.

60. 488 U.S. 469 (1989).

61. 490 U.S. 755 (1989).

62. 497 U.S. 547 (1990).

63. 515 U.S. 200 (1995).

64. *Grutter v. Bollinger,* 539 U.S. 306 (2003).

65. *Gratz v. Bollinger,* 539 U.S. 244 (2003).

66. The surveys and studies we review use different questions to tap attitudes toward the Supreme Court, use varying sampling techniques, sometimes make

generalizations based on small sample sizes, and may be susceptible to race-of-interviewer effects. These methodological issues make it difficult to draw hard and fast conclusions from the data.

67. This assertion is predicated on a cohort analysis by Gibson and Caldeira (1992) and a similar analysis conducted on the 2003 BSCS data. In both analyses, an examination of respondents with high levels of diffuse support for the Court finds the greatest share in the Warren Court–era cohort.

CHAPTER 3. ESTABLISHING THE
SUPREME COURT'S LEGITIMIZING CAPACITY

1. Our measure of political interest focused on interest in politics generally. The NBES does not contain a question on general political interest, but it does include an item measuring interest in political campaigns. Thus, this comparison should be viewed with some caution, since the question is a bit different, as are the number of response options.

2. The overrepresentation of males is not surprising given the gender breakdown at Purdue University: 58% male and 42% female.

3. There is some slippage in this comparison because we measured political interest on a 7-point scale, while the National Election Study used a 4-point scale.

4. The Cronbach's alpha for the black diffuse support scale is .60 (mean = 3.6, sd = .60, n = 123); for the white scale, .67 (mean = 4.1, sd = .64, n = 95).

5. The predicted probability of the dichotomous experimental condition was computed by allowing the variable to range from 0 to 1, while holding the remaining variables constant at their means. For all continuous variables, predicted probabilities were computed by allowing the variable of interest to range ± one standard deviation about its mean while holding the remaining variables at their mean values.

6. See Cook and Barrett (1992) for an example of research using similar items to measure behavioral support for social welfare policies.

7. The Cronbach's alpha for the behavioral intention scale is .80 (mean = 1.63, sd = .51, n = 69).

8. A reviewer suggested a counterhypothesis: that people protesting for purely symbolic reasons might be *more likely* to challenge the legitimate authority—the Supreme Court. We did not find this to be the case.

CHAPTER 4. DIFFERENT PRESSES, DIFFERENT FRAMES

1. The following discussion is drawn from Wolseley (1990).

2. 515 U.S. 200 (1995).

3. The Court's most demanding standard of review. In effect, the application of the "strict scrutiny" standard is often fatal.

4. *City of Richmond v. J. A. Croson Co.* (488 U.S. 469 [1989]).

5. Two years later, a federal district court in Denver, Colorado, concluded that the subcontracting clause in question failed to met the Court's strict scrutiny standard and was therefore unconstitutional (*Adarand Constructors, Inc. v. Frederico Pena,* 965 F. Supp. 1556 [1997]).

6. "Another Blow to Affirmative Action," *St. Louis Post-Dispatch,* June 14, 1995, sec. B.

7. There are also important differences between mainstream print and television coverage. See Slotnick and Segal (1998).

8. Anthony W. McCarthy, "Justice Thomas Does It to Us Again," *Baltimore Afro-American,* June 17, 1995, sec. A.

9. "Cong. Owens Calls Clarence Thomas a Danger to African-Americans," *New York Amsterdam News,* July 15, 1995.

10. Julianne Malveaux, "Malveaux at Large: What a Fool Believes: Clarence Thomas and Affirmative Action," *Sun Reporter,* June 22, 1995.

11. "Thomas, An Embarrassment," *Cleveland Call & Post,* June 29, 1995, sec. A.

12. "Thomas, An Embarrassment."

13. Malveaux, "Malveaux at Large: What a Fool Believes."

14. David G. Savage, "High Court Deals Severe Blow to Federal Affirmative Action Rights: Justices Hold That Race-Based Preferential Treatment Is Almost Always Unconstitutional. But an Opening Is Left for Narrow, Specific Bias Remedies," *Los Angeles Times,* June 13, 1995, sec. A.

15. 539 U.S. 244 (2003) and 539 U.S. 306 (2003), respectively.

16. After a careful reading of the articles in our sample, we developed these four frames: No Preferential Treatment, Dramatic Setback, Policy Implementation, and Affirmative Action Is Not Dead. A graduate student coded all of the stories, and the first author coded a subset of 24 articles to conduct a reliability test. Our intercoder reliability was 92%.

17. Scholars have demonstrated the impact of the NPT frame on public opinion (see, for example, Nelson and Kinder 1996), but that research has not considered the legitimacy-conferring capacity of the Supreme Court.

CHAPTER 5. MEDIA FRAMING AND THE SUPREME COURT'S LEGITIMIZING CAPACITY

1. 515 U.S. 200.

2. Using an experimental design, Mondak (1994) has taken a turn at analyzing this question. Manipulating the context of the media's coverage of three Supreme Court decisions, he found that "variance in media reports does not limit the Supreme Court's power of legitimation" (689). Whatever impact the media have is indirect: "Information reported in news stories can shape policy agreement, and thus bring indirect impact on policy legitimacy" (689). We do not believe, however, that his analysis completely addresses the possible consequences of media coverage. Mondak's experimental stimuli do not capture the systematic

differences in the black and mainstream presses' construction of a Court decision, since his stimuli are drawn from mainstream coverage of the Court. Indeed, where possible he used the exact wording of the *New York Times* story (685). Since mainstream coverage likely complements preexisting levels of institutional credibility (see, for example, Gibson, Caldeira, and Baird 1998), it is little wonder that the effect of the media's content on policy legitimacy is quite minimal.

3. In a study using data from 1992, Kuklinski and Hurley (1994) showed that blacks used race, rather than ideology, as a cue for interpreting political messages from elites. That is, *both* Jesse Jackson and Clarence Thomas were more influential than Ted Kennedy. We think this finding is time-bound, however. Because of his race, many blacks were willing to give Justice Thomas the benefit of the doubt and were quite hopeful that his "true" attitudes would emerge once he had life tenure on the bench and was no longer beholden to Republican interests (Edley 1998; Mansbridge and Tate 1992). More than a decade later, Thomas's track record is clear, and liberal blacks no longer give him the time of day, let alone the benefit of the doubt. A quick analysis of data from the 1996 National Black Election Study (NBES) shows that liberal citizens are significantly less "warm" toward Thomas than conservative ones.

4. The black students' survey included three additional questions: two asking about attitudes toward the Supreme Court ruling in *Bush v. Gore* and one asking about attention to the "war on terror." We asked about *Bush v. Gore* because black citizens had such a strong negative reaction to that case, some even likening it to the *Dred Scott* decision. We were afraid that a lingering distaste for the Court might hinder our ability to assess its legitimizing capacity. We were also concerned that our experiment might be affected by its timing, just a few months after the September 11 terrorist attacks. In initial analyses, we included these items as control variables; however, they did not have a significant impact on black support for the Court's rulings or black attitudes toward the implementation of the ruling against affirmative action. For that reason we do not include these variables in the models presented here.

5. Diffuse support was used as an independent variable only in the analysis of the white subjects. For some reason, a significant percentage of black subjects (13%) did not answer the diffuse support questions.

6. We refer to this battery of items as "racial resentment" even when blacks are the respondents in order to make it clear that the same set of items was used for both black and white subjects.

7. Although the coefficient misses statistical significance, we consider it substantively important as well as statistically important, given the small sample size ($n = 55$).

8. Ideally, we would analyze moderates and conservatives separately. Unfortunately (and not surprisingly), there are only 14 conservatives in our sample, leading us to lump them in with the moderates ($n = 68$).

9. We do not present this analysis here, but the results are available from the authors upon request.

10. In contrast, whites' ideological leanings do not moderate their responses. These results are available from the authors upon request.

11. Although we do not present this analysis here, we came to this conclusion by examining the impact of the Frame by Racial Resentment and the Frame by Individualism interaction terms on attitudes toward the policy's implementation. The results are available from the authors upon request.

12. 539 U.S. 558 (2003).

13. We are not the first to comment on the biases that result from the mainstream media's emphasis on objectivity. See Bennett's (1988) discussion of the ways in which objectivity leads to bias in the news. Entman and Rojecki (2000) argue, "For the news, it is clear that conventions of objectivity, the relatively simple techniques used to ensure balance and avoid bias, are not up to the task of covering issues in a racialized culture" (211). Iyengar and McGrady (2007, 67–68) provide an insightful analysis of how the norm of objectivity influenced coverage of the infamous Willie Horton ad during the 1988 presidential campaign. Ansolabehere, Behr, and Iyengar (1993) summarize research on campaign news by stating, "Campaign reporting may be objective, but the consequences of campaign reporting for the candidates is [sic] far from neutral" (64). Curran (2005) bemoans the emphasis on objective journalism in the mainstream media and suggests that adversarial media can provide "liberating access to alternative ideas and arguments" (126). Finally, Bennett and Serrin (2005) argue that objective reporting undermines the watchdog role of journalists. In short, a number of scholars have pointed out the limitations of the mainstream media's focus on objectivity and neutrality.

14. As is typical with cross-sectional data, the specific causal direction of the relationship between diffuse support and exposure to black media is difficult to pin down. In the final analysis, it is possible that the causal direction of the relationship we are modeling runs in the opposite direction. That is, exposure to black media sources is at least partly a function of attitudinal forces that include support for white social and political institutions, such as the Supreme Court. Given the weight of the circumstantial evidence linking knowledge of the Court, the nature of the mainstream media's portrayal of the Court, and attitudes toward the Court, however, we believe that our specification of the causal direction is more persuasive.

CHAPTER 6. THE SUPREME COURT'S LEGITIMIZING CAPACITY AMONG AFRICAN AMERICANS

1. 410 U.S. 113 (1973).

2. 481 U.S. 279 (1987).

3. 408 U.S 238 (1972).

4. These statistics are available on the Death Penalty Information Center website: http://www.deathpenaltyinfo.org/article.php?scid=5&did=184#defend, accessed on June 3, 2008. Despite these statistics, some readers may question

whether capital punishment is, in fact, a particularly racially charged issue. Certainly at the time *McCleskey* was decided (and our data were gathered), capital punishment was presented in racial terms. *Every* article on *McCleskey* appearing in the *Washington Post, New York Times,* and *Los Angeles Times* around the time of the decision (i.e., between March 23 and June 21, 1987) specifically addresses the issue of racial bias in the death penalty's implementation. Clearly, capital punishment is *perceived* in racial terms.

5. To locate these polling data, we conducted a Lexis-Nexis search of their "Polls & Surveys" using the terms "death penalty and black" for all available years.

6. The accession number for the *L.A. Times* survey is 0219354.

7. The accession number for the Princeton Survey Research Associates/*Newsweek* poll is 0280519.

8. The accession number for the Gallup Poll is 0322054.

9. To locate these polling data, we conducted a Lexis-Nexis search of their "Polls & Surveys" using the terms "affirmative action and black" for all available years. The accession number for the CBS News/*New York Times* poll is 0288624.

10. The accession number for this question in the CBS News/*New York Times* poll is 0288643.

11. The accession number for the NBC/*Wall Street Journal* poll is 0246471.

12. *Gregg v. Georgia* (428 U.S. 153 [1976]); *Proffitt v. Florida* (428 U.S. 242 [1976]); *Jurek v. Texas* (428 U.S. 262 [1976]).

13. *Coker v. Georgia* (433 U.S. 584 [1977]); *Barefoot v. Estelle* (463 U.S. 880 [1980]); *Spaziomo v. Florida* (468 U.S. 447 [1984]); *Ford v. Wainwright* (477 U.S. 399 [1986]); *Tison v. Arizona* (481 U.S. 137 [1987]); *McCleskey v. Kemp* (481 U.S. 279 [1987]).

14. *Gratz et al. v. Bollinger et al.* (539 U.S. 306 [2003]); *Grutter v. Bollinger et al.* (539 U.S. 244 [2003]).

15. This conundrum about the causal relationship between institutional support for the Supreme Court and specific support for its outputs is reminiscent of the classic efforts of scholars of voting behavior to sort out the causal relationships among party identification, issue positions, candidate evaluations, and vote choice (Markus and Converse 1979; Page and Jones 1979).

16. 531 U.S. 98 (2000).

17. Here we are using the concept of "race consciousness" to refer to a wide body of literature. Some of the research focuses specifically on racial identification, while other studies examine components of race consciousness, such as power discontent and system blame.

18. This expectation is similar to the finding made by Hoekstra and Segal (1996) concerning the susceptibility of public opinion to the persuasive effect of a Court ruling. Examining local public opinion, they found that those individuals for whom a case is especially salient are less susceptible to the Court's persuasive effect.

19. The GSS is a full probability sample. The response rate for the 1987 black oversample was 79.9%.

20. A principal components factor analysis indicates that the structure is unidimensional. The first and only factor emerging accounts for 40% of the variance; Cronbach's alpha = .64. Admittedly, this is a somewhat crude measure of race consciousness; however, these were the best items available in the 1987 GSS. The question tapping perceptions of black influence has been used in previous research to measure one aspect of group consciousness: power discontent (Gurin, Hatchett, and Jackson 1989; Miller et al. 1981; Reese and Brown 1995). The other three items measure black opposition to restrictions on basic freedoms: what Gurin, Hatchett, and Jackson in their classic study of group consciousness refer to as "rejection of legitimacy of race stratification" (1989, 77).

21. To ensure that our findings are robust across different model specifications, we also conducted the analysis using the mean, rather than the factor scores, of these four items. This modification did not change the substantive interpretation of our results. The results we report in Table 6.1 and Figure 6.1 are derived from the specification using the factor scores.

22. Whether the Court's power of judicial review should be eliminated, whether the Court itself should be eliminated, whether the U.S. Constitution should be rewritten to reduce the Court's powers, whether the Court's jurisdiction should be limited, and whether people should work to prevent the Court from being abolished. A principal components factor analysis indicates that the structure is unidimensional. The first and only factor emerging accounts for 51% of the variance; Cronbach's alpha = .75.

23. To ensure that our findings are robust across different model specifications, we also conducted the analysis using the mean, rather than the factor scores, of these four items. This modification did not change the substantive interpretation of our results. The results we report in Table 6.1 and Figure 6.1 are derived from the specification using the factor scores.

24. *Gender*: 1 = female. *Partisanship*: 1 = Democrat, 2 = Independent, 3 = Republican. *Ideology*: 1 = liberal, 2 = moderate, 3 = conservative. *Attendance* is measured as the frequency of church attendance: 0 = never, 4 = once a month, 8 = more than once a week. *Suburban*: 1 = lives in suburban area, 0 = otherwise. *Children*: 1 = yes, 0 = no. *Trust*: 1 = almost never, 2 = sometimes, 3 = most of the time, 4 = almost always. In earlier analyses we also included age, education level, region, and marital status. None of these forces, however, even approached statistical security, and on the rule of parsimony, we excluded them from the final model.

25. In contrast, research on white support for capital punishment shows that white women are *less likely* than white men to favor the death penalty (see Peffley and Hurwitz 2002).

26. We computed the predicted probabilities for the capital punishment model by varying the variable of interest one standard deviation below and above its mean, while holding the remaining variables constant at their mean values.

27. To identify high and low group-centrism, we divided our measure at its mean.

28. We computed these impacts by varying the independent variable of interest from its minimum to its maximum value while holding the remaining independent variables constant at their mean. We discuss diffuse support's effect in terms of the percentage change in the likelihood of a black respondent's supporting capital punishment, given a change in the independent variable. For instance, the likelihood for a black respondent with low group-centrism and high levels of diffuse support for the Court is .61, compared with .33 when diffuse support is low. Computing the difference between the two likelihoods (.28) and dividing by the likelihood of a respondent's supporting capital punishment when levels of diffuse support are low (.33) yields .848, or 85%.

29. The overall response rate for the 1996 NBES is 65%.

30. *Gender:* 1 = female. *Partisanship:* 0 = strong Republican, .5 = Independent, 1 = strong Democrat. *Ideology:* 0 = strong liberal, .5 = moderate, 1 = strong conservative. *Income:* 0 = < $10K, .1 = $10K–15K, .2 = $15K–20K, .3 = $20K–25K, .4 = $25K–30K, .5 = $30K–40K, .6 = $40K–50K, .7 = $50K–75K, .8 = $75K–90K, .9 = $90k–105K, 1 = > $105K. *Education:* 0 = < high school, .125 = some high school, .250 = high school, .375 = some college, .5 = AA, .625 = BA, .75 = some graduate school, .825 = MA, 1 = PhD. *Trust:* 0 = never, .33 = sometimes, .66 = most of the time, 1 = almost always. As in our examination of black attitudes on the death penalty, we included a number of other demographic variables in earlier analyses. None of these forces approached statistical significance, and again on the rule of parsimony, we excluded them from the final model.

31. To derive the probabilities for the affirmative action model, we computed the likelihood of moving from the "support" to the "oppose" categories by varying the variable of interest 1 standard deviation above and below its mean, while holding the remaining variables constant at their mean value.

32. Because our measure of black group-centrism is skewed to the left, we divided it at the 10th percentile.

33. These analyses are available from the authors upon request.

34. We are indebted to an anonymous reviewer for bringing this parallel to our attention.

CHAPTER 7. THE CAUSAL RELATIONSHIP BETWEEN PUBLIC OPINION TOWARD THE COURT AND ITS POLICIES

1. Hoekstra (2000) does perform a longitudinal study, allowing her to estimate the effect of rulings on subsequent evaluations of the Court. As Gibson, Caldeira, and Spence (2003b) note, however, her analysis does not make use of the most valid soundings of the Court's institutional support.

2. 539 U.S. 244 (2003); 539 U.S. 306 (2003).

3. *Regents of the University of California v. Bakke* (438 U.S. 265 [1978]).

4. *Lawrence v. Texas* (539 U.S. 558 [2003]).

5. Interviews were also completed with a small sample of non-black respondents. In the analysis presented in this chapter, we do not draw on the non-black data.

6. With survey data generally, and panel data in particular, a key criterion used to gauge the data's generalizability is the response rate. There are a variety of ways to calculate these rates. We chose to use a formula that takes into account the fact that a certain percentage of the undetermined telephone numbers will not belong to black subscribers. Thus, we use the formula: Completed Interviews + Partial Interviews/(Completed + Partial + [Incidence × Undetermined Numbers] + Eligible Refusals). Two alternative measures of response rate are the incidence rate and the combined incidence rate. The former yields a response rate of 29.8%; the latter, 41.3%.

7. Our measure of diffuse support for the Court is a modified version of the instrument originally developed by Caldeira and Gibson (1992).

8. To provide some comparative leverage, we followed the same approach to compute diffuse support for the Court among black Americans using data originally collected by Gibson and Caldeira (1992; see also Caldeira and Gibson 1992). This resulted in a diffuse support measure of 3.52 on a 5-point scale. Rescaling to a 4-point index yields a diffuse support measure of 2.82.

9. To analyze this model, we use AMOS software, with all available data used to compute the estimates (Arbuckle and Wothke 1999).

10. In more technical language, we are testing a two-wave model with synchronous effects (Finkel 1995). In our model, we allow the pre-ruling diffuse support and affirmative action latent variables to covary. We also estimate the covariance between the error terms associated with the structural equations. Both of these relationships are negative, but neither reaches statistical significance. We also examined an alternative model specification: a two-wave model with cross-lagged effects. The substantive and statistical conclusions we would draw from the results of the cross-lagged model are comparable to those presented here.

11. 531 U.S. 98 (2000).

12. The χ^2 difference between the two models, $120.030 - 119.014 = 1.016$, with two degrees of freedom. This nonsignificant difference indicates that the results displayed in Table 7.8 hold across levels of race consciousness.

CHAPTER 8. CONCLUSION

1. To be sure, black Americans' present-day share of the "American dream" remains unacceptably small, but when it is compared with the size of their share prior to the 1950s, it is clear that tangible gains have been made.

2. *Parents Involved in Community Schools v. Seattle School District, No. 1, et al.; Meredith v. Jefferson County Board of Education, et al.* (127 S. Ct. 2738 [2007]).

3. *Yick Wo v. Hopkins* (118 U.S. 356 [1886]).

4. *Shaare Tefila Congregation v. Cobb* (481 U.S. 614 [1987]).

5. *St. Francis College v. Al-Khazraq* (481 U.S. 604 [1987]).

6. A fairly recent example is *Burlington Northern and Santa Fe Railway Company v. White* (548 U.S. 53 [2006]). The case concerned a female employee's allegation that her employer unlawfully reassigned her for making a sexual harassment complaint. The Court found for the employee.

7. 539 U.S. 558 (2003).

8. For example, *Havens Reality Corp. v. Coburn* (455 U.S. 363 [1982]).

9. Quoted in David S. Broder, "Female Voters Courted in Affirmative-Action Fight," *Washington Post,* November 2, 2006.

References

Adamany, David W., and Joel B. Grossman. 1983. "Support for the Supreme Court as a National Policymaker." *Law and Policy Quarterly* 5:405–37.

Allen, Richard L., Michael C. Dawson, and Ronald E. Brown. 1989. "A Schema-Based Approach to Modeling African-American Racial Belief Systems." *American Political Science Review* 83:421–41.

Ansolabehere, Stephen, Roy Behr, and Shanto Iyengar. 1993. *The Media Game.* New York: Macmillan.

Arbuckle, James L., and Werner Wothke. 1999. *Amos 4.0 User's Guide.* Chicago: SmallWaters Corporation.

Aronson, Elliot, Phoebe C. Ellsworth, J. Merrill Carlsmith, and Marti Hope Gonzales. 1990. *Methods of Research in Social Psychology.* New York: McGraw-Hill.

Baldus, David C. 1995. "The Death Penalty: Dialogue between Law and Social Science." *Indiana Law Journal* 70:1033–41.

Barkan, Steven E., and Steven F. Cohn. 1994. "Racial Prejudice and Support for the Death Penalty by Whites." *Journal of Research in Crime and Delinquency* 31:202–9.

Barnum, David G. 1985. "The Supreme Court and Public Opinion: Judicial Decisionmaking in the Post New Deal Period." *Journal of Politics* 47:652–65.

Barrett-Howard, Edith, and Tom R. Tyler. 1986. "Procedural Justice as a Criterion in Allocation Decisions." *Journal of Personality and Social Psychology* 50:296–304.

Bartels, Brandon L. 2003. "A Top-Down Model of Specific Support for the U.S. Supreme Court." Paper presented at the annual meeting of the Midwest Political Science Association, Chicago, April 3–6.

Bennett, W. Lance. 1988. *News: The Politics of Illusion*. 2nd ed. New York: Longman.

Bennett, W. Lance, and William Serrin. 2005. "The Watchdog Role." In *The Press*, ed. Geneva Overholser and Kathleen Hall Jamieson. Oxford: Oxford University Press, 169–88.

Bobo, Lawrence, and Franklin D. Gilliam, Jr. 1990. "Race, Sociopolitical Participation, and Black Empowerment." *American Political Science Review* 84:377–93.

Boninger, David S., Jon A. Krosnick, and Matthew K. Berent. 1995. "Origins of Attitude Importance: Self-Interest, Social Identification, and Value Relevance." *Journal of Personality and Social Psychology* 68:61–80.

Boykoff, Maxwell T., and Jules M. Boykoff. 2004. "Balance as Bias: Global Warming and the U.S. Prestige Press." *Global Environmental Change* 14:125–36.

Bratton, Kathleen A., and Kerry L. Haynie. 1999. "Agenda Setting and Legislative Success in State Legislatures: The Effects of Gender and Race." *Journal of Politics* 61:658–79.

Browne, Michael W., and Robert Cudek. 1993. "Alternative Ways of Assessing Model Fit." In *Testing Structural Equation Models*, ed. Kenneth A. Bollen and J. Scott Long. Newbury Park, CA: Sage, 136–62.

Burns, Nancy, Donald R. Kinder, Steven J. Rosenstone, Virginia Sapiro, and the National Election Studies. 2002. AMERICAN NATIONAL ELECTION STUDY, 2000: PRE- AND POST-ELECTION SURVEY [Computer file]. 2nd ICPSR version. Ann Arbor: University of Michigan, Center for Political Studies [producer], 2001; Inter-university Consortium for Political and Social Research [distributor], 2002.

Caldeira, Gregory A. 1986. "Neither the Purse nor the Sword: Dynamics of Public Confidence in the Supreme Court." *American Political Science Review* 80:1209–26.

Caldeira, Gregory A. 1991. "Courts and Public Opinion." In *The American Courts: A Critical Assessment*, ed. John B. Gates and Charles A. Johnson. Washington, DC: CQ Press, 303–34.

Caldeira, Gregory A., and James L. Gibson. 1992. "The Etiology of Public Support for the Supreme Court." *American Journal of Political Science* 36:635–64.

Casey, Gregory. 1974. "The Supreme Court and Myth: An Empirical Investigation." *Law and Society Review* 8:385–419.

Clawson, Rosalee A., Elizabeth R. Kegler, and Eric N. Waltenburg. 2001. "The Legitimacy-Conferring Authority of the U.S. Supreme Court: An Experimental Design." *American Politics Review* 29:566–91.

Clawson, Rosalee A., Elizabeth R. Kegler, and Eric N. Waltenburg. 2003. "Supreme Court Legitimacy and Group-Centric Forces: Black Support for Capital Punishment and Affirmative Action." *Political Behavior* 25:289–311.

Clawson, Rosalee A., Katherine Tate, and Eric N. Waltenburg. 2003. *Blacks and the U.S. Supreme Court Survey*. National Science Foundation SES #0331509.

Clawson, Rosalee A., Katherine Tate, and Eric N. Waltenburg. 2004. "'For Better and for Worse?' Black Opinion on the U.S. Supreme Court since *Brown*."

Paper prepared for presentation at America's Second Revolution: The Path to and from *Brown v. Board of Education,* sponsored by the Benjamin L. Hooks Institute for Social Change, University of Memphis, March 12–14.

Clawson, Rosalee A., and Eric N. Waltenburg. 2004. "The U.S. Supreme Court's Legitimizing Capacity among Blacks and Latinos." Paper presented at the annual meeting of the Southern Political Science Association, New Orleans, January 8–10.

Conover, Pamela Johnston. 1988. "The Role of Social Groups in Political Thinking." *British Journal of Political Science* 18:51–76.

Conover, Pamela, and Stanley Feldman. 1981. "The Origins and Meanings of Liberal/Conservative Self-Identifications." *American Journal of Political Science* 25:617–45.

Converse, Philip E. 1964. "The Nature of Belief Systems in Mass Publics." In *Ideology and Discontent,* ed. David E. Apter. New York: Free Press, 206–61.

Cook, Fay L., and Edith J. Barrett. 1992. *Support for the American Welfare State: The Views of Congress and Public.* New York: Columbia University Press.

Coyle, Marcia. 1995. "Supreme Court Ponders Racial Set-Aside Case: New Era or Step Backward?" *National Law Journal,* January 23, A1.

Craig, Stephen C. 1993. *The Malevolent Leaders: Popular Discontent in America.* Boulder, CO: Westview Press.

Curran, James. 2005. "What Democracy Requires of the Media." In *The Press,* ed. Geneva Overholser and Kathleen Hall Jamieson. Oxford: Oxford University Press, 120–40.

Cushman, Barry. 1994. "Rethinking the New Deal Court." *Virginia Law Review* 80:201–61.

Dahl, Robert. 1957. "Decisionmaking in a Democracy: The Supreme Court as a National Policymaker." *Journal of Public Law* 6:279–95.

Davis, Darren, and Christian Davenport. 1997. "The Political and Social Relevancy of *Malcolm X*: The Stability of African American Political Attitudes." *Journal of Politics* 59:550–64.

Davis, James Allan, and Tom W. Smith. 1972–1998. *General Social Surveys, 1972–1998* [machine-readable data file]. Principal investigator, James A. Davis; director and co-principal investigator, Tom W. Smith; co-principal investigator, Peter V. Marsden; sponsored by National Science Foundation. NORC ed. Chicago: National Opinion Research Center [producer]; Storrs, CT: Roper Center for Public Opinion Research, University of Connecticut [distributor].

Davis, Michael D., and Hunter R. Clark. 1994. *Thurgood Marshall: Warrior at the Bar, Rebel at the Bench.* Rev. ed. New York: Citadel Press.

Davis, Richard. 1994. *Decisions and Images: The Supreme Court and the Press.* Englewood Cliffs, NJ: Prentice-Hall.

Dawson, Michael C. 1994. *Behind the Mule.* Princeton: Princeton University Press.

Dawson, Michael C. 2001. *Black Visions.* Chicago: University of Chicago Press.

Druckman, James N. 2001. "On the Limits of Framing Effects: Who Can Frame?" *Journal of Politics* 63:1041–66.

Eagly, Alice H., and Shelly Chaiken. 1993. *The Psychology of Attitudes.* Fort Worth, TX: Harcourt Brace Jovanovich.

Easton, David. 1965. *A Systems Analysis of Political Life.* New York: Wiley.

Easton, David, and Jack Dennis. 1969. *Children in the Political System: Origins of Political Legitimacy.* New York: McGraw-Hill.

Edley, Christopher, Jr. 1998. *Not All Black and White: Affirmative Action and American Values.* New York: Hill and Wang.

Entman, Robert M. 1993. "Framing: Toward Clarification of a Fractured Paradigm." *Journal of Communication* 43(4):51–58.

Entman, Robert M., and Andrew Rojecki. 2000. *The Black Image in the White Mind.* Chicago: University of Chicago Press.

Epstein, Lee, Jeffrey A. Segal, Harold J. Spaeth, and Thomas G. Walker. 1994. *The Supreme Court Compendium.* Washington, DC: Congressional Quarterly Press.

Feldman, Stanley. 1993. "Economic Individualism and Mass Belief Systems." *American Politics Quarterly* 11:3–29.

Finkel, Steven E. 1995. *Causal Analysis with Panel Data.* Thousand Oaks, CA: Sage Publications.

Fiske, Susan, and Shelley Taylor. 1991. *Social Cognition.* 2nd ed. New York: McGraw-Hill.

Fox, James Allen, Michael L. Radelet, and Julie L. Bonsteel. 1990–91. "Death Penalty Opinion in the Post-*Furman* Years." *Review of Law and Social Change* 18:499–528.

Franklin, Charles H., and Liane C. Kosaki. 1989. "Republican Schoolmaster: The U.S. Supreme Court, Public Opinion, and Abortion." *American Political Science Review* 83:751–71.

Franklin, Charles, and Liane C. Kosaki. 1995. "Media, Knowledge, and Public Evaluations of the Supreme Court." In *Contemplating Courts,* ed. Lee Epstein. Washington, DC: Congressional Quarterly Books, 352–75.

Franklin, Charles H., Liane C. Kosaki, and Herbert M. Kritzer. 1993. "The Salience of Supreme Court Decisions." Paper presented at the annual meeting of the American Political Science Association, Washington, DC, September 2–5.

Gamson, William A. 1992. *Talking Politics.* New York: Cambridge University Press.

Gamson, William A., and Katherine E. Lasch. 1983. "The Political Culture of Social Welfare Policy." In *Evaluating the Welfare State,* ed. Shimon E. Spiro and Ephraim Yuchtman-Yaar. New York: Academic Press.

Gamson, William A., and Andre Modigliani. 1987. "The Changing Culture of Affirmative Action." *Research in Political Sociology* 3:137–77.

Gans, Herbert J. 1979. *Deciding What's News.* New York: Pantheon Books.

Gibson, James L. 1989. "Understandings of Justice: Institutional Legitimacy, Procedural Justice, and Political Tolerance." *Law and Society Review* 23:469–96.

Gibson, James L., and Gregory A. Caldeira. 1992. "Blacks and the U.S. Supreme Court: Models of Diffuse Support." *Journal of Politics* 54:1120–45.

Gibson, James L., Gregory A. Caldeira, and Vanessa A. Baird. 1998. "On the Legitimacy of National High Courts." *American Political Science Review* 92: 343–58.

Gibson, James L., Gregory A. Caldeira, and Lester Kenyatta Spence. 2003a. "Measuring Attitudes toward the United States Supreme Court." *American Journal of Political Science* 47:354–67.

Gibson, James L., Gregory A. Caldeira, and Lester Kenyatta Spence. 2003b. "The Supreme Court and the U.S. Presidential Election of 2000: Wounds, Self-Inflicted or Otherwise?" *British Journal of Political Science* 33:535–56.

Gilliam, Franklin D., Jr. 1996. "Exploring Minority Empowerment: Symbolic Politics, Governing Coalitions and Traces of Political Style in Los Angeles." *American Journal of Political Science* 40:56–81.

Gilliam, Franklin D., Jr., and Shanto Iyengar. 2000. "Prime Suspects: The Influence of Local Television News on the Viewing Public." *American Journal of Political Science* 44:560–73.

Glendon, Mary Ann. 1991. *Rights Talk*. New York: Free Press.

Graber, Doris. 1993. *Mass Media and American Politics*. 4th ed. Washington, DC: Congressional Quarterly Press.

Grosskopf, Anke, and Jeffery J. Mondak. 1998. "Do Attitudes toward Specific Supreme Court Decisions Matter? The Impact of *Webster* and *Texas v. Johnson* on Public Confidence in the Supreme Court." *Political Research Quarterly* 51:633–54.

Gurin, Patricia, Shirley Hatchett, and James S. Jackson. 1989. *Hope and Independence: Blacks' Response to Electoral and Party Politics*. New York: Russell Sage Foundation.

Handberg, Roger, and William S. Maddox. 1982. "Public Support for the Supreme Court in the 1970s." *American Politics Quarterly* 10:333–46.

Haynie, Kerry L. 2001. *African American Legislators in the American States*. New York: Columbia University Press.

Herring, Mary. 1990. "Legislative Responsiveness to Black Constituents in Three Deep South States." *Journal of Politics* 52:740–58.

Higginbotham, A. Leon, Jr. 1996. *Shades of Freedom: Racial Politics and Presumptions of the American Legal System*. New York: Oxford University Press.

Hirsch, Herbert, and Lewis Donohew. 1968. "A Note on Negro-White Differences in Attitudes toward the Supreme Court." *Social Science Quarterly* 49:556–62.

Hoekstra, Valerie J. 1995. "The Supreme Court and Opinion Change: An Experimental Study of the Court's Ability to Change Public Opinion." *American Politics Quarterly* 23:109–29.

Hoekstra, Valerie J. 2000. "The Supreme Court and Local Public Opinion." *American Political Science Review* 94:89–100.

Hoekstra, Valerie J., and Jeffrey A. Segal. 1996. "The Shepherding of Local Opinion: The Supreme Court and *Lamb's Chapel*." *Journal of Politics* 58:1079–1102.

Huspek, Michael. 2004. "Black Press, White Press, and Their Opposition: The Case of the Police Killing of Tyisha Miller." *Social Justice* 31:217–41.

Iyengar, Shanto. 1991. *Is Anyone Responsible?* Chicago: University of Chicago Press.

Iyengar, Shanto, and Jennifer A. McGrady. 2007. *Media Politics: A Citizen's Guide.* New York: W. W. Norton.

Jacobs, Ronald N. 2000. *Race, Media, and the Crisis of Civil Society: From Watts to Rodney King.* Cambridge: Cambridge University Press.

Jaros, Dean, and Robert Roper. 1980. "The U.S. Supreme Court: Myth, Diffuse Support, Specific Support, and Legitimacy." *American Politics Quarterly* 8:85–105.

Jeffries, Judson L. 2000. *Virginia's Native Son: The Election and Administration of Governor L. Douglas Wilder.* West Lafayette, IN: Purdue University Press.

Johnson, Timothy R., and Andrew D. Martin. 1998. "The Public's Conditional Response to Supreme Court Decisions." *American Political Science Review* 92:299–310.

Johnston, John. 1972. *Econometric Methods.* 2nd ed. New York: McGraw-Hill.

Kellstedt, Paul M. 2000. "Media Framing and the Dynamics of Racial Policy Preferences." *American Journal of Political Science* 44:239–55.

Kelly, Alfred H., Winfred A. Harbison, and Herman Belz. 1991. *The American Constitution: Its Origins and Development.* 7th ed. New York: W. W. Norton.

Kinder, Donald R., and Thomas R. Palfrey. 1993. "On Behalf of an Experimental Political Science." In *Experimental Foundations of Political Science,* ed. Donald R. Kinder and Thomas R. Palfrey. Ann Arbor: University of Michigan Press, 1–39.

Kinder, Donald R., and Lynn M. Sanders. 1996. *Divided by Color.* Chicago: University of Chicago Press.

Kinder, Donald R., and David O. Sears. 1981. "Prejudice and Politics: Symbolic Racism Versus Racial Threats to the Good Life." *Journal of Personality and Social Psychology* 40:414–31.

Kinder, Donald R., and Nicholas Winter. 2001. "Exploring the Racial Divide: Blacks, Whites, and Opinion on National Policy." *American Journal of Political Science* 45:439–53.

King, Gary, Robert O. Keohane, and Sidney Verba. 1994. *Designing Social Inquiry.* Princeton: Princeton University Press.

Kluger, Richard. 1975. *Simple Justice: The History of Brown v. Board of Education and Black America's Struggle for Equality.* New York: Knopf.

Krosnick, Jon A., David S. Boninger, Yao C. Chuang, Matthew K. Berent, and Catherine G. Carnot. 1993. "Attitude Strength: One Construct or Many Related Constructs?" *Journal of Personality and Social Psychology* 65:1132–51.

Kuklinski, James H., and Norman L. Hurley. 1994. "On Hearing and Interpreting Political Messages: A Cautionary Tale of Citizen Cue-Taking." *Journal of Politics* 56:729–51.

Lee, Taeku. 2002. *Mobilizing Public Opinion: Black Insurgency and Racial Attitudes in the Civil Rights Era*. Chicago: University of Chicago Press.

Leuchtenburg, William E. 1995. *The Supreme Court Reborn: The Constitutional Revolution in the Age of Roosevelt*. New York: Oxford University Press.

Lowenberg, Gerhard. 1971. "The Influence of Parliamentary Behavior on Regime Stability: Some Conceptual Clarifications." *Comparative Politics* 3:177–200.

Lublin, David. 1997. *The Paradox of Representation: Racial Gerrymandering and Minority Interests in Congress*. Princeton: Princeton University Press.

Luks, Samantha, and Laurel Elms. 2005. "African-American Partisanship and the Legacy of the Civil Rights Movement: Generational, Regional, and Economic Influences on Democratic Identification, 1973–1994." *Political Psychology* 26:735–54.

Mansbridge, Jane. 1999. "Should Blacks Represent Blacks and Women Represent Women? A Contingent 'Yes.'" *Journal of Politics* 61:628–57.

Mansbridge, Jane, and Katherine Tate. 1992. "Race Trumps Gender: The Thomas Nomination in the Black Community." *PS: Political Science & Politics* 25: 488–92.

Marcus, George E., John L. Sullivan, Elizabeth Theiss-Morse, and Sandra L. Wood. 1995. *With Malice toward Some*. Cambridge: Cambridge University Press.

Markus, Gregory B., and Philip E. Converse. 1979. "A Dynamic Simultaneous Equation Model of Electoral Choice." *American Political Science Review* 73:1055–70.

Marshall, Thomas. 1989. *Public Opinion and the Supreme Court*. Boston: Unwin.

Martindale, Carolyn. 1986. *The White Press and Black America*. New York: Greenwood Press.

McAdam, Doug. 1982. *Political Process and the Development of Black Insurgency, 1930–1970*. Chicago: University of Chicago Press.

McClerking, Harwood K., and Ismail White. 1999. "Black Media and Black Linked Fate." Paper presented at the annual meeting of the Southern Political Science Association, Savannah, GA, November 3–7.

McCloskey, Robert G. 1994. *The American Supreme Court*. 2nd ed. Chicago: University of Chicago Press.

Miller, Arthur, Patricia Gurin, Gerald Gurin, and Oksana Malanchuk. 1981. "Group Consciousness and Political Participation." *American Journal of Political Science* 25:494–511.

Mondak, Jeffery J. 1990. "Perceived Legitimacy of Supreme Court Decisions: Three Functions of Source Credibility." *Political Behavior* 12:263–84.

Mondak, Jeffery J. 1991. "Substantive and Procedural Aspects of Supreme Court Decisions as Determinants of Institutional Approval." *American Politics Quarterly* 19:174–88.

Mondak, Jeffery J. 1992. "Institutional Legitimacy, Policy Legitimacy, and the Supreme Court." *American Politics Quarterly* 20:457–77.

Mondak, Jeffery J. 1994. "Policy Legitimacy and the Supreme Court: The Sources and Contexts of Legitimation." *Political Research Quarterly* 47:675–92.

Mondak, Jeffery J., and Shannon I. Smithey. 1997. "The Dynamics of Public Support for the Supreme Court." *Journal of Politics* 59:1114–42.

Morris, Aldon D. 1984. *The Origins of the Civil Rights Movement: Black Communities Organizing for Change.* New York: Free Press.

Murphy, Walter F., James E. Fleming, Sotirios A. Barber, and Stephen Macedo. 2003. *American Constitutional Interpretation.* 3rd ed. New York: Foundation Press.

Murphy, Walter F., and Joseph Tanenhaus. 1968. "Public Opinion and the United States Supreme Court: A Preliminary Mapping for Some Prerequisites for Court Legitimation of Regime Changes." *Law and Society Review* 2:357–82.

Murphy, Walter F., Joseph Tanenhaus, and Daniel Kastner. 1973. *Public Evaluations of Constitutional Courts: Alternative Explanations.* Beverly Hills: Sage.

Nelson, Thomas E., Rosalee A. Clawson, and Zoe M. Oxley. 1997. "Media Framing of a Civil Liberties Conflict and Its Effect on Tolerance." *American Political Science Review* 91:567–83.

Nelson, Thomas E., and Donald R. Kinder. 1996. "Issue Frames and Group-Centrism in American Public Opinion." *Journal of Politics* 58:1055–78.

Nelson, Thomas E., Zoe M. Oxley, and Rosalee A. Clawson. 1997. "Toward a Psychology of Framing Effects." *Political Behavior* 19:221–46.

O'Brien, David M. 1995. *Constitutional Law and Politics,* vol. 2: *Civil Rights and Civil Liberties.* 2nd ed. New York: W. W. Norton.

O'Brien, David M. 1996. *Storm Center: The Supreme Court in American Politics.* 4th ed. New York: W.W. Norton.

O'Callaghan, Jerome, and James O. Dukes. 1992. "Media Coverage of the Supreme Court's Caseload." *Journalism Quarterly* 69:195–203.

Orfield, Gary, and Chungmei Lee. 2004. *Brown at 50: King's Dream or Plessy's Nightmare?* Cambridge, MA: Civil Rights Project, Harvard University; available from http://www.eric.ed.gov/ERICDocs/data/ericdocs2sql/content _storage_01/0000019b/80/1b/b8/82.pdf (accessed December 17, 2007).

Owens, Reginald. 1996. "Entering the Twenty-First Century: Oppression and the African American Press." In *Mediated Messages and African-American Culture,* ed. Venise T. Berry and Carmen L. Manning-Miller. Thousand Oaks, CA: Sage Publications, 96–116.

Page, Benjamin I., and Calvin C. Jones. 1979. "Reciprocal Effects of Policy Preferences, Party Loyalties, and the Vote." *American Political Science Review* 73:1071–90.

Pan, Zhongdang, and Gerald M. Kosicki. 1993. "Framing Analysis: An Approach to News Discourse." *Political Communication* 10:55–75.

Patterson, James T. 2001. *Brown v. Board of Education: A Civil Rights Milestone and Its Troubled Legacy.* New York: Oxford University Press.

Peffley, Mark, and Jon Hurwitz. 2002. "The Racial Component of 'Race-Neutral' Crime Policy Attitudes." *Political Psychology* 23:59–74.

Peffley, Mark, Todd Shields, and Bruce Williams. 1996. "The Intersection of Race and Crime in Television News Stories: An Experimental Study." *Political Communication* 13:309–27.

Pitkin, Hanna Fenichel. 1967. *The Concept of Representation.* Berkeley: University of California Press.

Pritchett, C. Herman. 1948. *The Roosevelt Court: A Study in Judicial Politics and Values, 1937–1947.* New York: Macmillan.

Pritchett, C. Herman. 1984. *Constitutional Civil Liberties.* Englewood Cliffs, NJ: Prentice-Hall.

Reese, Laura, and Ronald E. Brown. 1995. "The Effects of Religious Messages on Racial Identity and System Blame among African Americans." *Journal of Politics* 57:24–43.

Reeves, Keith. 1997. *Voting Hopes or Fears?* New York: Oxford University Press.

Rodgers, Harrell R., Jr., and Charles S. Bullock III. 1972. "School Desegregation: A Policy Analysis." *Journal of Black Studies* 2:409–37.

Rosenberg, Gerald. 1991. *The Hollow Hope: Can Courts Bring About Social Change?* Chicago: University of Chicago Press.

Sandys, Marla, and Edmund F. McGarrell. 1995. "Attitudes toward Capital Punishment: Preference for the Penalty or Mere Acceptance?" *Journal of Research in Crime and Delinquency* 32:191–213.

Schudson, Michael. 1998. *The Good Citizen.* Cambridge, MA: Harvard University Press.

Schwartz, Bernard. 1993. *A History of the Supreme Court.* New York: Oxford University Press.

Sears, David O. 1986. "College Sophomores in the Laboratory: Influences of a Narrow Data Base on Social Psychology's View of Human Nature." *Journal of Personality and Social Psychology* 51:515–30.

Sears, David O., Colette van Laar, Mary Carrillo, and Rick Kosterman. 1997. "Is It Really Racism? The Origins of White Americans' Opposition to Race-Targeted Policies." *Public Opinion Quarterly* 61:877–86.

Secret, Philip E., James B. Johnson, and Susan Welch. 1986. "Racial Differences in Attitudes toward the Supreme Court's Decision on Prayer in the Public Schools." *Social Science Quarterly* 67:877–86.

Segal, Jeffrey A., Harold J. Spaeth, and Sara C. Benesh. 2005. *The Supreme Court in the American Legal System.* New York: Cambridge University Press.

Shaw, David. 1981. "Media Coverage of the Court: Improving but Still Not Adequate." *Judicature* 65:18–24.

Shingles, Richard. 1981. "Black Consciousness and Political Participation: The Missing Link." *American Political Science Review* 75:76–91.

Sigelman, Lee. 1979. "Black-White Differences in Attitudes toward the Supreme Court: A Replication in the 1970s." *Social Science Quarterly* 60:113–19.

Simon, James G. 1996. *The Center Holds: The Power Struggle inside the Rehnquist Court.* New York: Touchstone.

Slotnick, Elliot E., and Jennifer A. Segal. 1998. *Television News and the Supreme Court: All the News That's Fit to Air?* New York: Cambridge University Press.

Spaeth, Harold J. 1999. UNITED STATES SUPREME COURT JUDICIAL DATA-BASE, 1953–1997 TERMS [Computer file]. 9th ICPSR version. East Lansing: Michigan State University, Department of Political Science [producer], 1998; Inter-university Consortium for Political and Social Research [distributor], 1999.

Spill, Rorie L., and Zoe M. Oxley. 2003. "Philosopher Kings or Political Actors: How the Media Portray the Supreme Court." *Judicature* 87:22–29.

Steeh, Charlotte, and Maria Krysan. 1996. "Trends: Affirmative Action and the Public, 1970–1995." *Public Opinion Quarterly* 60:128–58.

Stoker, Laura. 1998. "Understanding Whites' Resistance to Affirmative Action: The Role of Principled Commitments and Racial Prejudice." In *Perception and Prejudice: Race and Politics in the United States,* ed. Jon Hurwitz and Mark Peffley. New Haven: Yale University Press, 135–70.

Stoutenborough, James W., Donald P. Haider-Markel, and Mahalley D. Allen. 2006. "Reassessing the Impact of Supreme Court Decisions on Public Opinion: Gay Civil Rights Cases." *Political Research Quarterly* 59:419–33.

Tate, Katherine. 1994. *From Protest to Politics: The New Black Voters in American Elections,* enlarged ed. Cambridge, MA: Harvard University Press and Russell Sage Foundation.

Tate, Katherine. 1996. NATIONAL BLACK ELECTION STUDY [Computer file]. ICPSR version. Columbus: Ohio State University [producer], 1997; Ann Arbor: Inter-University Consortium for Political and Social Research [distributor], 1998.

Tate, Katherine. 2003. *Black Faces in the Mirror: African Americans and Their Representatives in the U.S. Congress.* Princeton: Princeton University Press.

Thornton, Leslie T. 2003. "With Friends Like These—The Weight of 90-plus Amicus Briefs in the Michigan Case Out to Influence the Court." *Legal Times,* March 31.

Towner, Terri L., Rosalee A. Clawson, and Eric N. Waltenburg. 2006. "Media Coverage of the University of Michigan Affirmative Action Decisions: The View from Mainstream, Black, and Latino Journalists." *Judicature* 90:120–28.

Tuch, Steven A., and Lee Sigelman. 1997. "Race, Class, and Black-White Differences in Social Policy Views." In *Understanding Public Opinion,* ed. Barbara Norrander and Clyde Wilcox. Washington, DC: CQ Press.

Tushnet, Mark V. 1987. *The NAACP's Legal Strategy against Segregated Education, 1925–1950.* Chapel Hill: University of North Carolina Press.

Tyler, Tom R. 1990. *Why People Obey the Law.* New Haven: Yale University Press.

Tyler, Tom R., and Gregory Mitchell. 1994. "Legitimacy and the Empowerment of Discretionary Legal Authority: The United States Supreme Court and Abortion Rights." *Duke Law Journal* 43:703–815.

Tyler, Tom R., and Renee Weber. 1982. "Support for the Death Penalty: Instrumental Response to Crime or Symbolic Attitude? *Law and Society Review* 17:21–45.

Vose, Clement E. 1967. *Caucasians Only: The Supreme Court, the NAACP, and the Restrictive Covenant Cases.* 2nd ed. Berkeley: University of California Press.

Waltenburg, Eric N. 2002. *Choosing Where to Fight: Organized Labor and the Modern Regulatory State, 1948–1987.* Albany: State University Press of New York.

Weisberg, Herbert F., Jon A. Krosnick, and Bruce D. Bowen. 1989. *An Introduction to Survey Research and Data Analysis.* 2nd ed. Glenview, IL: Scott, Foresman.

Wills, Gary, ed. 1982. *The Federalist Papers by Alexander Hamilton, James Madison and John Jay.* New York: Bantam Books.

Wilson, Clint C., II. 1991. *Black Journalists in Paradox: Historical Perspectives and Current Dilemmas.* Westport, CT: Greenwood.

Wolseley, Roland E. 1990. *The Black Press, U.S.A.* 2nd ed. Ames: Iowa State University Press.

Young, Robert L. 1992. "Religious Orientation, Race, and Support for the Death Penalty." *Journal for the Scientific Study of Religion* 31:76–87.

Zaller, John R. 1992. *The Nature and Origins of Mass Opinion.* Cambridge: Cambridge University Press.

Zanna, Mark P., and John K. Rempel. 1988. "Attitudes: A New Look at an Old Concept." In *The Social Psychology of Knowledge,* ed. Daniel Bar-Tal and Arie W. Kruglanski, vol. 5, 151–63. Hillsdale, NJ: Erlbaum.

Index

Remedial Action frame, 79–80
Representation, 8–10, 56, 63–65
Republican Court, 35–41, 163
Reverse discrimination, 15, 84, 87–89, 155
Rights revolution, 160
Rigid scrutiny, 26
Roe v. Wade (410 U.S. 113 [1973]), 111, 133
Rojecki, Andrew, 191n13
Roosevelt, Franklin Delano, 23–24, 161, 185n11
Rosenberg, Gerald, 133–134, 159

San Antonio Independent School District v. Rodriquez (411 U.S. 1 [1973]), 36
Sanders, Lynn M., 89–90
Scalia, Antonin, 76–77, 103, 112
School desegregation, 31–32, 34, 37–38, 57, 161–162
Schudson, Michael, 160
Schwartz, Bernard, 26, 32–33
Sears, David O., 12
Segal, Jeffrey A., 56, 58, 192n18
Segal, Jennifer A., 69, 189n7
Separate but equal doctrine, 21, 24, 31–32, 184n7
Serrin, William, 191n13
Shelley v. Kraemer (334 U.S. 1 [1948]), 30, 186n28
Sigelman, Lee, 43
Slaughterhouse Cases (83 U.S. 36 [1873]), 19
Slotnick, Elliot E., 69, 189n7
Smith v. Allwright (321 U.S. 649 [1944]), 27
Social desirability, 63
Socialization. *See* Political socialization
Source credibility, media, 88, 103
Souter, David, 40, 76
South Carolina v. Katzenbach (383 U.S. 301 [1966]), 29
Spaeth, Harold J., 37, 56, 58
Specialized media, 69–70. *See also* Advocacy press; Black press; Black media

Specific support, 88, 94–95, 118–120, 128, 183n3
Spence, Lester Kenyatta, 44, 119, 128, 149, 151, 194n1
State-action theory, 20, 30
Stein, Trisha, 169
Stevens, John Paul 76
Stewart, Potter, 112
Stoker, Laura, 87
Stoutenborough, James W., 103, 142
Strict scrutiny, 39–41, 71–72, 75, 188n3, 189n5
Supreme Court Justices. *See names of specific justices*
Sweatt v. Painter (339 U.S. 629 [1950]), 31–32
Symbolic predispositions, 95, 100. *See also* Group attitudes; Group-centrism; Political predispositions; Racial Resentment
Symbolic representation, 9–10, 64–65

Tate, Katherine, 9, 113
Thirteenth Amendment, 19, 21–22
Thomas, Clarence, 40, 64, 163, 190n3; effects of media coverage of, 86–92, 94–102, 106, 156; media coverage of, 75–78, 82, 87, 104, 155
Towner, Terri L., 74–75, 78
Truman, Harry, 24, 161
Tushnet, Mark V., 24–25
Twenty-Fourth Amendment, 28

United Nations Charter (1948), 24
University of Michigan affirmative action cases: Court rulings, 40–41, 115, 137–138, 169; media coverage of, 74, 78; panel data and, 13, 16, 106, 136, 157; public opinion toward, 140–151. *See also* Affirmative action; Affirmative action policy; *Gratz v. Bollinger*; *Grutter v. Bollinger*
Urciolo v. Hodge 334 U.S. 24 (1948), 186n28

Rosalee A. Clawson is Associate Professor of Political Science at Purdue University and the co-author of *Public Opinion: Democratic Ideals, Democratic Practice*.

Eric N. Waltenburg is Associate Professor of Political Science at Purdue University and the author of *Choosing Where to Fight: Organized Labor and the Modern Regulatory State, 1948–1987*.